ESSENTIALS OF NONVERBAL COMMUNICATION

Mark L. Knapp

Purdue University

HOLT, RINEHART AND WINSTON

New York   Chicago   San Francisco   Atlanta   Dallas

Montreal   Toronto   London   Sydney

Library of Congress Cataloging in Publication Data
Knapp, Mark L.
    Essentials of nonverbal communication.

    Bibliography.
    Includes indexes.
    1. Nonverbal communication. I. Title.
BF637.C45K56   153   79-17769

ISBN 0-03-049861-9

Acknowledgments

Figures 1.1 and 1.2:   Reprinted from "Movements with Precise Meanings" by Paul Ekman, *Journal of Communication* 26:3.

Page 17:   Quotes from Joe McGinniss reprinted by permission of The Sterling Lord Agency, Inc. Copyright © 1969 by Joemac, Inc.

Table 3.1: L. B. Wexner, "The Degree to Which Colors (Hues) Are Associated with Mood-Tones," *Journal of Applied Psychology* 38 (1954):432-435. Copyright 1954 by the American Psychological Association. Reprinted by permission.

Figure 3.3:   From *The Realities of Teaching: Explorations with Video Tape* by Raymond S. Adams and Bruce J. Biddle. Copyright © 1970 by Holt, Rinehart and Winston, Inc. Reprinted by permission of Holt, Rinehart and Winston.

Figure 3.5: Reprinted from *Social Pressures in Informal Grops* by Leon Festinger, Stanley Schacter, and Kurt Back with the permission of the publishers, Stanford University Press. Copyright 1950, 1978 by the Board of Trustees of The Leland Stanford Junior University.

Tables 4.1 and 4.2:   From Robert Sommer, *Personal Space: The Behavioral Basis of Design*, © 1969, pp. 62–63. Adapted by permission of Prentice-Hall, Inc., Englewood Cliffs, New Jersey.

Page 103: J. B. Cortes and F. M. Gatti, "Physique and Self-Description of Temperament," Journal of Consulting Psychology 29 (1965):434. Copyright 1965 by the American Psychological Association. Reprinted by permission.

Figure 7.1: S. M. Jourard, "An Exploratory Study of Body-Accessibility," *British Journal of Social and Clinical Psychology* 5 (1966):221-231.

Figure 7.2: D. C. Barnlund, "Communicative Styles in Two Cultures: Japan and the United States," in A. Kendon, R. M. Harris, and M. R. Key (eds.) *Organization of Behavior in Face-to-Face Interaction* (Chicago: Aldine) 1975.

Figure 7.3: Reprinted from "The Meaning of Touch: Sex Differences," by T. Nguyen, R. Heslin, and M. L. Nguyen in the *Journal of Communication* 25:3.

Figure 8.10: Reprinted from M. Cline, "The Influence of Social Context on the

(Acknowledgments continued on p. 263)

PREFACE

The word *essentials* in this book's title clearly specifies what I have attempted to achieve—presenting the reader with only that information which I felt was absolutely necessary for developing a basic understanding of nonverbal behavior. For courses that examine nonverbal communication as only a part of a larger area of study, this relatively brief account may be especially useful as a supplementary text. These courses may be in any one of the fields that have contributed to the scientific study of nonverbal behavior: anthropology, child development and family relations, communication, counseling, dance, education, ethology, linguistics, psychiatry, social psychology, sociology, and speech science.

Most of the research summarized in this book emanated from scholars in these areas during the last thirty years. These relatively recent contributions were not without some important predecessors, however; Darwin's *The Expression of Emotion in Man and Animals* published in 1872 has been highly influential in the modern study of facial expressions; Kretschmer's *Physique and Character* in 1925 and Sheldon's *The Variations of Human Physique* in 1940 laid the foundation for work on body types; and Efron's 1941 classic, *Gesture and Environment,* introduced innovative ways of studying body language, set forth the important role of culture in shaping many of our gestures, and constructed a framework for classifying nonverbal behaviors which influences researchers today. Anthropologists Ray Birdwhistell (*Introduction to Kinesics,* 1952) and Edward T. Hall (*The Silent Language,* 1959) founded research programs in kinesics and proxemics. Psychiatrist Jurgen Ruesch and photographer Weldon Kees authored the first book to use the term nonverbal communication in its title in 1956 with *Nonverbal Communication: Notes on the Visual Perception of Human Relations*. The decades of the 1960s and 1970s are punctuated with important contributions from scholars such as Argyle, Davitz, Dittmann, Goldman-Eisler, Hess, Kendon, Mehrabian, Rosenthal, Scheflen, Sommer, Trager, and others whose work is documented throughout this book. In 1969 Ekman and Friesen detailed an important theoretical framework on the origins, usage and coding of nonverbal behavior. The 1970s began with a journalist's account of nonverbal study (Fast, *Body Language*) that caught the imagination of the public and was soon followed by a steady stream of books and magazine articles that attempted to make nonverbal findings understandable and usable for a popular audience. Some of these books and articles, in the interest of simplification and readability, misrepresented findings about the role of nonverbal communication in making a sale, detecting deception, obtaining a partner for sex, and the like. This book has attempted to maintain its interest for the reader without sacrificing important qualifications, contingencies, and complexities.

As with any relatively new area of study heavily promoted in the popular press, some common myths are associated with nonverbal communication. It is hoped that this book will help to dispel these myths, which include: (1) The Isolation Myth views the nonverbal system as an entity distinct and isolated from the total system of human communication. Although this book focuses almost exclusively on these nonverbal processes the reader is reminded that they are inextricably bound up with verbal and contextual aspects of communication. The separation is artificial because in actual daily interaction verbal and nonverbal systems are interdependent. (2) The Key to Success Myth argues that an understanding of nonverbal communication is somehow a magic elixir for success in interpersonal relations. Understanding "body language" is much like understanding the nuances of persuading, informing, entertaining, expressing emotions, and managing interaction through verbal behavior. It is only a part of understanding the total communication process, only a part of the skill necessary to become an effective communicator. It can be very important in some situations and not very important in others. A related myth concerns the fear that we will be totally transparent to people who have "broken" the nonverbal code, that some people will be able to know our deepest thoughts because we can't control these nonverbal signals. We are very much aware of and exert a great deal of control over some nonverbal behavior and once we are aware that someone is trying to use their knowledge of our nonverbal behavior in an unproductive or manipulative way, we will modify it and make adaptations. (3) The Single Meaning Myth is based on the assumption that when we see a particular nonverbal signal (a nod, for instance) we can confidently associate a certan meaning with that behavior (agreement). Nonverbal behavior, like verbal, may have many different meanings depending on the social context. Rapid nodding may mean you want the other person to hurry up and finish talking rather than agreement.

I would like to conclude this Preface by acknowledging my superbly talented editor, Roth Wilkofsky. The fact that editors and sales representatives from competing publishing companies have told me how lucky I am to be working with Roth is a good measure of his professional stature. Undertaking this book was largely due to his encouragement, so he will, of course, share the blame if it doesn't sell. I would also like to award the verbal equivalent of the *croix de guerre* to Marjorie Marks for her outstanding work as my production editor on this, our second book together.

Hazel Crest, Illinois   M.L.K.
January 1980

CONTENTS

NONVERBAL COMMUNICATION: BASIC PERSPECTIVES

"Those of us who keep our eyes open can read volumes into what we see going on around us."

E. T. HALL

Herr von Osten purchased a horse in Berlin, Germany, in 1900. When von Osten began training his horse, Hans, to count by tapping his front hoof, he had no idea that Hans was soon to become one of the most celebrated horses in history. Hans was a rapid learner and soon progressed from counting to addition, multiplication, division, subtraction, and eventually the solution of problems involving factors and fractions. As if this were not enough, von Osten exhibited Hans to public audiences, where the horse counted the number of people in the audience or simply the number who were wearing eyeglasses. Still responding only with taps, Hans could tell time, use a calendar, display an ability to recall musical pitch, and perform numerous other seemingly fantastic feats. After von Osten taught Hans an alphabet that could be coded into hoofbeats, the horse could answer virtually any question—oral or written. It seemed that Hans, a common horse, had a complete comprehension of the German language, the ability to produce the equivalent of words and numerals, and an intelligence beyond that of many human beings.

Even without the promotion of Madison Avenue, the word spread quickly, and soon Hans was known throughout the world. He was soon dubbed Clever Hans. Because of the obviously profound implications for several scientific fields and because some skeptics thought there was a gimmick involved, an investigating committee was established to decide, once and for all, whether there was any deceit involved in Hans' performances. A professor of psychology and physiology, the director of the Berlin Zoological Garden, a director of a circus, veterinarians, and cavalry officers were appointed to this commission of horse experts. An experiment with Hans from which von Osten was excluded demonstrated no change in the apparent intelligence of Hans. This was sufficient proof for the commission to announce that there was no trickery involved.

The appointment of a second commission was the beginning of the end for Clever Hans. Von Osten was asked to whisper a number into the horse's left ear while another experimenter whispered a number into the horse's right ear. Hans was told to add the two numbers—an answer none of the onlookers, von Osten, or the experimenter knew. Hans failed, and with further tests he continued to fail. The experimenter, Pfungst, discovered on further experimentation that Hans could only answer a question if someone in his visual field knew the answer.[1] When Hans was given the question, the onlookers assumed an expectant posture and increased their body tension. When Hans reached the correct number of taps, the onlookers would relax and make a slight movement of the head—which was Hans' cue to stop tapping.

The story of Clever Hans is frequently used in discussions concerning the capacity of an animal to learn verbal language. It also seems well suited to an introduction to the field of nonverbal communication. Hans's cleverness was not in his ability to verbalize or understand verbal commands, but in his ability to respond to almost imperceptible and unconscious movements on the part of those surrounding him. It is not unlike that perceptiveness or sensitivity to nonverbal cues exhibited by a Clever Carl, Chris, Frank, or Harriet when they are closing a business deal, giving an intelligent and industrious image to a professor, impressing a date, knowing when to leave a party, and in a multitude of other common situations. This book is written for the purpose of expanding your conscious awareness of the numerous nonverbal stimuli that confront you in your everyday dialogue. Each chapter summarizes behavioral science research on a specific area of nonverbal communication. It is first, however, necessary to develop a few basic perspectives—a common frame of reference, a lens through which we can view the remaining chapters.

PERSPECTIVES ON DEFINING NONVERBAL COMMUNICATION

Conceptually, the term *nonverbal* is subject to a variety of interpretations—just like the term *communication*. The basic issue seems to be whether the events that are traditionally studied under the heading *nonverbal* are literally nonverbal. Ray Birdwhistell, a pioneer in nonverbal research, is reported to have said that studying *nonverbal* communication is like studying *noncardiac* physiology. His point is well taken. It is not easy to dissect human interaction and make one diagnosis that concerns only verbal behavior and another that concerns only nonverbal behavior. The verbal dimension is so intimately woven and so subtly represented in so much of what we have previously labeled nonverbal that the term does not always adequately describe the behavior under study. Some of the most noteworthy scholars associated with nonverbal study refuse to segregate words from gestures and hence work under the broader terms *communication* or *face-to-face interaction*.

Another possible source of confusion in defining nonverbal communication is whether we are talking about the signal *produced* (nonverbal) or the internal code for *interpreting* the signal (frequently verbal). Generally, when people refer to nonverbal behavior they are talking about the signal(s) to which meaning will be attributed—not the process of attributing meaning.

The fuzzy line between verbal and nonverbal communication is augmented by an equally difficult distinction between vocal and nonvocal phenomena. Consider the following: (1) Not all acoustic phenomena are vocal—for example, knuckle-cracking; a gurgling stomach; farting; slapping one's thigh, another's back, or a desk top; snapping one's fingers; and clapping. (2) Not all nonacoustic phenomena are nonverbal—for example, some of the gestures used in American Sign Language used by many deaf people. (3) Not all vocal phenomena are the same—some are respiratory and some are not. A sigh or prespeaking inspiration of breath may be considered vocal and respiratory; a click or "tch, tch!" might be classified as vocal but nonrespiratory. (4) Not all words or "apparent" word strings are clearly or singularly verbal—for example, onomatopoetic words such as *buzz* or *murmur* and nonpropositional speech used by auctioneers and some asphasics. Neat categorization for each behavior under consideration is often difficult. Realistically, we should expect that there will be points of overlap—behaviors that fit some aspects of one category and some aspects of another.

Instead of trying to classify behavior as either nonverbal or verbal, Mehrabian chose instead to use an "explicit-implicit" dichotomy.[2] In other words, Mehrabian believed that it was the subtlety of a signal that brought it into the nonverbal realm—and subtlety seemed to be directly linked to a lack of explicit rules for coding. Mehrabian's work has focused primarily on the referents people have for various configurations of nonverbal and/or implicit behavior—that is, the meaning you attach to these behaviors. The results of extensive testing reveal a threefold perspective.[3] (1) Immediacy. Sometimes we react to things by evaluating them—positive or negative, good or bad, like or dislike. (2) Status. Sometimes we enact or perceive behaviors that indicate various aspects of status to us—strong or weak, superior or subordinate. (3) Responsiveness. This third category refers to our perceptions of activity—slow or fast, active or passive.

PERSPECTIVES ON CLASSIFYING NONVERBAL BEHAVIOR

The following classification schema was derived from an examination of writing and research currently being conducted in which the authors either explicitly or implicitly categorized their own work as being subsumable under the label *nonverbal*.

I. Body Motion or Kinesic Behavior

Body motion, or kinesic behavior, typically includes gestures, movements of the body, limbs, hands, head, feet and legs, facial expressions (smiles), eye behavior (blinking, direction and length of gaze, and pupil dilation), and posture. The furrow of the brow, the slump of a shoulder, and the tilt of a head—all are within the purview of kinesics. Obviously, there are different types of nonverbal behavior just as there are different types of verbal behavior. Some nonverbal cues are very specific, and some are more general. Some are intended to communicate, and some are expressive only. Some provide information about emotions, and others carry information about personality traits or attitudes. In an effort to sort through the relatively unknown world of nonverbal behavior, Ekman and Friesen[4] developed a system for classifying nonverbal behavior acts. These categories include:

A. Emblems. These are nonverbal acts that have a direct verbal translation or dictionary definition, usually consisting of a word or two or a phrase.[5] There is high agreement among members of a culture or subculture on the verbal "translation" of these signals. The gestures used to represent "A-OK" or "Peace" (also known as the victory sign) are examples of emblems for a large part of our culture. Mostly, these emblems are culture specific. For example, Figure 1.1 shows variations in suicide emblems depending on the popularity of a method (hanging, shooting, or stabbing) for a particular culture. However, some emblems portray actions that are common to the human species and seem to transcend a given culture. Eating (bringing hand up to mouth) and sleeping (tilting head in lateral position, almost perpendicular to the body, accompanied sometimes with eye closing and/or a hand or hands below the head like a pillow) are two examples of emblems that Ekman and his colleagues have observed in several cultures. Ekman also found that

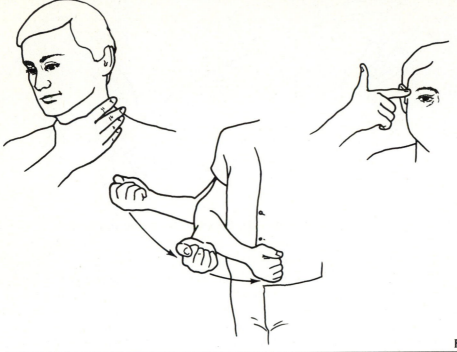

FIGURE 1.1

Emblems for suicide. Top left, the South Fore, Papua, New Guinea; Top right: the United States; Bottom: Japan.

different cultures also seem to have emblems for similar classes of messages, regardless of the gesture used to portray it, for example, insults, directions (come, go, stop), greetings, departures, certain types of responses (yes, no, I don't know), physical, state, and emotion. The number of emblems used within a given culture may vary considerably, from less than 100 (United States) to more than 250 (Israeli) students.

Emblems are often produced with the hands—but not exclusively. A nose wrinkle may say "I'm disgusted!" or "Phew! It stinks!" To say "I don't know" or "I'm helpless" or "I'm uncertain" one might turn both palms up, shrug shoulders, or do both simultaneously. Ekman believes that facial emblems probably differ from other facial expressions by being more stylized and being presented for longer or shorter durations. Facial emblems may also emphasize particular parts of the face; for example, the smile may be used to indicate happiness or surprise by mechanically dropping the jaw or dramatically raising the eyebrows.

Emblems are frequently used when verbal channels are blocked (or fail) and are usually used to communicate. Some of the sign language of the deaf, nonverbal gestures used by television production personnel, signs used by two underwater swimmers, or motions made by two peo-

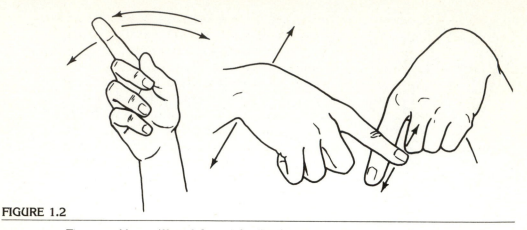

FIGURE 1.2

Finger emblems. (United States) for "No" (left) and "Shame on you" (right).

ple who are too far apart to make audible signals practical are all situations ripe for emblem production.

Our own awareness of emblem usage is about the same as our awareness of word choice. Also, like verbal behavior, context can sometimes change the interpretation of the signal; that is, giving someone "the finger" can be either humorous or insulting, depending on the other cues accompanying it. Ekman has also observed "emblematic slips," analogous to slips of the tongue. He gives an example of a woman who was subjected to a stress interview by a person whose status forbade free expressions of dislike. The woman, unknown to herself or the interviewer, displayed "the finger" on the arm of her chair for several minutes during the interview.

Unlike verbal behavior, emblems are not generally strung together like words, although there are exceptions. You may be talking on the phone when a visitor enters and you have to indicate "wait a minute," "come in," and "sit down" in succession. Finally, some emblems seem to be specifically adapted to particular subgroups within a given culture. For instance, Figure 1.2 shows two gestures, one which seems to be used primarily when adults are talking to children ("no-no") and one which seems primarily limited to usage by children ("shame on you").

B. Illustrators.   These are nonverbal acts that are directly tied to, or accompany, speech and serve to illustrate what is being said verbally. These may be movements that accent or emphasize a word or phrase, sketch a path of thought, point to present objects, depict a spatial relationship, depict the rhythm or pacing of an event, draw a picture of the referent, or depict a bodily action. They may also be emblems used to illustrate verbal statements, either repeating or substituting for a word or phrase. Illustrators seem to be within our awareness, but not as explicitly as emblems. They are used intentionally to help communication, but not as deliberately as emblems. Many factors can alter the frequency with which illustrators are displayed. We would expect to find more illustrators in face-to-face communication than when communicating over an intercom;[6] we would expect people who are excited and enthusiastic to display more illustrators than those who are not; and we would expect more illustrators during "difficult" communication situations; for example, not being able to find the right words to express a thought or being confronted by a receiver who either isn't paying attention or isn't comprehending what you're trying to say. Illustrators are probably learned by watching others.

C. Affect Displays. These are primarily facial configurations that display affective states. Although the face is the primary source of affect, the body can also be read for global judgments of affect; for example, a drooping, sad body. Affect displays can repeat, augment, contradict, or be unrelated to, verbal affective statements. Once the display has occurred, there is usually a high degree of awareness, but it can occur without any awareness. Affect displays are often not intended to communicate, but they can be intentional.

D. Regulators. These are nonverbal acts that maintain and regulate the back and forth nature of speaking and listening between two or more interactants. They tell the speaker to continue, repeat, elaborate, hurry up, become more interesting, give the other a chance to talk, and so forth. Some of the behavior associated with greetings and good-byes may be regulators to the extent that they indicate the initiation or termination of face-to-face communication.

In recent years the various nonverbal behaviors associated with turn-taking are the regulators that have been given the most attention.[7] Turn-taking refers to the cues we use: to tell another person we want to talk, to keep another person from getting the floor away from us, to give up a speaking turn and ask the other person to continue, and to show we are finished speaking and the other person can take a turn. Generally we don't say these things verbally; they are communicated by many nonverbal behaviors. Probably the most familiar regulators are head nods and eye behavior. If head nods occur frequently in rapid succession, the message may be "hurry up and finish," but if the nods follow points made by the speaker and appear slow, deliberate, and thoughtful they may signal "keep talking" or "I like what you're saying." We found people who were trying to terminate a conversation severely decreased the amount of eye contact with the other person.[8]

Regulators seem to be on the periphery of our awareness and are generally difficult to inhibit. They are like overlearned habits and are almost involuntary, but we are very much aware of these signals when they are sent by others.

E. Adaptors. These nonverbal behaviors are perhaps the most difficult to define and involve the most speculation. They are labeled adaptors because they are thought to develop in childhood as adaptive efforts to satisfy needs, perform actions, manage emotions, develop social contacts, or perform a host of other functions. Ekman and Friesen have identified three types of adaptors: self-, object-, and alter-directed.

Self-adaptors, as the term implies, refer to manipulations of one's own body, such as holding, rubbing, squeezing, scratching, pinching, or picking oneself. These self-adaptors will often increase as a person's anxiety level increases. Picking one's nose can be a self-adaptor; an adult who wipes the corner of his or her eye during times of sadness (as if to brush away tears) may be showing a response that reflects that person's early experiences with sadness. Ekman and his colleagues have found the "eye cover act" to be associated with shame and guilt, and the "scratch-pick act" to be associated with hostility—aggression toward oneself or toward another displaced onto oneself.

Alter-adaptors are learned in conjunction with our early experiences with interpersonal relations—giving and taking from another, attacking or protecting, establishing closeness or withdrawing, and the like. Leg movements may be adaptors, showing residues of kicking aggression, sexual invitation, or flight. Ekman believes that many of the restless movements of the hands and feet, which have typically been considered indicators of anxiety, may be residues of adaptors necessary for flight from the interaction. An example from the interaction behavior of baboons will help illustrate the nature of these alter-adaptors. When a young baboon is learning the fundamentals of attack and aggression, the mother baboon will watch from close by. The young baboon will enact aggressive behavior, but will also turn the head laterally to check whether the mother is still there. As an adult, the baboon may still perform this lateral head movement during threatening conditions even though the mother is no longer there and no functional purpose seems to be served by this movement.

Object-adaptors involve the manipulation of objects and may be derived from the performance of some instrumental task—such as smoking, writing with a pencil, and so on. Although we are typically unaware of performing these adaptor behaviors, we are probably most aware of the object-adaptors. These behaviors are often learned later in life, and there seem to be fewer social taboos associated with them.

Since there seem to be social constraints on displaying these adaptive behaviors, they are more often seen when a person is alone. At least, we would expect that we would see the full act rather than just a fragment of it. Alone you might pick your nose without inhibition; when other people are around you may just touch your nose or rub it "casually." Adaptors are not intended for use in communication, but they may be triggered by verbal behavior in a given situation associated with conditions occurring when the adaptive habit was first learned.

II. Physical Characteristics

Whereas the previous section was concerned with movement and motion, this category covers things that remain relatively unchanged during the period of interaction. They are influential nonverbal cues that are not movement bound. Included are such things as physique or body shape, general attractiveness, body or breath odors, height, weight, hair, and skin color or tone.

III. Touching Behavior

For some, kinesic study includes touch behavior; for others, however, actual physical contact constitutes a separate class of events. Some researchers are concerned with touching behavior as an important factor in the child's early development, and others are concerned with adult touching behavior. Subcategories of touch behavior may include stroking, hitting, holding, guiding another's movements, and other, more specific instances.

IV. Paralanguage

Simply put, paralanguage deals with how something is said and not what is said. It deals with the range of nonverbal vocal cues surrounding common speech behavior. Trager believed that paralanguage had the following components.[9]

A. Voice Qualities.   This includes such things as pitch range, pitch control, rhythm control, tempo, articulation control, resonance, glottis control, and vocal lip control.

B. Vocalizations.   (1) *Vocal characterizers*. This includes such things as laughing, crying, sighing, yawning, belching, swallowing, heavily marked inhaling or exhaling, coughing, clearing of the throat, hiccuping, moaning, groaning, whining, yelling, whispering, sneezing, snoring, stretching, and the like. (2) *Vocal qualifiers*. This includes intensity (overloud to oversoft), pitch height (overhigh to overlow), and extent (extreme drawl to extreme clipping). (3) *Vocal segregates*. These are such things as "uh-huh," "um," "uh," "ah," and variants thereof.

Related work on such topics as silent pauses (beyond junctures), intruding sounds, speech errors, and latency would probably be included in this category.

V. Proxemics

Proxemics is generally considered to be the study of our use and perception of social and personal space. Under this heading, we find a body of work called small group ecology, which is concerned with how people use and respond to spatial relationships in formal and informal group settings. Such studies deal with seating arrangements and spatial arrangements as related to leadership, communication flow, and the task at hand. The influence of architectural features on residential living units and even on communities is also of concern to those who study human proxemic behavior. On an even broader level, some attention has been given to spatial relationships in crowds and densely populated situations. Our personal space orientation is sometimes studied in the context of conversational distance, and how it varies according to sex, status, roles, cultural orientation, and so forth. The term *territoriality* is also frequently used in the study of proxemics to denote the human tendency to stake out personal territory—or untouchable space—much as wild animals and birds do.

VI. Artifacts

Artifacts include the manipulation of objects with the interacting persons that may act as nonverbal stimuli. These artifacts include perfume, clothes, lipstick, eyeglasses, wigs and other hairpieces, false eyelashes, eyeliners, and the whole repertoire of falsies and "beauty" aids.

VII. Environmental Factors

Thus far we have been concerned with the appearance and behavior of the persons involved in communicating. This category concerns those elements that impinge on the human relationship, but are not directly a part of it. Environmental factors include the furniture, architectural style, interior decorating, lighting conditions, smells, colors, temperature, additional noises or music, and the like, within which the interaction occurs. Variations in arrangements, materials, shapes, or surfaces of objects in the interacting environment can be extremely influential on the outcome of an interpersonal relationship. This category also includes what might be called traces of action. For instance, as you observe cigarette butts, orange peels, and wastepaper left by the person with whom you will soon interact, you are forming an impression that will eventually influence your meeting.

PERSPECTIVES ON NONVERBAL COMMUNICATION IN THE TOTAL COMMUNICATION PROCESS

We are constantly being warned against presenting material out of context. Although this book was written as a supplement to a treatment of verbal behavior, the book deals almost exclusively with nonverbal communication. There is a danger that the reader may forget that nonverbal communication cannot be studied in isolation from the total communication process. Verbal and nonverbal communication should be treated as a total and inseparable unit. Argyle states, "Some of the most important findings in the field of social interaction are about the ways that verbal interaction needs the support of nonverbal communications."[10] What are some of the ways in which verbal and nonverbal systems interrelate?

Before outlining some of the verbal/nonverbal interrelationships, we should recall that there may be nonverbal interrelationships as well—that is, nonverbal channels interacting others. An example of a nonverbal interrelationship is a loud "Well!" preceding a handshake, which makes you anticipate a firm handshake. Odors can shorten or lengthen distance, interaction distance can affect vocal loudness, and so on. Argyle has identified the primary uses of nonverbal behavior in human communication as: (1) expressing emotion, (2) conveying interpersonal attitudes (like/dislike, dominance/submission, and the like), (3) presenting one's personality to others, and (4) accompanying speech for the purposes of managing turn-taking, feedback, attention, and the like.[11] None of these functions of nonverbal behavior is limited to nonverbal behavior alone—that is, emotions and attitudes can be expressed and interaction can be managed verbally, as well. In some cases, however, we rely more heavily on verbal behavior for some purposes and on nonverbal behavior for others. Like words and phrases, nonverbal signals can have multiple meanings and multiple uses—for example, a smile can be part of an emotional expression, an attitudinal message, part of a self-presentation, or a listener response to manage the interaction. Nonverbal behavior can repeat, contradict, substitute for, complement, accent, or regulate verbal behavior.[12]

Repeating.   Nonverbal communication can simply repeat what was said verbally. For instance, if you told someone that he or she had to go north to find a newspaper stand and then pointed in the proper direction, this would be considered repetition.

Contradicting. Nonverbal behavior can contradict verbal behavior.[13] A classic example is the parent who yells to his or her child in an angry voice, "Of course I love you!" Or the not-so-confident person about to make a public speech who, despite trembling hands and knees and beads of perspiration on the brow, says, "I'm not nervous." If there is no reason to suspect that conflicting cues might be present, we probably rely mainly on verbal messages. It has been said that when we receive contradictory messages on the verbal and nonverbal levels, we are more likely to trust and believe in the nonverbal message.[14] It is assumed that nonverbal signals are more spontaneous, harder to fake, and less apt to be manipulated. It is probably more accurate to say, however, that some nonverbal behaviors are more spontaneous and harder to fake than others, and that some people are more proficient than others at nonverbal deception.[15] With two contradictory cues, both of which are nonverbal, we predictably place our reliance on the cues we consider harder to fake. Sometimes we choose to be more direct with nonverbal cues because we know that they will be perceived as being less direct.

Young children seem to give less credence to certain nonverbal cues than do adults when they are confronted with conflicting verbal and nonverbal messages.[16] Conflicting messages in which the speaker smiled while making a critical statement were interpreted more negatively by children than by adults. This was particularly true when the speaker was a woman. Other work casts a further shadow on the "reliance on nonverbal cues in contradictory situations" theory.[17] Shapiro found student judges to be extremely consistent in their reliance on either linguistic or facial cues when they were asked to select the affect being communicated from a list of incongruent faces (sketched) and written messages. Vande Creek and Watkins extended Shapiro's work by using real voices and moving pictures. The stimulus persons were portraying inconsistencies in the degree of stress in verbal and nonverbal channels. Again they found that some respondents tended to rely primarily on verbal cues, some on nonverbal cues, and some responded to the degree of stress in general—regardless of the channels manifesting it. The cross-cultural research of Solomon and Ali suggests that familiarity with the verbal language may affect the reliance that one has on verbal or nonverbal cues. They found, for instance, that persons who were not as familiar with the language used to construct the contradictory message would rely on the content for judgments of affective meaning. Those who knew the language well were more apt to rely on the vocal intonation for the affective meaning. It thus appears that some people will rely more on the verbal message whereas others will rely on the nonverbal. We do not know all the conditions that would affect these preferences. Although one source of our preferences for verbal or nonverbal cues may be learned experiences, others believe that there may also be an even more basic genesis—such as right-left brain dominance.

Although there are times when inconsistent messages are produced to achieve a particular effect, such as sarcasm, there are some who believe that a constant barrage of inconsistent messages can contribute to a psychopathology for the receiver. This may be particularly true when people have a close relationship and the receiver has no other people to whom he or she can turn for discussion and possible clarification of the confusion. Some research finds that parents of disturbed children produce more messages with conflicting cues,[18] whereas other work suggests that the differences are not in conflicting cues, but in negative messages; that is, parents with disturbed children sent more negative messages.[19] Either situation is undesirable and the combination of negativity, confusion, and punishment can be very harmful.

Substituting. Nonverbal behavior can substitute for verbal messages. When a dejected and downtrodden executive (or janitor) walks into his or her house after work, a facial expression substitutes for the statement, "I've had a rotten day." With a little practice, people soon learn to identify a wide range of these substitute nonverbal displays—all the way from "It's been a fantastic, great day!" to "Oh, God, am I miserable!" We do not need to ask for verbal confirmation of our perception. Sometimes, when substitute nonverbal behavior fails, the communicator resorts back to the verbal level. Consider the woman who wants her date to stop "making out" with her. She may stiffen, stare straight ahead, or act unresponsive and cool. If the suitor persists, she is apt to say something like, "Look Larry, please don't ruin a nice friendship," and so on.

Complementing. Nonverbal behavior can modify, or elaborate on, verbal messages. An employee may nonverbally reflect an attitude of embarrassment when talking to his or her supervisor about a poor performance. Further, nonverbal behavior may reflect changes in the relationship between the employee and the supervisor. When the employee's slow, quiet verbalizations and relaxed posture change—when posture stiffens and the emotional level of the verbalized statement increases—this may signal changes in the overall relationship between the interactants. Complementary functions of nonverbal communication serve to signal one's attitudes and intentions toward another person.

Accenting. Nonverbal behavior may accent parts of the verbal message much as underlining written words or *italicizing* them serves to emphasize them. Movements of the head and hands are frequently used to accent the verbal message. When a father scolds his son about staying out too late at night, he may accent a particular phrase with a firm grip on the son's shoulder and an accompanying frown on his face. In some instances, one set of nonverbal cues can accent other nonverbal cues. Ekman found that emotions are primarily exhibited by facial expressions, but that the body carries the most accurate indicators regarding the level of arousal.[20]

Regulating. Nonverbal behaviors are also used to regulate the communicative flow between the interactants. The way one person stops talking and another starts in a smooth, synchronized manner may be as important to a satisfactory interaction as the verbal content that is exchanged. After all, we do make judgments about people based on their regulatory skills—for example, "talking to him is like talking to a wall" or "you can't get a word in edgewise with her." When another person frequently interrupts or is inattentive we may feel that this is a statement about the relationship—perhaps one of disrespect. There are rules for regulating conversations, but they are generally implicit. It isn't written down, but we seem to "know" that two people shouldn't talk at the same time, that each person should get an equal number of turns at talking if he or she desires it, that a question should be answered, and so forth. Wiemann's research found that relatively minute changes in these regulatory behaviors (interruptions, pauses longer than three seconds, unilateral topic changes, and the like) resulted in sizable variations in how competent a communicator was perceived.[21] As listeners, we are apparently attending to, and evaluating a host of, fleeting, subtle, and habitual features of another's conversational behavior. There are probably differences in the actual behaviors used to manage conversational flow across cultures or with certain subcultural groups. We know that as children are first learning these rules they use less subtle cues—for example, tugging on clothing, raising a hand, and the like. Some of the behaviors used to facilitate this conversational regulation follow.[22]

When we want to indicate that we are finished speaking and the other person can start, we may increase our eye contact with the other person. This is often accompanied by the vocal cues associated with ending declarative or interrogative statements. If the other person still doesn't pick up the conversational "ball," we might extend silence or interject a "trailer," for example, "you know . . ." or "so, ah . . ." Keeping another from getting in the conversation requires us to keep long pauses from occurring, decrease eye contact, and perhaps raise our volume if the other person tries to "get in." When we do not want to take a speaking turn we might give the other person some reinforcing head nods and maintain attentive eye contact, and, of course, keep from speaking when the other begins to yield. When we do want the floor we might raise our index finger or enact an audible inspiration of breath with a straightening of the posture as if we were "ready" to take over. Rapid nodding may also signal the other person to hurry up and finish, but if we have trouble getting in we may have to talk simultaneously for a few words or engage in "stutter starts" that, hopefully, will be more easily observed cues to exemplify our desire to speak.

Conversational beginnings and endings also act as regulatory points. When greeting others, our eye contact signals that the channels of conversation are open. A slight head movement and an "eyebrow flash" (a barely detectable but distinct up-and-down movement of the eyebrows) may be present. The hands are also used in greetings for salutes, waves, handshakes, hand slaps, emblematic signals like the peace or victory sign, a raised fist, or thumbs up. Hands may also perform grooming activities (putting fingers through one's hair) or be involved in various touching activities like kissing, embracing, or hitting another on the arm. The mouth may form a smile or an oval shape as if one were ready to start talking.[23]

Saying good-bye in semiformal interviews brought forth many nonverbal behaviors, but the most common included the frequent breaking of eye contact and for increasingly longer periods of time, positioning one's body toward an exit, leaning forward, and rapidly nodding. Less frequent, but also very noticeable were accenting behaviors; for example, "This is the termination of our conversation and I don't want you to miss it!" These accenters included what we called *explosive* hand and foot movements—raising the hands and/or feet and bringing them down with enough force to make an audible slap while simultaneously using the hands and feet as leverage to catapult out of the seat. A less direct manifestation of this is to place your hands on your thighs or knees in a "leveraging" position (as if you were soon to catapult) and hope that the other person picks up the good-bye cue.[24]

It should be clear from the preceding that verbal and nonverbal behavior work together in many ways. In order to fully understand a communicative transaction we must analyze both types of behavior as an inseparable unit.

PERSPECTIVES ON NONVERBAL COMMUNICATION IN AMERICAN SOCIETY

The importance of nonverbal communication would be undeniable if sheer quantity were the only measure. Birdwhistell, who is generally considered as a noted authority on nonverbal behavior, makes some rather astounding estimates of the amount of nonverbal communication that takes place. He estimates that the average person actually speaks words for a total of only 10 to 11 minutes daily—the standard spoken sentence taking only about 2.5 seconds. He goes on to say that in a normal two-person conversation, the verbal components carry less than 35 percent of the social meaning of the situation; more than 65 percent of the social meaning is carried on the nonverbal band.

Another way of looking at the quantity of nonverbal messages is to note the various systems that humans use to communicate. Hall outlines ten separate kinds of human activity that he calls "primary message systems."[25] He suggests that only one involves language. Ruesch and Kees discuss at least seven different systems—personal appearance and dress, gestures or deliberate movements, random action, traces of action, vocal sounds, spoken words, and written words. Only two of the seven systems involve the overt use of words.[26]

It is not my purpose here to argue the importance of the various human message systems, but to put the nonverbal world in perspective. It is safe to say that the study of human communication has for too long ignored a significant part of the process.

Further testimony to the prevalence and importance of nonverbal communication is available if we scrutinize specific facets of our society. For example, consider the role of nonverbal signals in therapeutic situations; an understanding of "disturbed" nonverbal behavior would certainly help in diagnosis and treatment. Nonverbal cues are also important in certain situations in which verbal communication is constrained—for example, doctor-nurse interaction during an operation. The significance of nonverbal cues in the arts is obvious—dancing, theatrical performances, music, pictures, and so on. It is the nonverbal symbolism of various ceremonies and rituals that creates important and necessary responses in the participants—for example, the trappings of the marriage ceremony, the Christmas decorations, religious rituals, funerals, and the like. We can also see how an understanding of nonverbal cues would better prepare us for communicating across cultures, classes, or age groups—and with different ethnic groups within our culture. Teaching and understanding the blind and deaf is largely a matter of developing a sophistication with nonverbal signals. Every day matters like forming impressions of people you meet, getting through a job interview, understanding advertising or the audience/speaker relationship in a public speech are all heavily laden with nonverbal behavior. Nonverbal cues are also being analyzed in the hope of predicting future behavior of people.[27] One expert claims to have analyzed hand gestures of prospective jurors in eleven major trials in 1975, hoping to predict how they would vote on the defendant. A list of situations in which nonverbal communication is critical is interminable so that only three areas: televised politics, classroom behavior, and courtship behavior are briefly described.

Televised Politics.   The tired, overweight, physically unappealing political boss is slowly being replaced by the young, good-looking, vigorous candidate who can capture the public's vote with an assist from nonverbal attraction. We currently watch between thirty and forty hours of television each week. Television has certainly helped to structure some of our nonverbal perceptions, and more political candidates have come to recognize the tremendous influence that these perceptions may have on the eventual election outcome. Perhaps the most frightening and vivid example of the role of nonverbal communication in televised politics is found in McGinniss' book, *The Selling of the President 1968:*

> Television seems particularly useful to the politician who can be charming but lacks ideas. . . . On television it matters less that he does not have ideas. His personality is what the viewers want to share. He need be neither statesman nor crusader; he must only show up on time. Success and failure are easily measured: how often is he invited back? Often enough and he reaches his goal—to advance from "politician" to "celebrity," a status jump bestowed by grateful viewers who feel that finally they have been given a basis for making a choice.
>
> The TV candidate, then, is measured not against his predecessors—not against a standard of performance established by two centuries of democracy—but against Mike Douglas. How well does he handle himself? Does he mumble, does he twitch, does he make me laugh? Do I feel warm inside?
>
> Style becomes substance. The medium is the massage and the masseur gets the votes . . . (p. 29–30).
>
> The words would be the same ones Nixon always used—the words of the acceptance speech. But they would all seem fresh and lively because a series of still pictures would flash on the screen while Nixon spoke. If it were done right, it would permit Treleaven to create a Nixon image that was entirely independent of the words. Nixon would say his same old tiresome things but no one would have to listen. The words would become Muzak. Something pleasant and lulling in the background. The flashing pictures would be carefully selected to create the impression that somehow Nixon represented competence, respect for tradition, serenity, faith that the American people were better than people anywhere else, and that all these problems others shouted about meant nothing in a land blessed with the tallest building, strongest armies, biggest factories, cutest children, and rosiest sunsets in the world. Even better: through association with these pictures, Richard Nixon could become these very things . . . (p. 85).
>
> "You know," Sage said, "what we're really seeing here is a genesis. We're moving into a period where a man is going to be merchandised on television more and more. It upsets you and me, maybe, but we're not typical Americans. The public sits home and watches Gunsmoke and when they're fed this pap about Nixon they think they're getting something worthwhile. . . ." (p. 114–115).[28]

It did not surprise us, then, to see Ron Nessen, President Ford's press secretary, hosting the satirical "Saturday Night Live"; to recall former Mayor of New York, John Lindsay, making frequent visits to the "Johnny Carson Show"; to see Robert Finch, presidential advisor, appearing on an antidrug episode of "The Name of the Game"; and to find former Vice President Spiro T. Agnew introducing the 1970 fall season of the "Red Skelton Show." Fortunately, the media experts do not control all the variables. The batting average for the top public relations and media experts in 1970 for both Democrats and Republicans was only about .500—sufficiently low to jeopardize their major-league status. We do not have a full accounting of the 1976 presidential debates, but a former movie star was unable to take the nomination from the incumbent president. Newscasts are currently under scrutiny, that is, the extent to which news programs are guided by "entertainment" considerations.

Nonverbal symbols have long been important in political behavior—before television marketing became popular. Picketing, parades, music, flags, uniforms, torches, hairstyles, sit-ins, and demonstrations with a large number of people marching with linked arms—all these and more have been a part of our nonverbal political heritage.

Classroom Behavior. The classroom is a veritable gold mine of nonverbal behavior, which has been nearly untapped by scientific probes. Acceptance and understanding of ideas and feelings on the part of both teacher and student, encouraging and criticizing, silence, questioning, and the like—all involve nonverbal elements. Consider the following instances as representative of the variety of classroom nonverbal cues: (1) the frantic hand waver who is sure that he or she had the correct answer; (2) the student who is sure that he or she does not know the answer and tries to avoid any eye contact with the teacher; (3) the effects of student dress and hair length on teacher-student interaction; (4) facial expressions—threatening gestures, and tone of voice are frequently used for discipline in elementary schools; (5) the teacher who requests student questioning and criticism, but whose nonverbal actions make it clear that he or she will not be receptive; (6) a student's absence from class communicates; (7) a teacher's trust of students is sometimes indicated by the arrangement of seating and monitoring behavior during examinations; (8) the variety of techniques used by students to make sleeping appear to be studying or listening; (9) the professor who announces that he or she has plenty of time for student conferences, but whose fidgeting and glancing at a watch suggest otherwise; (10) teachers who try to assess visual feedback to determine student comprehension;[29] (11) even classroom design (wall colors, space between seats, windows) has an influence on student participation in the classroom.

The subtle nonverbal influences in the classroom can sometimes have dramatic results, as Rosenthal and Jacobson found out. They gave IQ tests to elementary school pupils prior to their entering for the fall term. Randomly (not according to scores) some students were labeled as high scorers on an "intellectual blooming test," which indicated that they would show unusual intellectual development during the following year. Teachers were given this information. These students' scores showed a sharp rise on IQ tests given at the end of the year. The experimenters attribute this to teacher expectations and to the way these "special" students were treated.

To summarize our speculations, we may say that by what she said, by how and when she said it, by her facial expressions, postures, and perhaps by her touch, the teacher may have communicated to the children of the experimental group that she expected improved intellectual performance. Such communications together with possible changes in teaching techniques may have helped the child learn by changing his self-concept, his expectations of his own behavior, and his motivation, as well as his cognitive style and skills.[30]

Courtship Behavior.   One commentary on nonverbal courtship behavior is found in the following excerpt from the Beatles' song "Something" (copyright © 1969 Harrisongs Ltd. Written by George Harrison. Used by permission. All rights reserved, International copyright secured):

Something in the way she moves
Attracts me like no other lover
Something in the way she woos me . . .

Something in her smile she knows
That I don't need no other lover
Something in her style that shows me . . .

You're asking me will my love grow. . . .

You stick around, now
It may show . . .

As the song suggests, we know there is "something" that is highly influential in our nonverbal courtship behavior. Like other areas of nonverbal study, however, we are still at a very early stage in quantifying these patterns of behavior. On a purely intuitive level, we know that there are some men and some women who can exude such messages as "I'm available," "I'm knowledgeable," or "I want you" without saying a word. For the male, it may be such things as his clothes, sideburns, length of hair, an arrogant grace, a thrust of his hips, touch gestures, extra long eye contact, carefully looking at the woman's figure, open gestures and movements to offset closed ones exhibited by the woman, gaining close proximity, a subtleness that will allow both parties to deny that either had committed themselves to a courtship ritual, making the woman feel secure and wanted, "like a woman," or showing excitement and desire in fleeting facial expressions. For the woman, it may be such things as sitting with her legs symbolically open, crossing her legs to expose a thigh, engaging in flirtatious glances, stroking her thighs, protruding her breasts, using an appealing perfume, showing the "pouting mouth" in her facial expressions, opening her palm to the male, using a tone of voice that has an "invitation behind the words," or any of a multitude of other cues and rituals—some of which vary with status, subculture, region of the country, and the like. A study by some students in Milwaukee of a number of singles' bars suggested that smoking a cigar was taboo for any male who wished to pick up a female in these places. Other particularly important behaviors for males operating in this context seemed to be looking the female in the eyes often; dressing slightly on the "mod" side, but generally avoiding extremes in dress; and staying with one woman for the entire evening.

Another group of Milwaukee undergraduate students focused on the nonverbal courtship behavior of homosexuals and found many similarities to heterosexual courtship rituals. Homosexuals were found to lavishly decorate their living quarters to impress their partners, to use clothing for attraction and identification, and to use eye behavior to communicate their intentions. Scheflen has outlined four categories of heterosexual nonverbal courtship behavior—courtship readiness, preening behavior, positional cues, and actions of appeal or invitation.[31] The Milwaukee students found these to be useful categories in analyzing homosexual nonverbal courtship behavior, as well. Contrary to a popular stereotype, most homosexuals do not have effeminate and lisping characteristics. This raises the question of what nonverbal cues are used for identification purposes between two homosexuals. Certainly the environmental context may be influential (gay bars), but other cues are also used. For instance, brief bodily contact (leg to leg) and other body movements, such as certain lilts of the head or hands, have been reported. In public places, however, the most common and effective signals used by homosexuals are extended eye glances. Uninterested males will most likely avoid these long, lingering glances whereas those males who maintain such eye contact suggest that they are open for further interaction.

Nielsen, citing Birdwhistell, described the "courtship dance" of the North American adolescent.[32] He claims to have identified twenty-four steps between the "initial contact between the young male and female and the coitional act." He explains that these steps have an order to them. By this he means that when a male begins holding a female's hand, he must wait until she presses his hand (signaling a go-ahead) before he can take the next step of allowing his fingers to intertwine with hers. Females and males are labeled "fast" or "slow" according to whether they follow the order of the steps. If a step is skipped or reversed in the order, the person who does so is labeled "fast." If a person ignores the signal to move on to the next step, or takes actions to prevent the next step, he or she is considered "slow." This ordering would suggest that only after the initial kiss may the male attempt to approach the female's breasts. She will probably block his approach with her upper arm against her side since protocol forbids approaching the breast from the front. The male really does not expect to reach the breast until after a considerable amount of additional kissing.

We have thus far concentrated on the nonverbal courtship behavior of unmarried men and women. Certainly additional volumes can be written on marital nonverbal courtship behavior patterns, as the whole repertoire of messages for inviting or avoiding sexual intercourse is largely nonverbal. For example, some observers have noted that "staying up to watch the late show" is a common method of saying "not tonight."

Morris believes that heterosexual couples in Western culture normally go through a sequence of steps, like the courtship patterns of other animals, on the road to sexual intimacy.[33] Notice the predominant nonverbal theme: (1) eye to body, (2) eye to eye, (3) voice to voice, (4) hand to hand, (5) arm to shoulder, (6) arm to waist, (7) mouth to mouth, (8) hand to head, (9) hand to body, (10) mouth to breast, (11) hand to genitals, (12) genitals to genitals and/or mouth to genitals. Morris, like Nielsen, believes that these steps generally follow the same order although he admits there are variations. One form of skipping steps or moving to a level of intimacy beyond what would be expected is found in socially formalized types of bodily contact—for example, a good-night kiss or a hand-to-hand introduction.

SUMMARY

The term *nonverbal* is commonly used to describe all human communication events that transcend spoken or written words. At the same time we should realize that these nonverbal events and behaviors can be interpreted through verbal symbols. When we consider a classification schema of vocal/nonvocal, verbal/nonverbal, acoustic/nonacoustic, respiratory/nonrespiratory we learn to expect something less than discrete category placement. Instead we might more appropriately put these behaviors on continua with some behaviors overlapping two continua.

The theoretical writings and research on nonverbal communication can be broken down into the following seven areas: (1) body motion or kinesics (emblems, illustrators, affect displays, regulators, and adaptors), (2) physical characteristics, (3) touching behavior, (4) paralanguage (vocal qualities and vocalizations), (5) proxemics, (6) artifacts, (7) environment. Nonverbal communication should not be studied as an isolated unit, but as an inseparable part of the total communication process. Nonverbal communication may serve to repeat, contradict, substitute, complement, accent, or regulate verbal communication. Nonverbal communication is important because of the role it plays in the total communication system, the tremendous quantity of informational cues it gives in any particular situation, and because of its use in fundamental areas of our daily life.

NOTES

1. O. Pfungst, *Clever Hans, The Horse of Mr. Von Osten* (New York: Holt, Rinehart and Winston, 1911).

2. A. Mehrabian, *Nonverbal Communication* (Chicago: Aldine-Atherton, 1972), p. 2.

3. In various verbal and nonverbal studies over the last three decades, dimensions similar to Mehrabian's have been consistently reported by investigators from diverse fields studying diverse phenomena. It is reasonable to conclude, therefore, that these three dimensions seem to be basic responses to our environment and are reflected in the way we assign meaning to both verbal and nonverbal behavior. Cf. A. Mehrabian, "A Semantic Space for Nonverbal Behavior," *Journal of Consulting and Clinical Psychology* 35 (1970): 248–257; and A. Mehrabian, *Silent Messages* (Belmont, Calif.: Wadsworth, 1971).

4. P. Ekman and W. V. Friesen, "The Repertoire of Nonverbal Behavior: Categories, Origins, Usage and Coding," *Semiotica* 1 (1969): 49-98. Also see the following for updated reports with specific research foci: P. Ekman and W. V. Friesen, "Hand Movements," *Journal of Communication* 22 (1972): 353–374 and P. Ekman and W. V. Friesen, "Nonverbal Behavior and Psychopathology," in R. J. Friedman and M. M. Katz (eds.), *The Psychology of Depression: Contemporary Theory and Research* (Washington, D.C.: Winston & Sons, 1974).

5. One treatment of emblems per se can be found in P. Ekman, "Movements with Precise Meanings," *Journal of Communication* 26 (1976): 14–26. Figures 1.1, 1.2, and the research reported in this section are drawn primarily from this work. Additional information on American emblems can be found in Chapter 6.

6. A. A. Cohen and R. Harrison, "Intentionality in the Use of Hand Illustrators in Face-to-Face Communication Situations," *Journal of Personality and Social Psychology* 28 (1973):276–279. See also A. A. Cohen, "The Communicative Functions of Hand Illustrators," *Journal of Communication* 27 (1977):54–63.

7. For a summary of these efforts, see J. M. Wiemann and M. L. Knapp, "Turn-Taking in Conversations," *Journal of Communication* 25 (1975): 75–92.

8. M. L. Knapp, R. P. Hart, G. W. Friedrich, and G. M. Shulman, "The Rhetoric of Goodbye: Verbal and Nonverbal Correlates of Human Leave-Taking," *Speech Monographs* 40 (1973): 182–198. A more complete elaboration of this and related studies dealing with regulators can be found in Chapter 6.

9. G. L. Trager, "Paralanguage: A First Approximation," *Studies in Linguistics* 13 (1958):1–12.

10. M. Argyle, *Social Interaction* (New York: Atherton Press, 1969), pp. 70–71.

11. M. Argyle, *Bodily Communication* (New York: International Universities Press, 1975).

12. See, P. Ekman, "Communication Through Nonverbal Behavior: A Source of Information About an Interpersonal Relationship," in *Affect, Cognition*

and Personality, edited by S. S. Tomkins and C. E. Izard (New York: Springer, 1965).

13. A sometimes subtle inconsistency can also be perceived within verbal communications. When you are trying to express an idea with which you basically disagree, the linguistic choices may reflect differences in directness—for example, "John has done good work" is less direct than "John does good work." See M. Wiener and A. Mehrabian, *Language Within Language* (New York: Appleton-Century-Crofts, 1968).

14. Some evidence to support this notion is found in the following two sources: E. Tabor, "Decoding of Consistent and Inconsistent Attitudes in Communication" (Ph.D. diss., Illinois Institute of Technology, 1970); and A. Mehrabian, "Inconsistent Messages and Sarcasm," in A. Mehrabian, *Nonverbal Communication* (Chicago: Aldine-Atherton, 1972), pp. 104–132. For an understanding of the cognitive processes used in interpreting inconsistent messages, see: D. E. Bugental, "Interpretations of Naturally Occurring Discrepancies Between Words and Intonation: Modes of Inconsistency Resolution," *Journal of Personality and Social Psychology* 30 (1974): 125–133.

15. See pages 4-9 for a discussion of our level of awareness of various nonverbal behaviors.

16. D. E. Bugental, J. W. Kaswan, L. R. Love, and M. N. Fox, "Child Versus Adult Perception of Evaluative Messages in Verbal, Vocal, and Visual Channels," *Developmental Psychology* 2 (1970): 367–375. Also see D. E. Bugental, L. R. Love, and R. M. Gianette, "Perfidious Feminine Faces," *Journal of Personality and Social Psychology* 17 (1971): 314–318.

17. J. G. Shapiro, "Responsivity to Facial and Linguistic Cues," *Journal of Communication* 18 (1968): 11–17; L. Vande Creek and J. T. Watkins, "Responses to Incongruent Verbal and Nonverbal Emotional Cues," *Journal of Communication* 22 (1972): 311–316; and D. Solomon and F. A. Ali, "Influence of Verbal Content and Intonation on Meaning Attributions of First-And-Second-Language Speakers," *Journal of Social Psychology* 95 (1975): 3–8.

18. D. E. Bugental, L. R. Love, J. W. Kaswan, and C. April, "Verbal-Nonverbal Conflict in Parental Messages to Normal and Disturbed Children," *Journal of Abnormal Psychology* 77 (1971): 6–10.

19. N. G. Beakel and A. Mehrabian, "Inconsistent Communications and Psychopathology," *Journal of Abnormal Psychology* 74 (1969): 126–130.

20. P. Ekman, "Body Position, Facial Expression and Verbal Behavior During Interviews," *Journal of Abnormal and Social Psychology* 68 (1964): 194–301. Also P. Ekman and W. V. Friesen, "Head and Body Cues in the Judgment of Emotion: A Reformulation," *Perceptual and Motor Skills* 24 (1967): 711–724.

21. J. M. Wiemann, "An Exploration of Communicative Competence in Initial Interactions: An Experimental Study" (Ph.D. diss., Purdue University, 1975).

22. Vocal cues involved in the turn-taking mechanism are treated in Chapter 10 and kinesic signals are listed in Chapter 6. For further reading in this area, see S. Duncan, "Some Signals and Rules for Taking Turns in Con-

versations," *Journal of Personality and Social Psychology* 23 (1972): 283–292; S. Duncan, "Toward a Grammar for Dyadic Conversation," *Semiotica* 9 (1973): 29–46; and J. M. Wiemann, "An Exploratory Study of Turn-Taking in Conversations: Verbal and Nonverbal Behavior," (M.S. thesis, Purdue University, 1973).

23. P. D. Krivonos and M. L. Knapp, "Initiating Communication: What Do You Say When You Say Hello?" *Central States Speech Journal* 26 (1975): 115–125.

24. Knapp, Hart, Friedrich, and Shulman, "The Rhetoric of Goodbye: Verbal and Nonverbal Correlates of Human Leave-Taking."

25. E. T. Hall, *The Silent Language* (Garden City, N.Y.: Doubleday, 1959).

26. J. Ruesch and W. Kees, *Nonverbal Communication: Notes on the Visual Perception of Human Relations* (Berkeley and Los Angeles, Calif.: University of California Press, 1956).

27. M. J. Saks, "Social Scientists Can't Rig Juries," *Psychology Today* 9 (1976): 48–50, 55–57. Also see R. T. Stein, "Identifying Emergent Leaders from Verbal and Nonverbal Communications," *Journal of Personality and Social Psychology* 32 (1975): 125–135; and P. Ekman, R. M. Liebert, W. V. Friesen, R. Harrison, C. Zlatchin, E. J. Malmstrom, and R. A. Baron, "Facial Expressions of Emotion While Watching Televised Violence as Predictors of Subsequent Aggression" (report to the Surgeon General's Scientific Advisory Committee on Television and Social Behavior, June, 1971).

28. J. McGinniss, *The Selling of the President 1968.* © 1969 by Joemac, Incorporated. Reprinted by permission of The Sterling Lord Agency, Inc. and Simon & Schuster, Inc.

29. At least one study suggests that even experienced teachers are not very successful at this. Cf. J. Jecker, N. Maccoby, M. Breitrose, and E. Rose, "Teacher Accuracy in Assessing Cognitive Visual Feedback from Students," *Journal of Applied Psychology* 48 (1964): 393–397.

30. R. Rosenthal and L. Jacobson, *Pygmalion in the Classroom* (New York: Holt, Rinehart and Winston, 1968).

31. A. E. Scheflen, "Quasi-Courtship Behavior in Psychotherapy," *Psychiatry* 28 (1965): 245–257.

32. G. Nielsen, *Studies in Self-Confrontation* (Copenhagen: Munksgaard; Cleveland: Howard Allen, 1962), pp. 70–71.

33. D. Morris, *Intimate Behavior* (New York: Random House, 1971), pp. 71–101.

ADDITIONAL READINGS

Theories, Summaries, and Overviews

Ekman, P. and W. V. Friesen. "The Repertoire of Nonverbal Behavior: Categories, Origins, Usage, and Coding." *Semiotica* 1 (1969): 49–98.

Henley, N. M. *Body Politics: Power, Sex, and Nonverbal Communication*. Englewood Cliffs, N.J.: Prentice-Hall, 1977.

Knapp, M. L., J. M. Wiemann, and J. A. Daly. "Nonverbal Communication: Issues and Appraisal." *Human Communication Research* 4 (1978): 271–80.

Ruesch, J. and W. Kees, *Nonverbal Communication: Notes on the Visual Perceptions of Human Relations*. Berkeley and Los Angeles, Calif.: University of California Press, 1956.

Sebeok, T. A., A. S. Hayes, and M. C. Bateson (eds.). *Approaches to Semiotics*. The Hague: Mouton, 1964.

Siegman, A. W. and S. Feldstein (eds.) *Nonverbal Behavior and Communication*. Hillsdale, N.J.: Lawrence Erlbaum, 1978.

Weiner, M., S. Devoe, S. Rubinow, and J. Geller. "Nonverbal Behavior and Nonverbal Communication." *Psychological Review* 79 (1972): 185–214.

Bibliographies

Davis, M. *Understanding Body Movement: An Annotated Bibliography*. New York: Arno Press, 1972.

Key, M. R. *Nonverbal Communication: A Research Guide and Bibliography*. (Metuchen, N.J.: Scarecrow Press, 1977).

Textbooks

Argyle, M. *Bodily Communication*. New York: International Universities Press, 1975.

Bosmajian, J. (ed.). *The Rhetoric of Nonverbal Communication*. Glenview, Ill.: Scott-Foresman, 1971.

Burgoon, J. K. and T. Saine. *The Unspoken Dialogue*. Boston: Houghton-Mifflin, 1978.

Harper, R. G., A. N. Wiens, and J. D. Matarazzo. *Nonverbal Communication: The State of the Art*. New York: John Wiley & Sons, 1978.

LaFrance, M. and C. Mayo *Moving Bodies*. Monterey, Calif.: Brooks/Cole, 1978.

Mehrabian, A. *Silent Messages*. Belmont, Calif.: Wadsworth, 1972.

Rosenfeld, L. B. and J. M. Civikly. *With Words Unspoken*. New York: Holt, Rinehart and Winston, 1976.

Weitz, S. (ed.). *Nonverbal Communication: Readings with Commentary*. New York: Oxford University Press, 1974.

Popularized Books for Mass Communication

Davis, F. *Inside Intuition*. New York: McGraw-Hill, 1971.

Morris, D. *Manwatching: A Field Guide to Human Behavior*. New York: Harry N. Abrams, 1977.

NONVERBAL COMMUNICATION: DEVELOPMENTAL PERSPECTIVES

There are no universal gestures. As far as we know, there is no single facial expression, stance or body position which conveys the same meaning in all societies.

R. L. BIRDWHISTELL

As we look back on a long phylogenetic history, which has determined our present day anatomical, physiological, and biochemical status, it would be simply astounding if it were found not to affect our behavior also. *T. K. PITCAIRN and I. EIBL-EIBESFELDT*

Children have been known to put their parents "on the spot" momentarily and to cause a fleeting frustration by innocently asking "Where did I come from?" When these same children reach adulthood, other questions of origin may be of interest—for example, "Am I doing this because of how I was raised or do all human beings do this?" The answers to these latter questions are often rapid, definite, and expressed with missionary zeal. On one side we hear scholars saying that behavior is innate, instinctive, inborn, or genetic; whereas other scholars argue that behavior is acquired, learned, culturally taught, imposed, imitated, or environmentally determined. It is the familiar nature/nurture dichotomy. The quotations that began this chapter aptly illustrate these differing points of view. In the course of this chapter we examine this issue concerning the origins of nonverbal behavior from two perspectives: (1) the roots of nonverbal behavior in human evolutionary history and (2) the roots of nonverbal behavior in our current lifetime.

First, let's look at the dichotomy between innate and learned. As with most dichotomies, proponents of each side lose some of their capacity to explain things by supporting a polarized and inflexible position—trying to squeeze all observations into a single point of view. Instead of looking for a single origin, we might more productively look at the contribution of each side to the manifestation of any given behavior. No doubt much of our nonverbal behavior has both innate and learned (including imitation) aspects to it. Ekman and Friesen, whose work in this area is discussed in detail later, have outlined three primary sources of our nonverbal behavior: (1) inherited neurological programs, (2) experiences common to all members of the species—for example, regardless of culture the hands are used to place food in the mouth, and (3) experience that varies with culture, class, family, or individual.[1]

Biological and cultural forces overlap in many important ways. Some very common biological processes are later used to communicate—for example, breathing becomes a sigh of relief, grief, or boredom; a hiccough becomes an imitation of a drunk's behavior; audible blowing through one's nose may be interpreted as a snort of scorn; coughing becomes "ahem"; and so on. Studies are discussed later in this chapter that suggest that some aspects of our facial expressions or emotion are inherited and are common to other members of the human species. This, however, does not mean that our cultural learning does not also play an important part in these expressions. The neurological program for any given facial expression can be altered or modified by learning display rules that are specific to our culture—for example, men should not cry. Different stimuli may trigger a given facial expression—again depending on one's cultural training. A snake may evoke an expression of fear in one culture and bring out an expression of joy to those who see it as an important source of food. The society we grow up in is also largely responsible for the way we blend two or more emotional expressions— for example, showing some features of surprise and some features of anger at the same time. Lack's study of robins further illustrates this interrelationship between instinct and environment.[2] It seems that the European male robin will attack strange robins that enter its territory during the breeding season. Lack was able to demonstrate with stuffed models that the red breast alone will trigger this attack mechanism. The female robin who shared the nest, however, also had a red breast and was not attacked. Thus, this aggressive behavior, which is believed to be innate, is modified by certain conditions in the environment or the situation that calls forth the response. According to Thorpe, some birds instinctively sing a song common to their own species without ever having heard another bird sing the song.[3] These birds may, upon hearing the songs of their particular group, develop a variation on the melody that reflects a local dialect. And, even though a bird's song may not be learned, the bird may have to learn to whom the call should be addressed, under what circumstances it is to be used, and how to recognize signals from other birds. Much of the inherited components of human behavior can be similarly modified. It is like our human *predisposition for* or *capacity to learn* verbal language.[4] We are born with this capacity to learn language, but language will not be learned without cultural training. Children who have been isolated from human contact have not developed linguistic competence. Some nonverbal signals are probably primarily dependent on inherited neurological programs, whereas others probably depend primarily on environmental learning; of course, many behaviors are influenced by both. Furthermore, some behaviors that are primarily culturally taught at this time in human history may later be transmitted genetically if the behavior plays an important role in the continuance and survival of the species.

Finally, the answer to the nature/nurture issue concerning nonverbal behavior will vary with the behavior under consideration. We've already discussed the multiple origins of facial expressions of emotion. Adaptors may also have an inherited and learned derivation. You will recall that adaptors are habits associated with one's early coping with sensation, excretion, ingestion, grooming, and affect; early experiences in maintaining interpersonal relationships; and performing certain instrumental tasks. Illustrators and regulators, on the other hand, seem to be primarily learned by imitating others. Hence, we would expect to find variations in these behaviors across cultural, class, and ethnic lines. And, although emblems seem to be found in several cultures, most seem to be very culture-specific; that is, they are taught very much as verbal language is taught. Emblems that are observed in more than one culture may occasionally have similar meanings, but usually they have very different ones, for example, the circle made with the index finger and thumb, which communicates "A-OK" to Americans, may signify female genitalia to members of another culture.

THE DEVELOPMENT OF NONVERBAL BEHAVIOR IN HUMAN HISTORY

Human beings, like other species, adapt to changing conditions around them. Some of these adaptations are important to human survival and are passed on from generation to generation. What are the nonverbal behaviors that have ancient roots in human history? On what basis do scientists conclude that a behavior or behavior pattern has an inherited component to it? It is not an easy task. Some of our current behavior displays are only fragments of larger patterns that are no longer enacted in their entirety; some behaviors which are not embedded in rituals have little to do with the original function of the behavior; and some behavior which seems to serve one function may be associated with something completely different—for example, grooming behavior may be the result of confusion or frustration in achieving a goal—rather than being enacted for some self-presentation, courtship, or cleanliness goals. Despite these and other difficult questions, researchers have made some important discoveries. Inferences about whether any given behavior has been inherited and is genetically transmitted to every member of the human species have been made primarily from three research strategies: (1) evidence from sensory deprivation—that is, noting the manifestation of a behavior in blind and/or deaf people who could not have learned it through visual or auditory channels; (2) evidence from nonhuman primates—that is, showing an evolutionary continuity of a behavior up to and including our closest relatives, nonhuman primates; and (3) evidence from multicultural studies, that is, observing the manifestation of similar behaviors used for similar purposes in other cultures around the world—literate and preliterate. Obviously, if we are able to compile evidence in all three categories our confidence in an inherited dimension reaches the highest level of confidence. At present, few behaviors have been studied with such thoroughness, nor do we know much about how innate and learned factors combine and interact during infancy. Nevertheless, we can derive some important inferences from studies in each area.

Evidence from Sensory Deprivation.   Many have observed the early appearance of nonverbal behavior in children. These behaviors may just be learned quickly. In order to verify this hypothesis, we need to examine children who, because of their being blind and deaf at birth, could not learn these behaviors from visual or auditory cues. Eibl-Eibesfeldt began filming the behavior of several blind/deaf children in 1966.[5] His conclusions are similar to those of others who systematically compared the behavior of blind/deaf children with sighted/hearing children. In short, the spontaneous expressions of sadness, crying, laughing, smiling, pouting, anger, surprise, and fear are not significantly different in blind/deaf children as compared to sighted hearing children. Smiling, crying and laughing sequences of blind/deaf children filmed by Eibl-Eibesfeldt are shown in Figures 2.1, 2.2, and 2.3.

Some might argue that such expressions could be learned by touching or by a slow reinforcement program. Eibl-Eibesfeldt points out, however, that even thalidomide babies who had no arms and children who could hardly be taught to raise a spoon to their mouth showed similar expressions.

In addition to facial expressions, these blind/deaf children sought contact with others by stretching out one or both hands and they wanted to be embraced and caressed when distressed. As the pictures in Figure 2.4 reveal, these children showed a remarkably familar sequence of refusal gestures.

Eibl-Eibesfeldt also reports some interesting eye patterns of blind

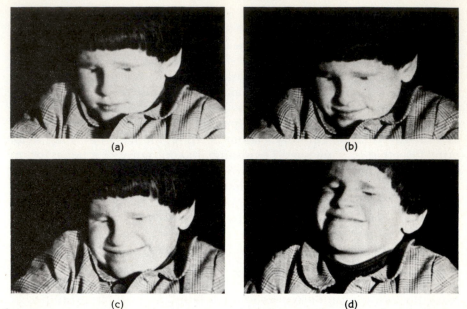

(a) (b)

(c) (d)

FIGURE 2.1

Eibl-Eibesfeldt's film of a blind/deaf smiling response. The head is lifted and tilted back as the intensity increases. From I. Eibl-Eibesfeldt, "The Expressive Behavior of the Blind-and-Deaf-Born," in M. von Cranach and I. Vine (eds.), *Social Communication and Movement* (New York: Academic Press, 1973).

children. When he complimented a ten-year-old girl on her piano playing, she looked at him, coyly looked down and away and then looked at him again. A similar sequence was recorded for an eleven-year-old blind boy when asked about his girl friend. This sequence of turning toward and away is also seen in sighted children under similar circumstances.

Naturally, blind/deaf children also show differences. The blind/deaf children do not show subtle gradations in expressions—for example, an expression may appear and suddenly disappear leaving the face blank. Some have noted that the expressions of blind/deaf children are more restricted or restrained—for example, softer crying, and laughing that resembles a giggle. Blind/deaf children also show fewer facial expressions generally, with facial blends being notably absent. Finally, when blind/deaf children are asked to act out or mimic certain facial expressions they show less ability than sighted/hearing children.

After reviewing an extensive body of literature dealing with studies of normal, feral, isolated, institutionalized, and blind/deaf children, Charlesworth and Kreutzer conclude:

. . . both the environment and innate factors have effects on expressive behavior. The environment may influence the time at which a behavior appears (many smiling individuals around a newborn may accelerate the

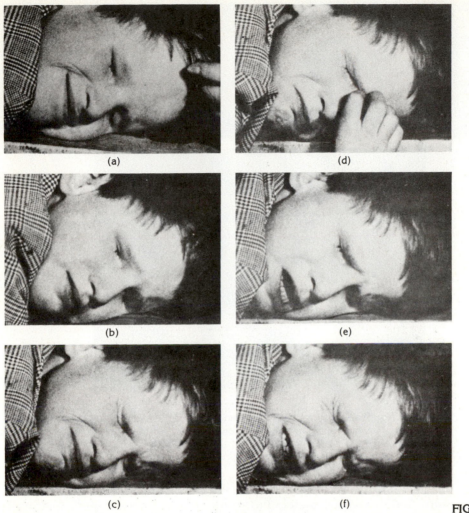

FIGURE 2.2

Blind/deaf crying response filmed by Eibl-Eibesfeldt. From T. K. Pitcairn and I. Eibl-Eibesfeldt, "Concerning the Evolution of Nonverbal Communication in Man," in M. E. Hahn and E. C. Simmel (eds.), *Communicative Behavior and Evolution* (New York: Academic Press, 1976).

appearance of the first social smile and may determine how often the behavior occurs once it first appears). The innate factors, on the other hand, seem to be mainly responsible for the morphological characteristics of expressive behaviors (and hence the fact that they occur at all as such) and for the connections such behaviors have to the emotional states associated with them.[6]

Evidence from Nonhuman Primates. Human beings are primates, but so are apes and monkeys. If we observe our nonhuman primate relatives

31

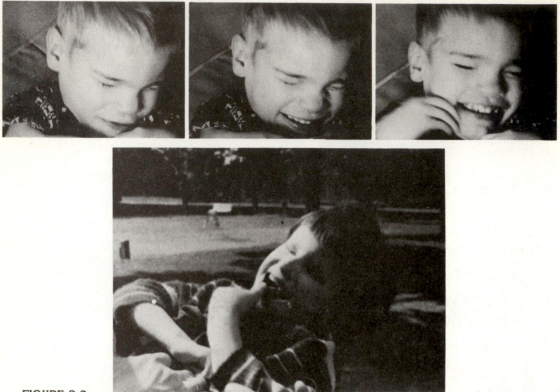

FIGURE 2.3

Laughing response of blind/deaf children filmed by Eibl-Eibesfeldt. From I. Eibl-Eibesfeldt in M. von Cranach and I. Vine (eds.), *Social Communication and Movement* (New York: Academic Press, 1973).

who manifest behaviors similar to ours in similar situations, we have more confidence that such behavior has origins in our evolutionary past.

Before we emphasize the similarities, we should acknowledge some important differences in the behavior of human and nonhuman primates. Humans make little use of changes in body color, but have an extensive repertoire of gestures that attend their verbal language. Humans also seem to have a greater variety of facial blends. Our response repertoire is not nearly so limited to immediate and direct stimuli. And, although other animals are capable of complex acts, the level of complexity, control, and modification shown by humans may be hard to match, for example, smiling for purposes of ingratiation as well as to show pleasure.

Behavioral similarities are often linked to common biological and social problems that confront human and nonhuman primates—for example, mating, grooming, avoiding pain, expressing emotional states, rearing children, cooperating in groups, developing leadership hierarchies, defending, establishing contact, maintaining relationships, and so

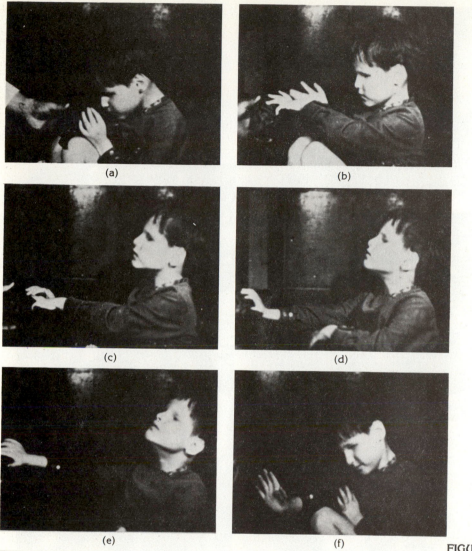

(a) (b)

(c) (d)

(e) (f)

FIGURE 2.4

A blind/deaf child refusing an offer of a tortoise. The child sniffs at the object and pushes it back while simultaneously lifting her head in a movement of withdrawal. Finally she puts out her hand in a gesture of warding off. Filmed by Eibl-Eibesfeldt. From I. Eibl-Eibesfeldt, in M. von Cranach and I. Vine (eds.), *Social Communication and Movement* (New York: Academic Press, 1973).

on. Figure 2.5 shows some of these similarities in grooming and bodily contact. Many behaviors might be explored for evolutionary roots.[7] We will focus on facial expressions of emotion.

Table 2.1 provides both written and visual descriptions of probable evolutionary paths for facial displays of anger in four living primates. Only those expressions that show some continuity are pictured. Other

33

FIGURE 2.5

Upper left: Sonjo children clasping each other in fright; Middle left: Rhesus monkey mother with child; Upper right: An approximately four-year-old female with an older male chimpanzee; Middle right: A human couple; Lower left: Social grooming of vervet monkeys; Lower right: Social grooming among Bali women. All photographs except the two chimpanzees were taken by I. Eibl-Eibesfeldt. From I. Eibl-Eibesfeldt, *Ethology: The Biology of Behavior,* 2nd ed. (New York: Holt, Rinehart and Winston, 1975). Photograph of the chimpanzees by Baron Hugo van Lawick, © National Geographic Society. Originally published in Jane Goodall, *My Friends the Wild Chimpanzees,* National Geographic Society, p. 86.

anger and threat expressions made by nonhuman primates do not seem to appear in human behavior. Chevalier-Skolnikoff has proposed similar evolutionary chains for expressions of happiness (smiling and laughter) and sadness (with crying and without).[8] Although humans have smaller and more discrete facial muscles, some of the similarities in the facial displays of humans to the nonhuman primates are striking. The activity that evokes the facial expression may also have similarities among the primates, for example, aggression, play, and the like. Like humans, nonhuman primates may accompany their emotional displays in the face with complementary cues in other body regions—for example, raised hair, muscle tenseness, and the like. And varying degrees of intensity (and blending) can be produced by nonhuman primates as well. Like humans, other primates can have the same facial display decoded in very different ways in different contexts, for example, a subordinate male monkey being chased by a dominant one can get the dominant monkey to leave by showing an expression of fear, but if the dominant male shows this fear expression while approaching a subordinate male, the subordinate may approach and embrace him. Finally, similarities can be observed in primate brains, that is, the parts of the brain that seem to mediate emotional responses in humans also seem to mediate facial expressions in nonhuman primates.

Many of the facial expressions in humans have evolved from non-communicative behaviors such as attacks, movements toward or away from things, self-protective movements, and movements associated with respiration and vision. Chevalier-Skolnikoff argues, for instance, that "threat postures of most primates contain elements derived from attack (mouth open and ready for biting) and locomotion toward (body musculature tense and ready to advance), while the submissive postures contain elements derived from protective responses (retraction of lips and ears) and locomotion away from the sender." Thus, a behavior such as flight from an enemy, which was originally critical to survival, may eventually become associated with feelings of fear and/or anger. It is possible, then, that an expression of fear and/or anger may appear even if the original behavior (fleeing) is unnecessary, for example, a monkey that feels fearful when approaching a female to copulate. The facial display has, over time, become associated with a particular feeling state and appears when that feeling state is aroused. Those animals who substituted facial expressions of threat for actual attack and fighting probably had a higher survival rate and, in turn, passed on this tendency to succeeding generations. In like manner, our heavy dependence on signals received visually (rather than through smell, for instance) may have been especially adaptive as our ancestors moved into open areas and increased in physical size.

Evidence from Multicultural Studies. If we can observe human beings in different environments with different cultural guidelines encoding and/

35

TABLE 2.1
A Between-Species Analysis and Probable Evolutionary Paths for
Facial Expressions of Anger

LEMURS	MACAQUES	CHIMPANZEES	HUMAN BEINGS
	Confident Dominant Threat; Anger Type I; "Stare" Eyes wide open; direct gaze; frequently with eye-to-eye contact. Brow often raised and lowered. Ears forward. Jaws closed; lips tightly closed.	Confident Dominant Threat; Anger; Type I; "Glare" Direct gaze. Jaw closed; lips closed.	Anger; Type I: "Angry Face" Direct gaze, frequently with eye-to-eye contact; no sclera (white part of eye) showing above and below iris (colored part of eye); upper lids sometimes tense and squared; lower lids sometimes tense and squared; lower lids raised and tensed, often producing a squint. Brows lowered and pulled together. Jaws clenched; lips contracted vertically and tightly pressed together.

or decoding certain nonverbal behaviors in a similar manner, we develop increasing confidence that inherited components of the species may be responsible.

Because human beings around the world share certain biological and social functions, it should not be surprising to find areas of similarity among them. We've already mentioned the multicultural observations of emblems dealing with eating, sleeping, overeating, and pointing. Beier and Zautra report the decoding of vocal cues of emotion to have agreement across cultures.[9] Eibl-Eibesfeldt suggests that we might find entire sequences of behavior to manifest cross-cultural similarities—for example, coyness, flirting, embarrassment, openhanded greetings, a low-

TABLE 2.1
A Between-Species Analysis and Probable Evolutionary Paths for
Facial Expressions of Anger *(continued)*

LEMURS	MACAQUES	CHIMPANZEES	HUMAN BEINGS
Subordinate Threat; Fear-Anger	Subordinate Threat; Fear-Anger; "Bared-Teeth Stare."	Subordinate Threat; Fear-Anger; "Scream Calls"	"Anger; Type II; "Anger Face"
Alternation of jaws open and lips contracted, covering the teeth and lips retracted horizontally producing a "grin." Invariably accompanied by "shrieks."	Eyes wide open; alternation of direct gaze, often with eye-to-eye contact, and gaze avoidance. Brow lowered; forehead retracted. Ears back. Jaws and teeth repeatedly opened and closed; lips retracted vertically and horizontally, displaying the teeth. Often accompanied by "high-pitched scream."	Jaws half or wide open; lips retracted vertically and horizontally, displaying the teeth. Often accompanied by "screams."	Direct gaze; frequently with eye-to-eye contact; no sclera showing; upper lids appearing lowered; upper lids sometimes tense and squared; lower lids raised and tensed, often producing a squint. Brows lowered and pulled together. Jaws moderately open; lips moderately contracted vertically and horizontally and extended, forming a rectangular opening with teeth showing.

The information and drawings in Table 2.1 can be found in S. Chevalier-Skolnikoff, "Facial Expression of Emotion in Nonhuman Primates," in P. Ekman (ed.), *Darwin and Facial Expression* (New York: Academic Press, 1973). Drawn by Eric Stoelting.

ered posture for communicating submission, and so on. On the other hand, the role of one's culture will surely contribute heavily to differences in nonverbal behavior because the circumstances that elicit the behavior will vary and the cultural norms and rules that govern the management of behavior will differ. Here we detail two behaviors that seem to have widespread documentation in a variety of cultures.

Eibl-Eibesfeldt has identified what he calls the "eyebrow-flash."[10]

He has observed this rapid raising of the eyebrows (maintained for about one-sixth of a second before lowering) among Europeans, Balinese, Papuans, Samoans, South American Indians, Bushmen, and others (see Figure 2.6). Although it can often be seen in friendly greeting behavior, this behavior has also been seen when people are giving approval or agreeing, seeking confirmation, flirting, thanking, and when beginning and/or emphasizing a statement. The common denominator seems to be a yes to social contact—requesting or approving such contact. Smiles and nods sometimes accompany this gesture. Some Japanese, however, are reported to suppress the gesture as an indecent behavior. There are, however, other instances of eyebrow raising that seem to indicate disapproval, indignation, or admonishment. These "no" eyebrow signals are

a   b   c   d

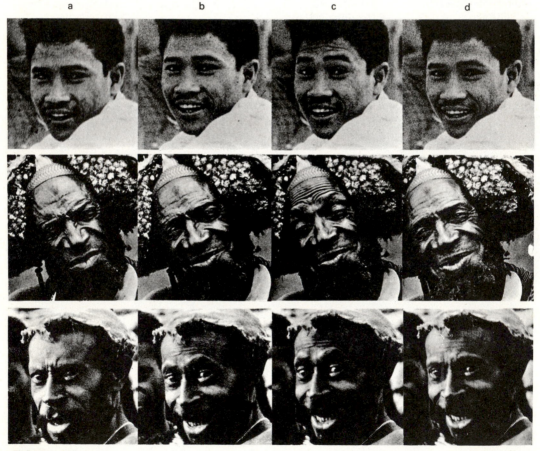

FIGURE 2.6

Eyebrow-flash during friendly greetings. Filmed by I. Eibl-Eibesfeldt. From I. Eibl-Eibesfeldt, *Ethology: The Biology of Behavior,* 2nd. ed. (New York: Holt, Rinehart and Winston, 1975).

often accompanied by a stare and/or head lift with a lowering of the eyelids—signaling a shutting off of contact. When Eibl-Eibesfeldt first observed eyebrow lifting in some Old World monkeys, he began to speculate on the possible evolutionary development. He reasoned that in both the yes and no displays a similar purpose was being served, that is, calling attention to someone or letting someone know (for sure) that he or she was being looked at. When we display the expression of surprise, for instance, we raise our eyebrows and call attention to the object of our surprise. It may be a friendly surprise or an annoyed surprise.

Perhaps the most conclusive evidence supporting the universality of facial expressions is found in the work of Ekman and his colleagues.[11] Photographs of thirty faces expressing happiness, fear, surprise, sadness, anger, and disgust/contempt were presented to people in five literate cultures. Faces were selected on the basis of meeting specific criteria for facial musculature associated with such expressions. As shown in Table 2.2, there was generally high agreement among the respondents regarding which faces fit which emotions. Ekman also asked his subjects to rate the intensity of each emotion and found no significant differences between the five cultures. Because these people were exposed to the mass media, one might argue that they may have learned to recognize unique aspects of faces in other cultures. However, in several studies with preliterate people (New Guinea) who did not have contact with the mass media and who had been almost completely isolated from contact with Western culture, Ekman found results comparable to those found in literate Eastern and Western cultures. In these studies, stories were told to the subjects who were then asked to select one of three facial photographs that reflected the emotion of the story. Distinguishing fear from surprise was the most difficult discrimination to make. Perhaps, as Ekman says, fearful events in this culture are often surprising too. When Ekman obtained photographs of expressions made by these New Guineans and asked North Americans to judge them, the North Americans accurately decoded all the expressions with high levels of

TABLE 2.2
Judgments of Emotion in Five Literate Cultures

	JAPAN	BRAZIL	CHILE	ARGENTINA	UNITED STATES
Happiness	87%	97%	90%	94%	97%
Fear	71	77	78	68	88
Surprise	87	82	88	93	91
Anger	63	82	76	72	69
Disgust/Contempt	82	86	85	79	82
Sadness	74	82	90	85	73
NUMBER OF SUBJECTS	29	40	119	168	99

accuracy—with the exception of fear, which was often judged as surprise, and vice versa.

Finally, Ekman and his co-workers sought to answer the question of whether only posed expressions of emotions were universally understood and manifested. Thus, spontaneous facial expressions were obtained from Japanese and North American subjects who watched a neutral and a stress-provoking film. The subjects showed similar facial configurations while they were alone watching the film, but during an interview with a member of their own culture the Japanese tended to mask their originally negative responses with polite smiles more than the North American subjects.

Although Ekman's program of research is perhaps the most complete, other studies of other cultures support his findings. Thus, there does seem to be a universal association between particular facial muscular patterns and discrete emotions. It should be noted that this is only a specific element of universality and does not suggest that all aspects of facial affect displays are universal. As Ekman and Friesen testify:

> . . . we believe that, while the facial muscles which move when a particular affect is aroused are the same across cultures, the evoking stimuli, the linked effects, the display rules and the behavioral consequences all can vary enormously from one culture to another.[12]

Thus far we've explored three areas of research, none of which singly offer "proof" of innate or inherited aspects for nonverbal behavior. When data is uncovered in each area, however, it provides the most conclusive evidence possible at this time. The primary facial expressions of emotion seem to meet this stringent test: They manifest themselves in children deprived of sight and hearing, in nonhuman primates, and in literate and preliterate cultures around the world. In view of such findings it would be hard to deny the existence of a genetic component passed along to members of the human species. Although the data supporting inherited aspects for other behaviors that have been reviewed is not currently as overwhelming, some strong indications have been noted. In keeping with the developmental perspective of this chapter, we now consider studies that have examined nonverbal behavior manifested during the early phases of the life span.

THE DEVELOPMENT OF NONVERBAL BEHAVIOR IN CHILDREN

The development of human speech has received considerably more attention than the development and origin of nonverbal behaviors. We do know that during the first few years of a child's life, an extensive repertoire of nonverbal signals is exhibited; we also know that shortly after birth the child is learning to interpret various nonverbal signals received from others. The following overview is not meant to be a comprehensive treatment of nonverbal behavior manifested by neonates, infants, children, and adolescents; instead we attempt to highlight only some of the research and thinking in each of the areas treated later in this book.

Body Movements.   Dittmann noticed that adults sometimes believe that children are not listening to them and badger them accordingly with questions like, "Did you hear me?" Dittmann reasoned that this common adult-child perception may be associated with what he calls "listener responses"—for example, head nods, some eyebrow raises, some types of smiles, "yeah," "I see," and so on.[13] His study of children in grades 1, 3, and 5 found these listener responses to be nearly absent except under "the strongest social pull" by the other interactant. Subsequent studies indicated the major deficiencies were in "m-hm" and head-nod responses. By the eighth grade a dramatic increase in these listener responses is found. Now the early adolescent's peers are beginning to lengthen their response duration (providing more opportunity for such listener responses); the "response pull" from adult interactants is increasing; and there is a continuing movement away from a purely self-orientation and toward imagining instead what others are going through.

Two research projects have focused on the use of emblems by children. Michael and Willis[14] asked children between the ages of four and seven to try to communicate the following messages without talking: "go away," "come here," "yes," "no," "be quiet," "how many," "how big," shape (for example, round or square), "I don't know," "good-bye," "hi," and "let me have your attention." They also tested the decoding ability of the children. In general, their results show that these children were better interpreters than senders, that children with a year of school experience were better than preschool children, and that middle-class children showed a proficiency that lower-class children didn't. Kumin and Lazar presented a videotape of thirty emblems to two groups.[15] One group was aged three to three and a half; whereas the ages in the other group ranged between four and four and a half. In addition, observations of these same children were made in a nursery school free-play setting to see what emblems they actually used. Generally, the ability to interpret emblems increased significantly from age three to three and a half to age four to four and a half. Boys seemed to accurately interpret a greater number of emblems in the younger group, but girls scored better in the older group. Four-year-old children of both sexes accurately interpreted the following emblems: "yes," "no," "come here," "quiet," "good-bye," "two," "I won't listen," blowing a kiss, "I'm going to sleep," and "I won't do it." None of the four-year-olds were able to accurately decode "crazy." Three children in the three to three-and-a-

TABLE 2.3
Emblems Most Frequently Observed in Children's Free Play

	3–3½ YEAR OLDS	4–4½ YEAR OLDS
BOTH GIRLS AND BOYS	"I don't know."	"I don't know."
	"Yes."	———
	"No."	"No."
	"I'm tired."	———
	"Come here."	"Come here."
	"Stop."	———
	"Naughty."	———
	"Quiet."	"Quiet."
	"Out."	"Out."
	"Hello."	"Hello."
	———	"I won't listen."
	———	Blow kiss.
	———	"I won't do it."
BOYS PRIMARILY	Fist shaking.	Fist shaking.
GIRLS PRIMARILY	"Go out."	———

half-year-old group could not interpret a single emblem. Older children did not seem to use more emblems than the younger age group, but girls at both age levels sent more emblems in free play. The most frequently used emblems by both groups are listed in Table 2.3.

Physical Appearance. At a very early age, children seem capable of making distinctions on the basis of physical appearance. Golomb found that most children at age two could not model a human figure out of clay, but by the end of the third year of life only a small percentage of children was unable to complete the task.[16] Before a child reaches age five, distinctions between skin color and incongruities in dress (for example, going barefoot in a wedding dress) are being made. Most of the research in this area has focused on general physical attractiveness and reactions to various body builds.

In Chapter 5 considerable evidence is cited to support the notion that people seem to agree generally on who is physically attractive and who isn't. When does this develop? According to Cavior and Lombardi, cultural guidelines for physical attractiveness are pretty well established by age six.[17] It is not surprising, then, to find peer popularity and physical attractiveness highly correlated in a number of elementary and secondary schools. Dion found that antisocial behavior (for example, throwing a brick through a window) was seen differently for attractive and unattractive children.[18] The transgression was seen as an enduring trait of the unattractive child, but only a temporary problem for the attractive one. The act was also evaluated more negatively for the unattractive child. It does not surprise us, then, to find that juvenile delinquents were also rated as lower on attractiveness. The perceptions of attractiveness in a child's world are not limited to his or her peers. Teachers tend to see attractive children as more intelligent, more socially adept, higher in educational potential, and more positive in their attitudes toward school—even though the unattractive children used in the study had similar academic performance records.

Perceptions of body builds (endomorphs, ectomorphs, and mesomorphs) have also been studied developmentally. As early as kindergarten, children seem to prefer the more muscular mesomorph to either the thin or fat body types.[19] Youngsters seem to have a particular aversion to the fat physiques. Older children who selected descriptive adjectives for these body types tended to see the mesomorph as "all things good," with ectomorphs and endomorphs attracting a host of unfavorable descriptors. Ten- and eleven-year-olds seemed to consider body build as a more important characteristic in judging physical appearance than such things as deformities, disfigurations, and handicaps.[20] The psychological aversion to chubby figures results in children maintaining a greater physical distance from them.[21] In turn, we find that chubby children often tend to have a negative perception of their own bodies, which may later generalize to a negative self-image.[22]

Eye Behavior. An infant responds positively to its mother's eyes very early. Eye-to-eye contact between mother and child may even occur as early as the fourth week of life.[23] During the first two months, a smiling response can be elicited from the infant with a mask that portrays the eyes with two dots; the same response, however, will not occur with a real face in which the eyes are covered.[24] It is not clear to what extent these eye patterns are innate, but it seems fair to conclude that the mutual gaze, the breaking of gaze, and facial responsiveness are crucial elements in establishing primitive bases for social relationships—even though the gaze duration may be fairly short. Pupil dilation has also been observed. At one month of age increased dilation occurs in response to faces; at four months the increased dilation is particularized to the mother's face.[25]

Although a number of researchers have been interested in eye behavior during infancy, childhood gazing patterns have received very little attention, and the two studies available seem to disagree on whether there is a gradually increasing or gradually decreasing trend in looking up to adolescence.[26] Data from both studies, however, do show that adolescence represents a low point for eye gazing. Finally, Levine and Sutton-Smith suggest that we may find children less likely than adults to look at the beginnings and ends of their utterances.

Personal Space. From birth, the developing child is exposed to gradually increasing distances for various communication situations. The first few years provide a familiarity with what Hall calls "intimate" distance (see Chapter 4); then the child learns appropriate conversational distances for an increasing number of acquaintances obtained from family, neighborhood, and school; and by about age seven the child may have incorporated the concept of "public" distance into his or her behavioral repertoire. Several studies tend to support this notion. For instance, when three-, five-, and seven-year-olds were asked to sit next to an unknown peer working on a task, the three-year-olds sat significantly closer—sometimes touching the unknown peer.[27] Other studies using simulations, laboratory observations, and field observations tend to find younger children seeking less interaction distance.[28] By around the third grade, however, the gradually increasing interaction distance seems to stabilize—more closely reflecting adult norms. Like any generalization, the preceding developmental pattern will be modified by many factors. A child may learn patterns of conversational spacing in an ethnic environment and incorporate patterns of the larger culture at a later time.[29]

The sex of the child may also influence early interaction distancing. Sometimes the different experiences of males and females will manifest themselves in different spatial needs. Some observers have suggested that the same stimuli may cause parents to put male infants on the floor or in a playpen, but to hug or put the females in a nearby high chair. Boys, too, are frequently given toys that seem to encourage activities which demand more space—often away from the confines of the home itself—for example, footballs, cars, trains, and the like. Girls, on the other hand, may receive dolls, dollhouses, and other domestic toys that require less space and encourage activity directed toward the home environment.[30] Observations of children at play tend to confirm the notion that many males learn the need for and use of greater territory at early ages. Boys spend more time outside, enter more areas than the girls, and maintain between 1.2 and 1.6 times the amount of space that females do.[31]

Studies that have examined interaction distances with specific others during childhood offer few surprises. Greater distances seem to be maintained with teachers and unknown adults, endomorphs, and unfriendly and/or threatening persons; closer distances are maintained with caretakers in unfamiliar environments. And, as social density increases, children tend to interact less and some may show increased aggressive tendencies.[32]

Vocalizations. Newborns begin making sounds almost immediately. The infant's first cries are undifferentiated and reflexive. But soon the influence of the infant's environment is shown and cries begin to show differences related to the motivation for crying, for example, pain, anger, and frustration. Other sounds, like laughter, cooing, and gurgling are produced, but our focus is on those sounds that are antecedent to and later attend spoken language—that is, pitch, pauses, loudness, and tempo.

At approximately three months of age, the child enters a stage called "babbling." Here the child is playfully experimenting with and exercising his or her sound-making equipment. Some sounds will be produced during this time that will not be reinforced by speakers of the child's native language and thus will receive minimal use later in life. Some believe that there is also an experimentation with intonation patterns at this stage—for example, expressing emotions, asking questions, and showing excitement through sounds alone. At the very least the child is imitating perceived differences in pitch levels. Lieberman, who recorded and analyzed samples of babbling for changes in pitch, noted that infant pitch levels varied with the sex of the parent—lower for the father and higher for the mother.[33] Further, pitch levels were lower when the child was "conversing" (parent present) than when babbling alone. Others have observed that when adults are talking to children their pitch level will rise; even older children will sometimes raise their pitch when interacting with younger children. At roughly six months, the infant begins to imitate his or her own sounds—again for pleasure and practice. At approximately eight months, the child increases his or her imitations of sounds made by others—and is rewarded accordingly. From this point on, the development of vocalizations necessary for human speech communication is a matter of practice and refinement.

Pitch goes through a number of changes from birth to puberty. A study of infants in their natural environments, using sophisticated recording equipment, found that during the first month of life pitch tended to decrease steadily.[34] During the second month pitch began to rise and kept rising until about four months. Generally, however, there is a gradual lowering of pitch that continues throughout childhood. At the onset of puberty, both male and female voices show a lowering of pitch—but the change for males is often dramatic.

Pause patterns seem to be well established when the child enters school. A study in which pause patterns in the speech of children five to twelve years of age were compared found no significant differences.[35] Tempo and loudness features also seem to be firmly established by the time children enter kindergarten.[36]

Thus far we have focused on the production of sounds. How do children interpret or respond to vocal cues? Perhaps the first indication of responsiveness to adult voices is in the seemingly synchronized movement of babies as young as twelve hours old with rhythmic adult speech.[37] It is believed that by the age of three months, infants behave as if they knew that they were the objects of the mothers' voices. And other work suggests that these first months are not too early for the infant to respond differently to friendly versus hostile voices, inflected versus noninflected voices, and baby talk versus normal talk.[38] Another study, using over two hundred children between five and twelve years old examined the ability of these youngsters to accurately interpret vocalized emotions. The words were the same; the vocal tone was varied. As the age of the child increased, the ability to accurately interpret vocal emotional expressions also increased. Sadness was most frequently identified correctly—followed by anger, happiness, and love. There was no marked pattern of correct or incorrect responses by age level, suggesting about the same rate of development, in terms of understanding, for all the emotions studied.[39]

Facial Expressions.   Exactly when the human infant begins to respond differentially to facial expressions in others is now well documented. At least two excellent reviews of this body of literature are available.[40] Recognition studies with infants usually rely on mean attention time and eye movement photography to form the bases for inferences about reactions. Although the infant does fixate on a few facial features, it is not until somewhere between two and five months that full facial scanning takes place. At about the middle of the infant's first year, it is making some discriminations of some aspects of facial expressions, and by the end of the first year facial expressions are probably recognized quite well—as long as they are pronounced and accompanied by the appropriate gestures and vocalizations. This generalization seems to be supported by a study of infants aged four, six, eight, and ten months.[41] The experimenter acted out angry, happy, sad, and "neutral" facial expressions—accompanied by the appropriate vocalizations. Videotapes were made of the infants' responses. At four months, reactions were indiscriminate; at six months (and beyond) infants seemed to discriminate between the expressions, sometimes mirroring the response given them. It is not clear from this research the extent to which the infants were responding to the face alone. An early recognition study conducted by Gates is reported because, although methodological problems did exist, the findings have not been seriously challenged.[42] This study also suggests that recognition of various expressions of emotion will occur at different ages with different expressions. Over four hundred children from age three to fourteen were shown adult photographs of emotional expressions. The youngest group could accurately identify only laughter. The majority were able to identify pain by the age of five or six, and anger at about age seven. Most of the children could not identify fear until nine or ten, and identification of surprise came a year later. At age fourteen a majority could still not identify scorn.

Tentatively, we can also suggest some approximate ages at which children will produce facial expressions of emotion. Generally, children express their emotions with more body parts in a less subtle fashion than adults. With increasing age we develop finer muscular control, our cognitive abilities become more complex, and we learn and respond to various social norms and pressures. As a result, we would expect to see a gradual increase in the ability to simulate facial expressions of emotion. Furthermore, the sudden shifts from one emotional display to another will likely decrease as age increases.

Smiling as a reflexive response occurs early in life. The first social smile, however, probably occurs between the second and fourth month. Laughing seems to appear later than smiling. Persons who are familiar to the child may elicit laughing by tactile stimulation (tickling) sooner, but laughing without tactile stimulation does not seem to occur until the end of the first year. Sroufe and Waters, observing about one hundred infants, had mothers employ numerous auditory, tactile, social, and visual stimuli to produce laughter in their children.[43] In children four months or younger, instances of laughter were not clearcut, but unambiguous cases appeared after four months and were clearly apparent in most infants by eight months. It is hard to tell when affection responses first appear, but it seems reasonable to assume that before the age of three years these responses will be directed primarily toward caretaking adults. During the third and fourth years we should see more peer-directed affection, which is frequently seen in role-played parental nurturing behavior with younger children. The child is now beginning experiences that may eventuate in the feeling that giving affection can be as satisfying as receiving it.

Expressions of anger seem to be well developed before six months of age, but increasing age seems to change the outward manifestations of this anger, for example, fewer explosive outbursts. As with affection, we would expect to see this anger directed primarily at parents first, with increasing anger displays directed toward peers as age increases. Environmental conditions will sometimes be very influential in the manifestations of this anger. In 69 percent of the angry outbursts that Ricketts observed in home settings, crying was involved; but crying was only a part of 39 percent of the anger responses at nursery school.[44]

Somewhere about the middle of the first year, expressions of fear seem to clearly manifest themselves, although some believe that there may be two types of fear displays—one of which occurs very early. It is no surprise that expressions of fear seem to occur most often in response to large dogs, snakes, and dark rooms. Expressions of surprise are extremely difficult to locate on a developmental continuum. The expression is infrequently seen during the second half of the first year. One reason for this may be the nature of the infant's face, which is smooth with very light eyebrows, making observation difficult. Furthermore, a young child has not developed strong expectations, which, when violated, produce a surprise reaction. The standard configuration of the face during surprise (mouth open, eyes opened wider, raised brows, and momentary freezing) described by Darwin does not seem to occur much in elementary school children and may not change much from infancy through the sixth grade.

Others have speculated on the occurrence of expressions of jealousy, sympathy, shyness, coyness, embarrassment, and shame, but credible data is not yet available. Many of these reactions will appear after infancy because they require the performer to cognitively consider the behavior of others. Sympathy, for instance, requires you to sense distress in another; embarrassment occurs only when you care what others think of you—a condition that does not exist with infants.

SUMMARY

The focus of this chapter has been on the origins and development of nonverbal behavior—development in the human species over geological time and development in the course of a single lifetime. With limited information available for points in the life span, our concern was mainly with the first part of the life span.

We took the point of view that neither nature nor nurture is sufficient to explain the origin of many nonverbal behaviors. In many instances we inherit a neurological program that gives us the capacity to perform a particular act or sequence of acts; the fact that a particular behavior occurs at all may be genetically based. Our environment and cultural training, however, may be responsible for when the behavior appears, the frequency of its appearance, and the display rules that accompany it. We looked at the three sources of evidence for inborn behavior: (1) blind/deaf children, (2) nonhuman primates, and (3) multi-cultural studies. A number of behaviors were examined, but facial expressions of emotion provided the consistent thread, deriving supporting data from all three categories.

Since the remainder of this book focuses on data that is heavily based on men and women between the ages of seventeen and twenty-five, this chapter presented some findings pertinent to infants and children. The development of touching behavior is treated fully in Chapter 7 and was not mentioned here. We did note some of the emblems used by children as young as three and a half and the fact that listener responses ("m-hm" and nodding) are infrequent in children until about the eighth grade. By the time children start school they have established preferences for body builds (mesomorphs) and general attractiveness. Teachers also seem to respond to children on the basis of attractiveness. The eyes seem to be a part of the human face that infants observe very early, but we seem to know very little about the development of eye gaze itself. The use of eye behavior to regulate the interaction flow seems infrequent in children. Most of the studies of personal space conducted thus far with children seem to confirm findings with adults. The stages of infant vocalizing, in preparation for using language, are pretty well known. We know less about when children begin to recognize and respond to various vocal expressions. One intriguing line of research suggests that there is a synchrony between the parent's voice and the infant's movements as soon as twelve hours after birth. Finally, we outlined some of the work on facial expressions, suggesting that a primitive type of discrimination begins at about six months but that recognition of an emotional expression in the face of another may be highly dependent on the emotion being portrayed (as well as other factors).

NOTES

1. P. Ekman and W. V. Friesen, "The Repertoire of Nonverbal Behavior: Categories, Origins, Usage, and Coding," *Semiotica* 1 (1969): 49–98.
2. D. Lack, "The Releaser Concept of Bird Behaviour," *Nature* 145 (1940): 107–108.
3. W. H. Thorpe, "Vocal Communication in Birds," in R. Hinde (ed.), *Nonverbal Communication* (Cambridge: Cambridge University Press, 1972).
4. E. Lennenberg, *Biological Foundations of Language* (New York: John Wiley & Sons, 1969).
5. I. Eibl-Eibesfeldt, *Ethology: The Biology of Behavior,* 2d ed. (New York: Holt, Rinehart and Winston, 1975); I. Eibl-Eibesfeldt, "The Expressive Behaviour of the Deaf-and-Blind-Born," in M. von Cranach and I. Vine (eds.), *Social Communication and Movement* (New York: Academic Press, 1973); and T. K. Pitcairn and I. Eibl-Eibesfeldt, "Concerning the Evolution of Nonverbal Communication in Man," in M. E. Hahn and E. C. Simmel (eds.), *Communicative Behavior and Evolution* (New York: Academic Press, 1976).
6. W. R. Charlesworth and M. A. Kreutzer, "Facial Expressions of Infants and Children," in P. Ekman (ed.), *Darwin and Facial Expression: A Century of Research in Review* (New York: Academic Press, 1973), p. 160.
7. A thorough description of chimpanzee behavior can be found in: J. A. R. A. M. van Hooff, "A Structural Analysis of the Social Behavior of a Semi-Captive Group of Chimpanzees," in M. von Cranach and I. Vine (eds.), *Social Communication and Movement.* For an extensive comparison of vocal cues, see W. H. Thorpe, "The Comparison of Vocal Communication in Animals and Man," in R. Hinde (ed.), *Non-verbal Communication* (Cambridge: Cambridge University Press, 1972).

    A major literature review of communication by nonhuman primates can be found in S. A. Altmann, "Primates," in T. A. Sebeok (ed.), *Animal Communication* (Bloomington, Ind.: Indiana University Press, 1968).
8. S. Chevalier-Skolnikoff, "Facial Expression of Emotion in Nonhuman Primates," in P. Ekman (ed.), *Darwin and Facial Expression* (New York:

Academic Press, 1973). Also see J. A. R. A. M. van Hooff, "A Comparative Approach to the Phylogeny of Laughter and Smiling," in R. Hinde (ed.), *Non-verbal Communication*.

9. E. G. Bier and A. J. Zautra, "Identification of Vocal Communication of Emotions Across Cultures," *Journal of Consulting and Clinical Psychology* 39 (1972): 166.

10. I. Eibl-Eibesfeldt, "Similarities and Differences Between Cultures in Expressive Movements," in R. Hinde (ed.), *Non-verbal Communication*.

11. This research was summarized in P. Ekman, "Cross-Cultural Studies of Facial Expression," in P. Ekman (ed.), *Darwin and Facial Expression* (New York: Academic Press, 1973).

12. P. Ekman and W. V. Friesen, "The Repertoire of Nonverbal Behavior: Categories, Origins, Usage and Coding," *Semiotica* 1 (1969): 49–98.

13. A. T. Dittmann, "Development Factors in Conversational Behavior," *Journal of Communication* 22 (1972): 404–423.

14. G. Michael and F. N. Willis, "The Development of Gestures as a Function of Social Class, Education and Sex," *Psychological Record* 18 (1968): 515–519; and G. Michael and F. N. Willis, "The Development of Gestures in Three Subcultural Groups," *Journal of Social Psychology* 79 (1969): 35–41.

15. L. Kumin and M. Lazar, "Gestural Communication in Preschool Children," *Perceptual and Motor Skills* 38 (1974): 708–710.

16. C. Golomb, "Evolution of the Human Figure in the Three Dimensional Medium," *Developmental Psychology* 6 (1972): 385–391.

17. N. Cavior and D. A. Lombardi, "Developmental Aspects of Judgments of Physical Attractiveness in Children," *Developmental Psychology* 8 (1973): 67–71; N. Cavior and P. R. Donecki, "Physical Attractiveness and Peer Perceptions Among Children," *Sociometry* 37 (1974): 1–12; K. K. Dion, "Young Children's Stereotypes of Facial Attractiveness," *Developmental Psychology* 9 (1973): 183–188; and J. F. Cross and J. Cross, "Age, Sex, Race and the Perception of Facial Beauty," *Developmental Psychology* 5 (1971): 433–439.

18. K. Dion, "Physical Attractiveness and Evaluations of Children's Transgressions," *Journal of Personality and Social Psychology* 24 (1972): 207–213; and N. Cavior and L. R. Howard, "Facial Attractiveness and Juvenile Delinquency Among Black and White Offenders," *Journal of Abnormal Child Psychology* 1 (1973): 202–213

19. R. M. Lerner and E. Gellert, "Body Builds Identification, Preference and Aversion in Children," *Developmental Psychology* 1 (1969) 456–462; J. R. Staffieri, "Body Build and Behavioral Expectancies in Young Females," *Development Psychology* 6 (1972): 125–127; R. M. Lerner and S. J. Kom, "The Development of Body Build Stereotypes in Males," *Child Development* 43 (1972): 908–920; R. M. Lerner and C. Schroeder, "Physique Identification, Preference and Aversion in Kindergarten Children," *Developmental Psychology* 5 (1971): 538; and P. A. Johnson and J. R. Staffieri, "Stereotypic Affective Properties of Personal Names and Somatypes in Children," *Developmental Psychology* 5 (1971): 176.

20. S. A. Richardson, N. Goodman, A. Hastorf, and S. Dornbusch, "Cultural Uniformities in Relation to Physical Disabilities," *American Sociological Review* 26 (1961): 241–247.

21. R. M. Lerner, S. A. Karabenick, and M. Meisels, "Effect of Age and Sex on the Development of Personal Space Schemata Towards Body Build," *Journal of Genetic Psychology* 127 (1975): 91–101; and R. M. Lerner, J. Venning, and J. R. Knapp, "Age and Sex Effects on Personal Space Schemata Toward Body Build in Late Childhood," *Developmental Psychology* 11 (1975): 855–856.

22. R. N. Walker, "Body Build and Behavior in Younger Children," *Child Development* 34 (1963): 1–23.

23. P. H. Wolff, "Observations on the Early Development of Smiling," in B. M. Foss (ed.), *Determinants of Infant Behaviour*, vol. 2 (London: Methuen, 1963).

24. R. A. Spitz and K. M. Wolf, "The Smiling Response: A Contribution to the Ontogenesis of Social Relationships," *Genetic Psychology Monographs* 34 (1946): 57–125.

25. H. E. Fitzgerald, "Autonomic Pupillary Reflex Activity During Early Infancy and Its Relation to Social and Non-Social Stimuli," *Journal of Experimental Child Psychology* 6 (1968): 470–482.

26. V. Ashear and J. R. Snortum, "Eye Contact in Children as a Function of Age, Sex, Social and Intellective Variables," *Developmental Psychology* 4 (1971): 479; and M. H. Levine and B. Sutton-Smith, "Effects of Age, Sex and Task on Visual Behavior During Dyadic Interaction," *Developmental Psychology* 9 (1973): 400–405.

27. J. Lomranz, A. Shapira, N. Choresh, and Y. Gilat, "Children's Personal Space as a Function of Age and Sex," *Developmental Psychology* 11: (1975) 541–545.

28. H. M. Bass and M. S. Weinstein, "Early Development of Interpersonal Distancing in Children," *Canadian Journal of Behavioral Science* 3 (1971): 368–376; J. C. Baxter, "Interpersonal Spacing in Natural Settings," *Sociometry* 33 (1970): 444–456; and C. J. Guardo and M. Meisels, "Factor Structure of Children's Personal Space Schemata," *Child Development* 42 (1971): 1307–1312.

29. S. Jones and J. Aiello, "Proxemic Behavior of Black and White First-, Third-, and Fifth-Grade Children," *Journal of Personality and Social Psychology* 25 (1973): 21–27.

30. H. L. Rheingold and K. V. Cook, "The Contents of Boys' and Girls' Rooms as an Index of Parents' Behavior," *Child Development* 46 (1975): 459–463.

31. L. Harper and K. M. Sanders, "Preschool Children's Use of Space: Sex Differences in Outdoor Play," *Developmental Psychology* 11 (1975): 119.

32. C. Hutt and M. J. Vaizey, "Differential Effects of Group Density of Social Behavior," *Nature* 209 (1967): 1371–1372; and C. Loo, "The Effects of Spatial Density on the Social Behaviour of Children," *Journal of Applied Social Psychology* 4 (1972): 172–181.

33. P. Lieberman, *Intonation, Perception, and Language* (Cambridge, Mass.: M.I.T. Press, 1966).

34. W. C. Sheppard and H. L. Lane, "Development of the Prosodic Features of Infant Vocalizing," *Journal of Speech and Hearing Research* 11 (1968): 94–108.

35. H. Levin, I. Silverman, and B. Ford, "Hesitations in Children's Speech During Explanation and Description," *Journal of Verbal Learning and Verbal Behavior* 6 (1967): 560–564.

36. B. Wood, *Children and Communication* (Englewood Cliffs, N.J.: Prentice-Hall, 1976), p. 224.

37. W. S. Condon and L. W. Sander, "Synchrony Demonstrated Between Movements of the Neonate and Adult Speech," *Child Development* 45 (1974): 456–462.

38. Lieberman, *Intonation, Perception, and Language.* Also see J. Kagan and M. Lewis, "Studies of Attention in the Human Infant," *Merrill-Palmer Quarterly* 4 (1965): 95–127.

39. L. Dimitrovsky, "The Ability to Identify the Emotional Meaning of Vocal Expression at Successive Age Levels," in J. R. Davitz (ed.), *The Communication of Emotional Meaning* (New York: McGraw-Hill, 1964), pp. 69–86; and A. Fenster and A. M. Goldstein, "The Emotional World of Children 'Vis-à-Vis' the Emotional World of Adults: An Examination of Vocal Communication," *Journal of Communication* 21 (1971): 353–362.

40. I. Vine, "The Role of Facial-Visual Signalling in Early Social Development," in M. Von Cranach and I. Vine (eds.), *Social Communication and Movement,* pp. 195-298; and W. R. Charlesworth and M. A. Kreutzer, "Facial Expression of Infants and Children," in P. Ekman (ed.), *Darwin and Facial Expression* (New York: Academic Press, 1973), pp. 91–168.

41. Charlesworth and Kreutzer, "Facial Expressions of Infants and Children," p. 122.

42. G. S. Gates, "An Experimental Study of the Growth of Social Perception," *Journal of Educational Psychology* 14 (1923): 449–461.

43. L. A. Sroufe and E. Waters, "The Ontogenesis of Smiling and Laughter," *Psychological Review* 83 (1976): 173–189.

44. A. F. Ricketts, "A Study of the Behavior of Young Children in Anger," in L. Jack et al. (eds.), *University of Iowa Studies: Studies in Child Welfare* 9 (1934): 163–171.

ADDITIONAL READINGS

Eibl-Eibesfeldt, I. *Ethology: The Biology of Behavior.* 2nd ed. New York: Holt, Rinehart and Winston, 1975.

Hahn, M. E. and E. C. Simmel, (eds.). *Communicative Behavior and Evolution.* New York: Academic Press, 1976.

Hinde, R. (ed.). *Non-verbal Communication.* Cambridge: Cambridge University Press, 1972.

Wood, B. *Children and Communication.* Englewood Cliffs, N.J.: Prentice-Hall, 1976.

THE EFFECTS OF
THE ENVIRONMENT

Every interior betrays the nonverbal skills of its inhabitants. The choice of materials, the distribution of space, the kind of objects that command attention or demand to be touched—as compared to those that intimidate or repel—have much to say about the preferred sensory modalities of their owners.

RUESCH AND KEES

The number of different places in which we communicate with others is limitless—buses, homes, apartments, public restaurants, offices, parks, hotels, sports arenas, factories, libraries, movie theaters, museums, and so on. Yet, despite this diversity, we probably see these environments along similar lines. Once we have perceived our environment in a certain way, we may incorporate our perceptions in the development of the messages we send. And, once that message has been sent, the environmental perceptions of the other person have been altered. Thus, we are both influenced by and influence our environments.

Mehrabian argues that we react emotionally to our surroundings and that the nature of our emotional reactions can be accounted for in terms of how arousing the environment made us feel, how pleasurable we felt, and how dominant we are made to feel.[1] Arousal refers to how active, stimulated, frenzied, or alert you are; pleasure refers to feelings of joy, satisfaction, or happiness; and dominance suggests that you feel in control, important—free to act in a variety of ways. Environments that are novel, surprising, crowded, and complex will probably produce feelings of higher arousal.

53

In another work, I proposed the following framework for classifying perceptions of interaction environments.[2] Although these perceptual bases are not intended to be completely relegated to emotional responses, it is not hard to see the overlap of this framework with Mehrabian's schema.

PERCEPTIONS OF OUR SURROUNDINGS

Perceptions of Formality. One familiar dimension along which environments can be classified is a formal/informal continuum. Our reaction may be based on the objects present, the people present, the functions performed, or any number of other characteristics. Individual offices may be more formal than a lounge in the same building; a year-end banquet may seem to take on more formality than a "come-as-you-are" party; an evening with one other couple in your home may be more informal than an evening with ten other couples; and so on. The greater the formality, the greater are the chances that the communication behavior will be less relaxed and more superficial, hesitant, and stylized.

Perceptions of Warmth. Environments that make us feel psychologically warm encourage us to linger, to feel relaxed, and to feel comfortable. It may be some combination of the color of the drapes or walls, or the paneling, carpeting, texture of the furniture, softness of the chairs, soundproofing, and so on. Fast-food chains try to retain some degree of warmth in their decor to remain inviting, but display enough coldness to encourage rapid customer turnover.

Perceptions of Privacy. Enclosed environments usually suggest greater privacy, particularly if they can accommodate a few people. As long as the possibility of other people's entering and/or overhearing your conversation is small (even if you are outdoors), there is a greater feeling of privacy. Sometimes the objects in the setting will add to the perceptions of privacy, for example, toilet articles and other personal items. With greater privacy, we will probably find close speaking distances and more personal messages that are designed and adapted for the specific other person rather than for "people in general."

Perceptions of Familiarity. When we meet a new person, we are typically cautious, deliberate, and conventional in our responses. The same is true when we are in unfamiliar environments, which are laden with ritual and norms we do not yet know. We are thus hesitant to move too quickly, and will probably go slowly until we can associate this unfamiliar environment with one we know. One interpretation for the rather stereotyped structures of quick-food stops is that they allow us (a mobile society) to readily find a familiar and predictable place that will guarantee minimum demands for active contact with strangers. In unfamiliar environments, the most likely topic of conversation will initially revolve around the environment itself—for example, "Have you ever been here before?" "What is it like?" "Who comes here?" "What's that for?" "Jeez, look at that!" and so on.

Perceptions of Constraint. Part of our total reaction to an environment is based on our perception of whether (and how easily) we can leave it. You might feel a distinct difference in the degree of confinement or constraint when your in-laws are visiting for an evening as compared to when they are visiting for a month. The intensity of these perceptions of constraint is closely related to the space available to us (and the privacy of this space) during the time we will be in the environment. Some environments seem to be only temporarily confining—for example, a long trip in an automobile; other environments seem more permanently confining—for example, prisons, spacecrafts, and nursing homes.

Perceptions of Distance. Sometimes our responses within a given environment will be influenced by how close or far away we must conduct our communication with another. This may reflect actual physical distance (an office on a different floor, a house in another part of the city), or it may reflect psychological distance (barriers clearly separating people who are fairly close physically). You may be seated close to someone and still not perceive it as a close environment—for example, interlocking chairs in an airport that face the same direction. When the setting forces us into close quarters with other people who are not known to us (elevators, crowded buses), we will probably see efforts to increase the distance between ourselves and the other people psychologically and to reflect a less intimate feeling—for example, less eye contact, body tenseness and immobility, cold silence, nervous laughter, jokes about the intimacy, and public conversation directed at all present.

The foregoing represent only some of the dimensions along which communication settings can be perceived. Generally, more intimate communication is associated with informal, unconstrained, private, familiar, close, and warm environments. In everyday situations, however, these dimensions combine in complex ways—for example, some formality may be combined with a lot of constraint and only a little bit of privacy. At present we do not know how these combinations affect the way we communicate. The mixture of intimate and nonintimate factors can be seen in an elevator if you perceive it as close, familiar, and temporarily confining, but it can also be public, formal, and cold.

The remainder of this chapter is devoted to the characteristics of environments—characteristics that go together to make up the perceptions that have just been outlined. Each environment is made up of three major components: (1) the natural environment—geography, location, atmospheric conditions; (2) the presence or absence of other people; and (3) architectural and design features, including movable objects.

THE NATURAL ENVIRONMENT

For many years, behavioral scientists have hypothesized that those who choose to live in urban rather than rural areas will have fewer close personal relations. In the United States, however, there is increasingly less evidence to support this theory. Greater mobility and the influence of the mass media tend to offset the possibility that these differences exist. There is evidence to suggest, however, that the more physical mobility you have in a city, the less social intimacy you will have within your own neighborhood. If you are a resident who is new to the community, you will very likely associate with your neighbors more than would an old resident who knew more people in other parts of town.

Some have even speculated on the effects of the moon and sunspots on human behavior. There is considerable skepticism of this work, partially because such forces seem too mystical to affect our behavior, and partially because the research studies along these lines show that behavior and the moon and sun seem to vary together, but fail to show that a particular moon position actually *causes* certain behaviors. Although this line of inquiry is not widely accepted, some of the findings are intriguing. For example, a group of scientists and engineers who study the use of nuclear energy for the Atomic Energy Commission published a report entitled, "Intriguing Accident Patterns Plotted Against a Background of Natural Environment Features."[3] The report maintains that accident rates (and presumably other human behavior) are influenced by phases of the moon, solar cycles, and other natural phenomena. An examination of accident patterns for the past twenty years suggested that people's susceptibility to accidents was highest during the lunar phase that was similar to or 180 degrees away from the one in which they were born. Accidents also tended to peak in cycles of the new moon in apogee, the point at which the moon was farthest away from the earth. The sun's rotation also seems to alter the strength of the earth's magnetic field—alterations that seem to coincide with increases and decreases in accidents. These scientists conclude that these natural features of our environment, in conjunction with other factors, help to create misjudgments, pressures, and situations that lead to accidents. Scientists who study wildlife have also found interesting covariations in an approximate ten-year lunar cycle and fluctuations in wildlife populations. Population peaks and declines appear to coincide with the nodal cycle of the moon, and this has been found in wildlife populations that were widely separated from each other.

A former director of climatology with the U.S. Weather Bureau was elected the president of an organization called the American Institute of Medical Climatology.[4] This is a group of meteorologists, physicists, and physicians who exchange findings regarding the effects of temperature fluctuations and changes in humidity and barometric pressure on various illness such as heart attacks, asthma, arthritis, migraine headaches, intestinal disorders, hypertension, mental illness, and even the common cold.

All of us sometimes feel unusually depressed during dark, overcast days. Others have noted that the right combination of atmospheric pressure and high temperatures may lead to restlessness, irritability, temper tantrums, and even aggressive acts. The National Advisory Commission on Civil Disorders reported, in 1968, that the hot summer nights added to an already explosive situation that eventually resulted in widespread rioting in ghetto areas: "In most instances, the temperature during the day on which the violence errupted was quite high."[5] Griffitt varied heat and humidity under controlled laboratory conditions for students and confirmed a relationship between these conditions and interpersonal responses. As the temperature and humidity increased, interpersonal attraction to another student decreased.[6] There may thus be more truth than fiction in the familiar explanation for a particularly unpleasant encounter, "Oh, he was just hot and irritable."

Obviously, the relationship between temperature and aggression is not a simple one. A number of things probably interact with the temperature to increase the chances of one's aggression, for example, prior provocation, presence of aggressive models, perceived ability to leave the environment, and so on. Laboratory studies by Baron and Bell provide some useful insights into this matter.[7] First, they had a confederate (an assistant to the experimenter) give some male students a rather harsh, negative evaluation, whereas other students received more positive feedback. Then, under the guise of another experiment, the students were given an opportunity to administer electric shocks to their partner—that is, the confederate who had evaluated them. The room temperatures were about 74 degrees F. for some of the students and about 94 degrees F. for others.

The results of the study were just the opposite of what was expected. The higher temperatures facilitated aggressive acts (shocks) by those who were given the positive evaluations, whereas those who received the negative messages were more inhibited. The explanation given by these researchers is that the subjects who had been treated harshly were apparently so uncomfortable that escape from the environment or minimization of the discomfort was the primary goal—rather than aggression. The subjects might have thought that if they gave strong electric shocks they would only prolong their already uncomfortable stay in this situation—delays caused either by protests from the person being shocked or censure by the experimenter. Furthermore, if they administered strong shocks they themselves might experience additional negative feelings such as guilt, empathizing with signs of pain in the victim, and the like. Thus, if we are to hypothesize a relationship between high temperatures and aggression, we need to consider the amount of negative affect the person is experiencing from all sources.

In the early twentieth century, Huntington advanced a seemingly bizarre theory that for mental vigor, an average outdoor temperature of 50 to 60 degrees F. is better than one above 70 degrees F.[8] More recently, scientists have suggested that (1) monotonous weather is more apt to affect your spirits; (2) seasonally, you do your best mental work in late winter, early spring, and fall; (3) a prolonged blue sky reduces your productivity; and (4) the ideal temperature should average about 64 degrees F. McClelland, in his analysis of folk stories in primitive societies, found that achievement motivation was highest in areas where the mean annual temperature ranged between 40 and 60 degrees F.[9] He also concluded that temperature variation was important in determining achievement motivation with a daily or seasonal variation of at least 15 degrees F. needed for high achievement motivation.

These reports on geography, climate, and celestial bodies provide us with little reliable and valid information. That our behavior is influenced by these factors seems a reasonable assumption, but the exact nature of this influence, the specific conditions under which this influence occurs, and the degree of the influence are still unknown.

OTHER PEOPLE IN THE ENVIRONMENT

In the next chapter we examine the reactions of people to environments that are overpopulated—that is, dense or crowded. For now, though, we merely point out that other people can be perceived as part of the environment—and will have an effect on your behavior. These people may be perceived as "active" or "passive" participants, depending on the degree to which they are perceived as "involved" (speaking or listening) in your conversation. In many situations these people will be seen as "active," especially if they are able to overhear what you are saying. There are, however, situations when we grant another person or persons the dubious status of "nonperson," and behave accordingly. This may occur in high-density situations, but it is also common with just one other person. Cab drivers, janitors, and children have been known to achieve nonperson status with some regularity. The presence of nonpersons allows the free uninhibited flow of interaction because, as far as the active participants are concerned, they are the only human interactants present. Parents will sometimes talk to others about very personal aspects of their child while the child is playing nearby. For the interactants, however, the child is perceived as "not here." Any relevant verbal or nonverbal responses on the part of the nonperson that are picked up by the interactants will immediately strip the person of the nonperson role.

When others are perceived as an active ingredient in the environment, it may facilitate or inhibit certain kinds of communication. The chief difference in communication with active others is that messages must be adapted to multiple audiences rather than to a single audience. Even telephone conversations, where the third party can hear only one of the interactants, are altered to account for the uninvited listener. Sometimes the existence of these additional audiences presents such a strain or threat that one or both communicators leave the scene. On the other hand, the appearance of a third party may provide an opportunity to ease out of a conversation with an undesirable other by "dumping" the focus of the interaction on this third party and making a polite exit.

The presence of others may increase our motivation to "look good" in what we say and do, which may either be detrimental (distorting information) or beneficial. The benefits of looking good in the presence of others is exemplified in the form of constructive approaches to conflict. For instance, the presence of others may prohibit overt fighting from arising at all. But such benefits may be temporary in nature. The other people in the environment have ensured a delay, which may act as a "cooling off" period or may further frustrate and aggravate the person who had to repress such feelings. If the people present are not highly interdependent on each other, the communication will probably be less personal and more conventional and stereotyped—a form of communication designed for broader, less specific audiences.

ARCHITECTURAL DESIGN AND MOVABLE OBJECTS

Sometimes we get very definite person-related messages from home environments. Our perception of the inhabitants of a home may be structured before we meet them—whether we think they decorated their house for themselves, for others, for conformity, for comfort, and so on. We may be influenced by the mood created by the wallpaper, by the symmetry and/or orderliness of objects displayed, by pictures on the walls, by the quality and apparent cost of the items placed around the house, and by many, many other things. Most of us have had the experience of being ushered into a living room, which we perceived as being more accurately labeled as an "unliving" room. We hesitate to sit down or touch anything because the room seems to say to us, "This room is for show purposes only; sit, walk, and touch carefully. It takes a lot of time and effort to keep this room neat, clean, and tidy; we don't want to clean it after you leave." The arrangement of other living rooms seems to say, "Sit down, make yourself comfortable, feel free to talk informally, and don't worry about spilling things." Interior decorators and product promotion experts often have experiential and intuitive judgments about the influence of certain colors, objects, shapes, arrangements, and the like, but few attempts have been made to empirically validate these feelings. Perhaps the best known empirical research into the influence of interior decoration on human responses are the studies of Maslow and Mintz.[10]

Maslow and Mintz selected three rooms for study: One was an "ugly" room (designed to give the impression of a janitor's storeroom in disheveled condition); one was a "beautiful" room (complete with carpeting, drapes, and the like); and one was an "average" room (a professor's office). Subjects were asked to rate a series of negative print photographs of faces. The experimenters tried to keep all factors, such as time of day, odor, noise, type of seating, and experimenter, constant from room to room so that any results could be attributed to the type of room. Results showed that subjects in the beautiful room tended to give significantly higher ratings to the faces than did participants in the ugly room. Experimenters and subjects alike engaged in various escape behaviors to avoid the ugly room. The ugly room was variously described as producing monotony, fatigue, headache, discontent, sleep, irritability, and hostility. The beautiful room, however, produced feelings of pleasure, comfort, enjoyment, importance, energy, and desire to continue the activity. In this instance, we have a well-controlled study that offers some evidence of the impact of visual-esthetic surroundings on the nature of human interaction. Similar studies have tested recall and problem solving in rooms similar to those used by Maslow and Mintz. In both cases, more effective performance was found in rooms that were well appointed or "beautiful."[11]

Color. Two newspaper accounts that appeared in 1972 reported that prisons were being repainted in order to "cut down on prisoner mischief." The walls of the city jail in San Diego were reportedly painted pink, baby blue, and peach on the assumption that pastel colors would have a calming effect on the inmates. In Salem, Oregon, the cell bars of Oregon's Correctional Institution were done in soft green, blues, and buffs; some cell doors were painted bright yellow, orange, green, and blue. In addition, the superintendent of the Salem institution said that the color schemes would be continually changed to keep the prison "an exciting place to work and live in." These are but two examples of organizations that have tried to use findings from environmental research, findings suggesting that colors, in conjunction with other factors, do influence moods and behavior.

According to Mehrabian, the most pleasant hues are, in order, blue, green, purple, red, and yellow, and the most arousing hues are red, followed by orange, yellow, violet, blue, and green.[12] Although these proposals are not completely comparable with the following paper-and-pencil research on colors and mood-tones, there are a number of similarities. Wexner presented eight colors and eleven mood-tones to ninety-four subjects. The results (see Table 3.1) show that for some mood-tones a single color is significantly related; for others there may be two or more colors.[13]

A real problem in interpreting such research concerns whether people pick colors that are actually associated with particular moods or whether they are responding using learned verbal stereotypes. Another problem with some of the color preferences research concerns the lack of association between color and objects. Pink may be your favorite color, but you may still dislike pink hair. Nevertheless, we cannot ignore the body of educational and design literature that suggests that carefully planned color schemes seem to have some influence on improving scholastic achievement. Obviously, we cannot make any final judgments about the impact of color on human interaction until behavioral studies link differently colored environments with different types of verbal behavior or communication patterns. That is, the configuration of circumstances that is necessary for environmental color to affect human interaction to any appreciable degree must first be clearly established.

TABLE 3.1
Colors Associated with Moods

MOOD TONE	COLOR	FREQUENCY OF TIMES CHOSEN
Exciting-Stimulating	Red	61
Secure-Comfortable	Blue	41
Distressed-Disturbed-Upset	Orange	34
Tender-Soothing	Blue	41
Protective-Defending	Red	21
	Brown	17
	Blue	15
	Black	15
	Purple	14
Despondent-Dejected-Unhappy-Melancholy	Black	25
	Brown	25
Calm-Peaceful-Serene	Blue	38
	Green	31
Dignified-Stately	Purple	45
Cheerful-Jovial-Joyful	Yellow	40
Defiant-Contrary-Hostile	Red	23
	Orange	21
	Black	18
Powerful-Strong-Masterful	Black	48

Sound.   The types of sounds and their intensity also seem to affect interpersonal behavior. We react very differently, however, to the drone of several people's voices, the overpowering sound of a nearby jackhammer, or the soothing or stimulating sounds of music. "Music" says Mehrabian, "can have a stronger and more immediate effect on arousal level and pleasure than, say, several cups of coffee."[14] That often unpleasant, arousing, and powerful sound of the morning alarm clock may have a good deal to do with some people's irritability on rising. Generally, the more pleasant the music, the more likely we are to engage in "approaching" rather than "avoiding" behavior. The effect of slow, simple, soft, and familiar music is to lower our arousal levels while maintaining pleasure—eliciting an easygoing and satisfying feeling.

In some environments we want to change the sound to change behavior, for example, raising the volume of music in a supermarket to stimulate more purchases in a shorter time. In other instances, we may want to reduce unproductive noise through structural changes. In one mental institution, floor tiles were replaced with carpeting, which it was believed made the patients less irritable and made the hospital seem warmer and more like a "home," which in turn encouraged the patients to spend more time taking care of their environment.[15]

Lighting.   Lighting also helps to structure our perceptions of an environment and these perceptions may very well influence the type of messages we send. If we enter a room that has dim lighting or candlelight, we may talk more softly and presume that more personal communication will take place. Bright lights, on the other hand, are more apt to be arousing—adding to initial discomfort in interacting with strangers—and indicative of less intimate interaction. Carr and Dabbs found that the combination of intimate questions and dim lighting with nonintimates caused a significant hesitancy in responding, a significant decrease in eye gaze, and a decrease in the average length of gaze.[16] All of these nonverbal behaviors appear to be efforts to create a greater psychological distance and to decrease the perceived inappropriateness of the intimacy created by the lighting and the questions.

Several attempts have been made to test the effects of various types of colored lighting on human performance. Birren cites evidence suggesting that human reactions are 12 percent faster than average under red lighting conditions. Green lights, on the other hand, seem to generate reactions that are slower than normal.[17] Colored lighting also seems to influence judgments of time, length, and weight. Under red lighting, these judgments tend to be overestimated, whereas a green or blue light appears to generate underestimation.[18]

Movable Objects.   If we know that the arrangement of certain objects in our environment can help structure the communication that takes place in that environment, it is not surprising that we often try to manipulate objects in order to bring about certain types of responses. Special, intimate evenings are often highlighted by candlelight, soft music, favorite drinks, fluffed pillows on the couch, and the absence of dirty dishes, trash, and other nonintimate material associated with daily living. Objects in our environment can also be arranged to reflect certain role relationships, to demarcate boundaries, or to encourage greater affiliation. The interior of an executive suite may clearly indicate the perceived status of the inhabitant—for example, expensive wall paintings, large desk, plush sofa and chairs, drapes, and the like. Such an atmosphere may be very inappropriate for a personal counseling situation, but it may be rearranged to make it more conducive to such a purpose. There are also times when we are able to communicate well in seemingly "inappropriate" settings, as when lovers say good-bye in the relatively cold and public environs of an airport terminal.

Desks seem to be an important object in the analysis of interpersonal communication. An experiment conducted in a doctor's office suggests that the presence or absence of a desk may significantly alter the patient's "at ease" state.[19] With the desk separating the doctor and patient, only 10 percent of the patients were perceived "at ease," whereas removal of the desk brought the figure of "at ease" patients up to 55 percent. Student-teacher relationships also seem to be affected by desk placement.[20] Faculty members were asked to sketch the furniture arrangement in their offices. These sketches were collected and analyzed with other information obtained from the professors in a school-wide teacher evaluation. Twenty-four out of thirty-three senior faculty members put their desks between themselves and their students, but only fourteen out of thirty junior faculty members did so. Furthermore, the "unbarricaded" professors were rated by students as more willing to "encourage the development of different viewpoints by students," as ready to give "individual attention to students who need it," and as less likely to show "undue favoritism." Even White House press briefings have apparently been affected by a barricade. During the Nixon administration, press briefings were formalized, and the press secretary stood behind a podium. Ron Nessen, President Ford's press secretary, believed that this arrangement contributed to an unproductive "us and them" feeling, which prompted him to conduct briefings without the obstacle.

Less obvious barriers also exist. For instance, if you find a delicate objet d'art placed in front of some books in a bookcase you will likely feel hesitant about using the books. Desks and other "barriers" are not inherently good or bad, but there will be some occasions when you want to keep a distant, formal relationship and the desk can help to create that feeling.

The arrangement of other items of furniture can facilitate or inhibit

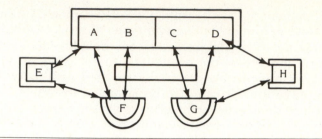

FIGURE 3.1

Conversation flow and furniture arrangement. Adapted from A. Mehrabian, *Public Places and Private Spaces* (New York: Basic Books, © 1976), p. 92.

communication. The location of the television set in a room will very likely affect the placement of chairs, and, in turn, the pattern of conversations that occur in that room. Sommer and Ross found that some residents in a geriatric ward were "apathetic" and had few friends in spite of a generally cheerful and bright environment. By rearranging the furniture to encourage interaction, they were able to double the frequency of resident conversations.[21] Even when you have tried to maximize the conversational possibilities, you may not get everyone to talk to everyone else. In the arrangement shown in Figure 3.1 the exchanges marked by arrows would likely be the most frequent, but the four people seated on the couch will probably talk to each other infrequently. The two groups of four on each end and the two people seated next to each other (F and G) are also likely to communicate infrequently. If the participants are periodically rearranged, the conversational groupings can be altered. Finally, there are no other chairs in this arrangement, which poses the question of where one goes when "bored stiff" with his or her current conversational grouping.

In at least one case, a furniture designer has deliberately designed a chair to exert disagreeable pressure on a person's spine when occupied for more than a few minutes. The Larsen chair was originally designed to keep patrons from becoming too comfortable and remaining in seats that could be occupied by other customers.[22] Hotel owners and airport designers apparently are also aware of the "too comfortable" phenomenon. Seating arrangements in some hotels and airports are thus deliberately made uncomfortable for long seating and conversations so that patrons will "move along" and perhaps drift into nearby shops where they can spend some of their money. Some environments seem to have an unwritten code that prohibits interaction. The lone men entering, sitting through, and leaving pornographic movies without a word are a case in point.

Structure and Design. We spend a lot of time in buildings. Most of us spend the day in a dwelling supposedly designed for the effective performance of our work; in the evening we enter another structure supposedly designed for the effective conduct of our personal or family life. The architecture can go a long way toward determining who shall meet whom, where, and perhaps for how long.

Office buildings in the United States are often constructed from a standard plan, which reflects a pyramidal organization, that is, a large number of people supervised by a few executives at the upper levels. And these executives generally have the most space, the most privacy, and the most desirable office locations, namely, on the highest floor of the structure. Achieving a height above the "masses" and acquiring a vast amount of space are only two indications of visible power. Corner offices, large picture windows, and private elevators are also associated with status and power, and an office right next to an important executive may also hold a formidable power base. The offices of top-level executives are often hard to reach, the assumption being that the more you have to walk to get to the executive, the more powerful he or she seems. Figure 3.2 is a hypothetical, but not farfetched, example of the long and circuitous route to a president's office. In order to get to the office, the visitor must be screened by a receptionist and a private secretary and in either or both places the visitor may be asked to sit and wait. So, although the status and power of an executive may be related to his or her inaccessibility, secretaries and receptionists may value open views that allow them to act as lookouts and defenders against unwanted intrusions on the executive. It is common for people on the lowest rungs of the organizational ladder to find themselves in a large open "pit," where their "offices" (desks) have little or no privacy, and complaints

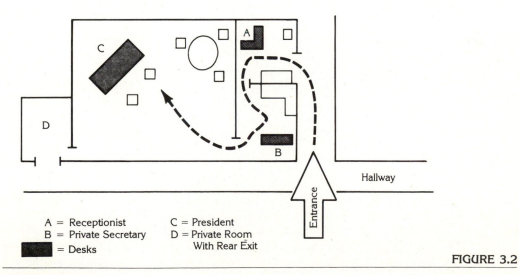

A = Receptionist C = President
B = Private Secretary D = Private Room
■ = Desks   With Rear Exit

Hallway

Entrance

FIGURE 3.2

Getting to the president's office.

are common. Although privacy is minimal at this location, communication opportunities are plentiful.

Some dormitories are built from floor plans resembling those in many office buildings and old hotels. Some have even speculated that these "corridor-type" dorms tend to encourage bureaucratic management approaches, which seem to fit the orderly and uniform structure. Rigid rules are easier to enforce in structures with these designs, but interaction among the residents is discouraged. The sense of community and the resulting responsibility for one's living space is difficult to achieve. Lounges are sometimes intended to facilitate such interaction, but their usefulness has been questioned by architects and behavioral scientists. Lounges, like any other design feature, must be integrated into the entire architectural plan developed from an analysis of human needs not inserted in places where they "fit nicely" or "look good" for parents and visitors.

Most classrooms in the United States are rectangular in shape with straight rows of chairs. They have wide windows that allow light to beam across the student's shoulder. This window placement determines the direction the students will face and thus designates the "front" of the classroom. Most classroom seats are also permanently attached to the floor for ease of maintenance and tidiness. Most classrooms have some type of partition (usually a desk) that separates the teacher from the students. Most students and teachers can provide a long list of "problems" encountered in environments designed for learning. These complaints center around poor lighting; poor acoustics; temperature that is too hot or too cold; outside construction noises; banging radiators; electrical outlets which do not work; seats which do not move; gloomy, dull, or distracting color schemes; unpleasant odors; and so on. The students and teachers complain because they recognize that such problems impede the purpose for gathering in these rectangular rooms, which is to increase one's knowledge through effective student-teacher communication. The whole question of the influence of the classroom environment on student-teacher behavior remains relatively unexplored.

Sommer selected six different kinds of classrooms for study. He found the odds of a student participating in class discussion are slightly greater for small classes. Student participation in the large classes seemed to involve questions of clarification or requests for repeating an idea—a type of participation that differs radically from the intellectual give and take between two people seeking to understand, to refine, to see ramifications and related ideas, and so on.

In the seminar rooms, Sommer noted that most participation came from students who were seated directly opposite the instructor. Students generally avoided the two chairs on either side of the instructor—even when all other seats were filled. When a student did occupy the seat next to the instructor, he or she was generally silent throughout the entire period. In straight-row rooms, the following observations were made: (1) Students within eye contact range of the instructor participated more. (2) There was a tendency for more participation to occur in the center sections of each row and for participation to generally decrease from the front to the back. This tendency, however, was not evident when interested students sat in locations other than those that provided maximum visual contact with the instructor. (3) Participation decreased as class size increased.[23]

A related research project offers additional support for Sommer's observations on participation in straight-row classrooms. Adams and Biddle noted a remarkably consistent pattern of interaction in grades one, six, and eleven, which indicated that most student participation comes from students sitting in the center of the room.[24] Sixty-three percent of the 1,176 behaviors observed came from students located in three positions, one behind the other down the center of the room. Almost all pupil-initiated comments came from the shadowed area in Figure 3.3. In no instance did teachers select special students for placement in these locations. As the authors point out "it is now possible to discriminate an area of the classroom that seems to be literally and figuratively the center of activity."

Koneya believed that some questions had not been sufficiently explored by Sommer and Adams and Biddle.[25] First, do high participators choose certain seats, or is there something about the dynamics of seat

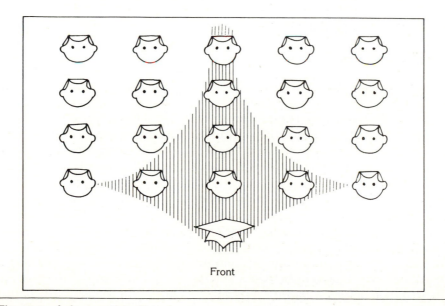

Front

FIGURE 3.3

The zone of class participation.

location that brings about high participation? In Koneya's study, after high and low participating students were identified, they were given the chance to choose a seat from a classroom diagram. High verbalizers did tend to select seats in the zone of participation more than low or moderate verbalizers. Second, Koneya wanted to put students who were previously identified as high, moderate, or low participators in different seats and observe their participation. These observations took place over seven class periods. Both the high and moderate participators talked more in the zone of participation than their counterparts in noncentral areas. Those who were low participators were consistently low—in or out of the central areas.

From these studies we can conclude that classroom seating is not random, that certain types of people do gravitate to central and noncentral areas, and that the zone of participation, heavily influenced by teacher-student visibility, will promote participation for everyone except initially low participators. Even then, we might find increased participation at some point after the seventh class period with a teacher who rewards and supports participation. Why is participation important? It may assist in clarifying difficult ideas to be learned and it may link teacher and student in a social bond that can create a better learning environment. And, to no student's surprise, "getting to know your instructor" may influence grades as well.

Sommer concludes his observations on classroom behavior and environmental influences by saying:

> At the present time, teachers are hindered by their insensitivity to and fatalistic acceptance of the classroom environment. Teachers must be "turned on" to their environment lest their pupils develop this same sort of fatalism.[26]

If you look carefully, you can see any number of environmental structures that inhibit or prohibit communication. Fences separating yards create obvious barriers even if they are only waist high; laundry rooms in apartment buildings and public housing located in dark, isolated places discourage use, particularly at night; homes with patios, which are only accessible through a bedroom, will probably discourage use; and so on.

Other environmental situations seem to facilitate interaction. Homes placed in the middle of a block seem to draw more interpersonal exchanges than those located in other positions on the block. Houses that have adjacent driveways seem to have a built-in structure drawing the neighbors together and inviting communication. Cavan reports that the likelihood of interaction between strangers at a bar varies directly with the distance between them.[27] As a rule, a span of three bar stools is the maximum distance over which patrons will attempt to initiate an encounter. Two men conversing with an empty bar stool between them are likely to remain that way since they would be too close if they sat next to each other. However, if a man is talking to woman and there is an empty stool between them, he will likely move onto it—to prevent someone else from coming between them. Most bars, however, are not designed for optimum interaction. The three bar designs in Figure 3.4 provide very different opportunities for facing your interaction partner, for mutual eye gaze, and for getting physically close. Most bars are similar to type B, the type that seems to discourage interaction the most.

Some recent designs for housing elderly people have taken into consideration the need for social contact. In these apartment dwellings the doors of the apartments on a given floor open into a common entranceway. The probabilities for social exchange are then greatly increased over the situation in which apartment doors are staggered on either side of a long hallway so that no doorways face one another. If you desire a structure to encourage social interaction, you must have human paths crossing, but if you want people to interact, there must be something that will encourage them to linger for a time. Furthermore, the nature of the design may encourage or discourage certain types of communication, that is, the structure may determine how much interaction takes place and what the general content of that interaction will be. Drew reports an unpublished study of three different designs for nursing stations within a mental hospital.[28] In one, interaction had to take place by opening a door; in another, interaction was conducted through a glass-enclosed counter; and in the third, interaction took place over an open counter. Although substantially more patients entered the nursing station through the door, interactions occurred less frequently than in the other two stations. An average of only one interaction per each fifteen-minute observation period occurred with the door; 5.3 interactions per period occurred in the glass-enclosed counter; and 8.7 occurred for the open counter. Although interaction was higher for the open counter, there was a preponderance of social conversation here, whereas the door design seemed to encourage more item requests and permission interactions. In short, the more inaccessible setting decreased interaction frequency and increased task-oriented messages; the more accessible setting increased interaction frequency and increased the amount of "small talk."

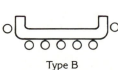

Type A   Type B   Type C

FIGURE 3.4

Designs for drinking.

A more complete analysis of physical proximity and spatial distance is provided in Chapter 4, but it is clearly relevant to this chapter on the environment as well. As Stouffer puts it:

> Whether one is seeking to explain why persons go to a particular place to get jobs, why they go to trade at a particular store, why they go to a particular neighborhood to commit a crime, or why they marry the particular spouse they choose, the factor of spatial distance is of obvious significance.[29]

Several studies have confirmed Stouffer's remarks. For instance, students tend to develop stronger friendships with students who share their classes or their dormitory or apartment building, or who sit near them, than with others who are geographically more distant. Workers tend to develop closer friendships with those who work close to them. Some research has concluded that increased proximity of white persons and blacks will assist in reducing prejudice.[30] Several studies show an inverse relationship between the distance separating potential marriage partners and the number of marriages. For example, in New Haven in 1940, Kennedy reports 76 percent of the marriages were between persons living within twenty blocks of each other and 35 percent of the marriages were between persons living within five blocks of each other.[31] Obviously, proximity allows us to obtain more information about the other person. The inescapable conclusion seems to be that as proximity increases, attraction is likely to increase. One might also posit that as attraction increases, proximity will tend to increase.

Perhaps the most famous study of proximity, friendship choice, and interpersonal contact was conducted by Festinger, Schachter, and Back in a housing development for married students.[32] Concern for what the authors called "functional distance" led to the uncovering of some data that clearly demonstrated that architects can have a tremendous influence on the social life of residents in these housing projects. Functional distance is determined by the number of contacts that are encouraged by position and design; for example, which way the apartments face, where the exits and entranceways are located, the location of stairways, and the like. Figure 3.5 shows the basic design of one type of building studied.

The researchers asked the residents of seventeen buildings (with the design of Figure 3.5) which people they saw most often socially and what friendship choices they made. Among the various findings from this study, the following are noteworthy: (1) There seemed to be a greater number of sociometric choices for those who were physically close to one another—on the same floor, in the same building, and so on. It was rare to find a friendship between people separated by more than four or five houses. (2) People living in apartments 1 and 5 gave

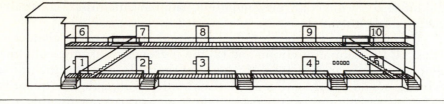

FIGURE 3.5

and received from the upper-floor residents more sociometric choices than the people living in any other apartment on the lower floor. (3) Apartments 1 and 6 exchanged more choices than apartments 2 and 7. Similarly, apartments 5 and 10 exchanged more choices than apartments 4 and 9. Although this represents the same physical distance, the functional distance differed. (4) Apartment 7 chose apartment 6 more than it chose apartment 8; apartment 9 chose apartment 10 more than it chose apartment 8. This relationship did not hold true for corresponding first-floor apartments. (5) Because of the mailboxes, apartment 5 chose more upper-level friends—more of those choices being apartments 9 and 10. There are many ways of making friends, but functional distance seems to be highly influential—and functional distance is sometimes the result of architectural design.

SUMMARY

The environment in which people communicate frequently contributes to the overall outcome of their encounters. We have seen that both the frequency and the content of our messages are influenced by various aspects of the setting in which we communicate. We have seen how the environment influences our behavior, but we also know that we can alter environments in order to elicit certain types of responses. Naturally, as our knowledge of environments increases, we may deliberately use them to help us obtain desired responses.

Throughout this chapter we referred to a number of different types of environments—the classroom, dormitories, offices, prisons, homes, and bars. We suggested that there were several different ways of looking at environments. Mehrabian, following research in other domains of human perception, suggested that all environments could profitably be examined by looking at our emotional reactions to them. These emotions, or feelings, says Mehrabian, can be plotted on three dimensions—arousing/nonarousing, pleasant/unpleasant, and dominant/submissive. Six perceptual bases were suggested for examining environments: formal/informal, warm/cold, private/public, familiar/unfamiliar, constraining/free, and distant/close.

Each environment seems to be composed of three major characteristics: (1) the natural environment, (2) the presence or absence of other people, and (3) architectural design and movable objects, including lighting, sound, color, and general visual-esthetic appeal. The quantity and quality of the research in each of these areas vary considerably, but it is clear that any analysis of human behavior must account for the influence of environmental features if it is to be a thorough analysis.

NOTES

1. A. Mehrabian, *Public Places and Private Spaces* (New York: Basic Books, 1976).
2. M. Knapp, *Social Intercourse: From Greeting to Goodbye* (Boston: Allyn and Bacon, 1978).
3. "Moonstruck Scientists," *Time* 48 (January 10, 1972).
4. T. K. Irwin, "Weather and You: Your Illness, Your Moods in Rain or Shine," *Family Weekly*, September 14, 1975, 4–6.
5. "Report of the National Advisory Commission on Civil Disorders" (Washington, D.C.: U.S. Government Printing Office, 1968), p. 71. Also see R. E. Goranson and D. King, "Rioting and Daily Temperature: Analysis of the U. S. Riots in 1967" (Unpublished manuscript, York University, Ontario, Canada, 1970).
6. W. Griffitt, "Environmental Effects of Interpersonal Affective Behavior: Ambient Effective Temperature and Attraction," *Journal of Personality and Social Psychology* 15 (1970): 240–244. Also see W. Griffitt and R. Veitch, "Hot and Crowded: Influence of Population Density and Temperature on Interpersonal Affective Behavior," *Journal of Personality and Social Psychology* 17 (1971): 92–98.
7. R. A. Baron and P. A. Bell, "Aggression and Heat: The Influence of Ambient Temperature, Negative Affect, and a Cooling Drink on Physical Aggression," *Journal of Personality and Social Psychology* 33 (1976): 245–255; Also see R. A. Baron and P. A. Bell, "Aggression and Heat: Mediating Effects of Prior Provocation and Exposure to an Aggressive Model," *Journal of Personality and Social Psychology* 31 (1975): 825–832.
8. E. Huntington, *Civilization and Climate* (New Haven: Yale University Press, 1915).
9. D. McClelland, *The Achieving Society* (New York: Van Nostrand Reinhold, 1961).
10. A. H. Maslow and N. L. Mintz, "Effects of Esthetic Surroundings: I. Initial Effects of Three Esthetic Conditions Upon Perceiving 'Energy' and 'Well-Being' in Faces," *Journal of Psychology* 41 (1956): 247–254. Also N. L. Mintz, "Effects of Esthetic Surroundings: II. Prolonged and Repeated Experience in a 'Beautiful' and 'Ugly' Room," *Journal of Psychology* 41 (1956): 459–466.

11. H. Wong and W. Brown, "Effects of Surroundings upon Mental Work as Measured by Yerkes' Multiple Choice Method," *Journal of Comparative Psychology* 3 (1923): 319–331; and J. M. Bilodeau and H. Schlosberg, "Similarity in Stimulating Conditions as a Variable in Retroactive Inhibition," *Journal of Experimental Psychology* 41 (1959): 199–204.
12. Mehrabian, *Public Places and Private Spaces*, p. 90.
13. L. B. Wexner, "The Degree to Which Colors (Hues) Are Associated with Mood-Tones," *Journal of Applied Psychology* 38 (1954): 432–435. Also see D. C. Murray and H. L. Deabler, "Colors and Mood-Tones," *Journal of Applied Psychology* 41 (1957): 279–283.
14. Mehrabian, *Public Places and Private Spaces*, p. 50.
15. F. E. Cheek, R. Maxwell, and R. Weisman, "Carpeting the Ward: An Exploratory Study in Environmental Psychiatry," *Mental Hygiene* 55 (1971): 109–118.
16. S. J. Carr and J. M. Dabbs, "The Effects of Lighting, Distance and Intimacy of Topic on Verbal and Visual Behavior," *Sociometry* 37 (1974): 592–600.
17. R. Birren, *Color Psychology and Color Therapy* (New York: University Books, 1965).
18. K. Goldstein, "Some Experimental Observations Concerning the Influence of Color on the Function of the Organism," *Occupational Therapy and Rehabilitation* 21 (1942): 147–151.
19. A. G. White, "The Patient Sits Down: A Clinical Note," *Psychosomatic Medicine* 15 (1953): 256–257.
20. R. Zweigenhaft, "Personal Space in the Faculty Office: Desk Placement and the Student-Faculty Interaction," *Journal of Applied Psychology* 61 (1976): 529–532.
21. R. Sommer and H. Ross, "Social Interaction in a Geriatric Ward," *International Journal of Social Psychiatry* 4 (1958): 128–133.
22. R. Sommer, *Personal Space* (Englewood Cliffs, N.J.: Prentice-Hall, 1969), p. 121.
23. Ibid., pp. 110–119. Also see: R. Sommer, *Tight Spaces* (Englewood Cliffs, N.J.: Prentice-Hall, 1974). Another report of the variance in classroom participation with seating arrangements is found in R. Sommer, "Classroom Ecology," *Journal of Applied Behavioral Science* 3 (1967): 487–503.
24. R. S. Adams and B. Biddle, *Realities of Teaching: Explorations With Video Tape* (New York: Holt, Rinehart and Winston, 1970).
25. W. Koneya, "The Relationship Between Verbal Interaction and Seat Location of Members of Large Groups" (Ph. D. diss., Denver University, 1973).
26. Sommer, *Personal Space*, p. 119.
27. S. Cavan, *Liquor License* (Chicago: Aldine Publishing Co., 1966).
28. C. J. Drew, "Research on the Psychological-Behavioral Effects of the Physical Environment," *Review of Educational Research* 41 (1971): 447–465. The study cited was R. L. Proctor, "An Investigation of Mental Hospital Nursing Station Design on Aspects of Human Behavior," the Environmental Research Foundation, Topeka, Kansas, 1966 (mimeograph).
29. S. A. Stouffer, "Intervening Opportunities: A Theory Relating Mobility and Distance," *American Sociological Review* 5 (1940): 845–867.

30. M. Deutsch and M. Collins, *Interracial Housing: A Psychological Evaluation of a Social Experiment* (Minneapolis, Minn.: University of Minnesota Press, 1951). It is interesting that some have attacked social legislation that was designed to eliminate segregation because the legislation did not change attitudes but only forced civil obedience. This study, and others, suggest that there are times when bringing those of different races together in close proximity will indeed bring about corresponding positive attitude changes. Caution should be exercised in the generalization of such an idea, however. If the two groups are extremely polarized, proximity may only serve to magnify the hostilities.

31. R. Kennedy, "Premarital Residential Propinquity," *American Journal of Sociology* 48 (1943): 580–584.

32. L. Festinger, S. Schachter, and K. Back, *Social Pressures in Informal Groups: A Study of Human Factors in Housing* (New York: Harper & Row, 1950). For another interesting example of how architecture structures interaction, see R. R. Blake, C. C. Rhead, B. Wedge, and J. S. Mouton, "Housing Architecture and Social Interaction," *Sociometry* 19 (1956): 133–139.

ADDITIONAL READINGS

Barker, R. G. "On the Nature of the Environment." *Journal of Social Issues* 19 (1963) 1–14.

Hall, E. T. *The Hidden Dimension*. Garden City, N.Y.: Doubleday, 1966.

Korda, M. "Office Power—You Are Where You Sit." *New York*, January 13, 1975, 36–44.

McLuhan, M. "Inside on the Outside, or the Spaced-Out American." *Journal of Communication* 26 (1976): 46–53.

Mehrabian, A. *Public Places and Private Spaces*. New York: Basic Books, 1976.

Newman, O. *Defensible Space*. New York: Macmillan Publishing Co., 1973.

Rohles, F. H. "Environmental Psychology: A Bucket of Worms." *Psychology Today* 1 (1967): 54–62.

Sommer, R. *Tight Spaces: Hard Architecture and How to Humanize It*. Englewood Cliffs, N.J.: Prentice-Hall, 1974.

THE EFFECTS OF
TERRITORY AND
PERSONAL SPACE

Spatial changes give a tone to a communication, accent it, and at times even override the spoken word.

E. T. HALL

"If you can read this, you're too close," announces a familiar automobile bumper sticker. This sign is an attempt to maintain a minimum safe amount of space between vehicles. Signs that read "Keep Out" and "Authorized Personnel Only" are similar attempts to regulate the amount of space between human beings. We don't put up signs in daily conversation, but we use other signals to avoid uncomfortable crowding and other perceived invasions of our personal space. Our use of space (our own and others') can dramatically affect our ability to achieve certain desired communication goals—whether they involve romance, diplomacy, or aggression. Any discussion of human spatial behavior should first consider the notion of territoriality. An understanding of this concept provides a useful perspective for our later examination of conversational space.

THE CONCEPT OF TERRITORIALITY

The term *territoriality* has been used for years in the study of animal and fowl behavior. Generally, the term has come to mean behavior that is characterized by identification with an area in such a way as to indicate ownership and defense of this territory against those who may "invade" it. There are many different kinds of territorial behavior, and frequently these behaviors perform useful functions for a given species. For instance, territorial behaviors may help coordinate activities; regulate density; ensure propagation of the species; provide places to hide; hold the group together; and provide staging areas for courtship, for nesting, or for feeding.

Most behavioral scientists agree that territoriality exists in human behavior, as well. It helps regulate social interaction, but it can also be the source of social conflict. Like animals, the more powerful, dominant humans seem to have control over more territory as long as the group or societal structure is stable. Some territorial behaviors around one's home are particularly strong, namely, Dad's chair, Mom's kitchen, Billy's stereo, or Barbara's phone.

TERRITORIALITY: INVASION AND DEFENSE

Instructions to police interrogators sometimes suggest that the interrogator sit close to the suspect and not allow a desk to intervene and provide any protection or comfort for the suspect. This theory of interrogation assumes that invasion of the suspect's personal territory (with no chance for defense) will give the police officer a psychological advantage over the suspect. Interestingly, as noted in the last chapter, a desk or similar office barrier could inhibit "friendly" interaction and perceptions of "closeness." What happens when somebody invades "your" territory? For instance, how do you feel when the car behind you is tailgating? How do you feel when you have to stand in a crowded theater lobby or crowded bus? How do you feel when somebody sits in "your" seat? Some researchers have asked similar questions, and their answers to them will help us understand further how we use the space around us.

Not all territorial encroachments are the same. Lyman and Scott[1] identify three types: (1) *Violation* involves the unwarranted use of another's territory. This may be done with the eyes (staring at someone trying to eat in a public restaurant); with the voice or other sounds (construction noise next to a home); or with the body (taking up two subway seats). (2) *Invasion* has a more all-encompassing and permanent nature. Here there is an attempt to take over another's territory. This may be an armed invasion of another country, or it may be the act of a wife who has turned her husband's den into a sewing room. (3) *Contamination* may occur when we defile another's territory not by our presence but by what we leave behind. When we take temporary occupancy of a hotel room, for instance, we do not want to find the previous "owner's" toilet articles and soiled sheets. Similarly, we are frequently upset by dog feces in our yard or food particles on "our" silverware in restaurants.

Although encroachments on one's territory will sometimes produce defensive maneuvers, this is not always the case. The intensity of one's reaction to encroachment on his or her territory will vary depending on a number of factors. Some of these include: (1) Who violated your territory? You may have very different reactions to friends as opposed to strangers; males as opposed to females; high-status individuals as opposed to low-status ones; objects as opposed to people; peers as opposed to the very old and very young. (2) Why did they violate your territory? If you feel that the violator "knew better" you might react more strongly than if you felt he or she "couldn't help it" or was "naive." (3) What type of territory was it? You may perceive a violation of your personal territory as far more serious than a violation of a public territory. (4) How was the violation accomplished? If your body is touched, you may be more aroused than if someone walked across your grass. (5) How long did the encroachment last? If the violation is perceived as temporary, your reactions may be less severe. (6) Where did the violation occur? The population density and opportunities for negotiating new territorial boundaries will surely affect your reaction. High-density situations and the way people react to them are discussed later in this chapter. This section primarily addresses low-density situations. On a public beach, for example, the territorial violations may not seem as important as those that occur in one's bathroom. On the beach there is more territory to negotiate, boundaries are easily redrawn, and it is considered public territory.

The two primary methods for territorial defense are *prevention* and *reaction*. Prevention is a means of staking out your territory so that others will recognize it as yours and go elsewhere. This may be done by actually occupying a place; asking another person to "watch" your territory while you are away; using "markers" such as umbrellas, coats, notebooks, and the like;[2] or using a special jargon or dialect to warn others that a particular space is reserved for those who "know the language."

People react in different ways when the prevention of territorial violations does not work. When people come close to us, we are physiologically aroused—our heart rate and galvanic skin responses increase.[3] Patterson observed that arousal also varies with eye gaze and touch as well as distance.[4] Once aroused, we need to label our state as "positive" (liking, love, relief) or "negative" (dislike, embarrassment, stress, anxiety). If the aroused state is labeled as a positive one, Patterson predicts we will reciprocate the behavior; if it is labeled a negative one, we will take measures to compensate. Thus, if someone is aroused by another person's approach and identifies it as an undesirable state, we would predict behavior designed to restore the "proper" distance between the interactants—looking away, changing the topic to a less personal one, crossing one's arms to form a frontal barrier to the invasion, covering one's body parts, rubbing one's neck (which makes the elbow protrude toward the invader), and so on.

Russo conducted a two-year study that consisted of invading the territory of female college students seated in a college library.[5] The study compared the responses of those invaded and a similar group that was not invaded. Several different invasion techniques were used—sitting next to subjects, sitting across from them, and so on. The quickest departure or flight was triggered when the researcher sat next to a subject and moved her chair closer (approximately one foot). After about thirty minutes, about 70 percent of the people whom Russo approached at the one-foot distance moved. Russo's work is summarized by Sommer:

> There were wide individual differences in the ways victims reacted—there is no single reaction to someone's sitting too close; there are defensive gestures, shifts in posture, and attempts to move away. If these fail or are ignored by the invader, or he shifts position too, the victim eventually takes to flight . . . There was a dearth of direct verbal responses to the invasions. . . . Only one of the eighty students asked the invader to move over.[6]

Barach conducted a study similar to Russo's, but the library invader's status was manipulated.[7] In this study, the students fled quickly from the more formally dressed "high-status" invaders. Knowles experimented with a type of invasion with which we are all familiar, talking to somebody in a hallway while other people decide whether to walk through or around the conversants.[8] Only 25 percent of the people in this study walked through, but when the conversants were replaced by barrels, 75 percent of the passersby walked through. The fewest intrusions occurred with four-person groups (rather than a dyad) and "high-status" conversants (older and more formally dressed). This study is reported to illustrate the fact that not only do we not want others to violate our territory, we generally do not like the role of invader either— as the mumbled apologies and bowed heads of some of Knowles' invaders testify.

Increasing the density of a species also results in territorial violations. The attention given to human overpopulation makes what happens when the population becomes so dense that one cannot exercise usual territorial behavior a particularly important concern.

DENSITY AND CROWDING

Let us first examine some interesting examples of animal behavior under conditions of high density or overpopulation. For years, scientists were intrigued by the large-scale suicides of lemmings, rabbits, and rats. The interest of these scientists was increased by the fact that at the time of the suicides, the animals seemed to have plenty of food, predators were not in evidence, and infection was not present. An ethnologist who had training in medical pathology hypothesized that the suicides were triggered by an endocrine reaction in the animals that resulted from stress built up in them during an increase of population.[9] This hypothesis was confirmed in a study of the deer population on James Island—an island one mile off the coast of Maryland in Chesapeake Bay. Careful histological studies over a period of years showed that the deer on James Island died from overactive adrenal glands—resulting from stress. The adrenal glands play an important part in the regulation of growth, reproduction, and the level of the body's defenses. Thus, overpopulation caused death, not by starvation, infection, or aggression from others but by a physiological reaction to the stress created.

Calhoun's experiments go even further to suggest peculiar modes of behavior under conditions of overpopulation.[10] Calhoun noted that with plenty of food and no danger from predators, Norway rats in a quarter-acre outdoor pen stabilized their population at about 150. His observations, made over a period of twenty-eight months, indicated that spatial relationships were extremely important. Calhoun then designed an experiment in which he could maintain a stressful situation through overpopulation while three generations of rats were reared. He labeled this experiment a "behavioral sink"—an area where most of the rats exhibited gross distortions of behavior. Some of Calhoun's observations are worth noting: (1) Some rats withdrew from social and sexual intercourse completely, whereas others began to mount anything in sight; courtship patterns were totally disrupted and females were frequently pursued by several males. (2) Nest-building patterns—ordinarily neat— became sloppy or nonexistent. (3) Litters of young rats became mixed; newborn and young rats were stepped on or eaten by invading hyperactive males. (4) Unable to establish spatial territories, the dominant males would fight over positions near the eating bins; "classes" of rats shared territories and exhibited similar behavior; the hyperactive males violated all territorial rights by running around in packs—disregarding any boundaries except those backed by force. (5) Pregnant rats frequently had miscarriages; disorders of the sex organs were numerous; and only one fourth of the 558 newborns in the sink survived to be weaned. (6) Aggressive behavior increased significantly.

Can we generalize from mice to men and women? Some early studies that found moderate correlations between various socially undesirable outcomes—such as crime, delinquency, and mental and physical disorders—and high population seemed to say yes. Others facetiously contend that the only generalization we can make from Calhoun's work is: "Don't crowd a rat!" On the basis of the research conducted thus far on human density and crowding, it is clear that we don't have a simple answer to the question of whether "crowding is good or bad."

One of the problems in interpreting this body of research concerns the many perspectives from which the subject has been studied. Density and crowding, for instance, are not the same. Density refers to the number of people per unit of space; whereas crowding is a feeling state that may develop in high- or low-density situations. Your perception of being crowded may be influenced by (1) environmental factors—for example, available space, noise, or the availability of resources and your access to them; (2) personal factors, such as personality and behavioral styles or prior experiences in high-density situations; and (3) social factors— for example, frequency and duration of contact, the nature of the contact (cooperative versus competitive), the people involved (friends versus strangers), or the number of people involved (one, several, or an entire community). Definitions of density are also complex and varied.

The Effects of High Density. Increased density does not automatically mean increased stress or antisocial behavior for human beings. Sometimes we even seek the pleasures of density, such as at football games and rock concerts. If we take responsibility for our presence in a highly populated situation and if we know that the condition will terminate in a matter of hours, the chances of negative effects seem to be minimal. Some studies have found results that might fit well into a "behavioral sink" theory—for example, aggression, stress, criminal activity, hostility toward others, and a deterioration of mental and physical health. However, in most cases we find other studies that do not find these effects. The difference usually lies in the fact that one of the variables mentioned earlier was influential in reducing the undesirable effects. Rohe and Patterson, for instance, found that if children are provided with enough of the toys they wanted, increased density would not produce the withdrawal and aggression suggested by previous studies.[11] Some high-density neighborhoods, which are highly cohesive, actually have a lower incidence of mental and physical health problems. Galle et al. looked at a number of density measures that have previously been associated with high criminal activity.[12] But unlike their predecessors, this research team tried to control for educational level, ethnic background, occupational status, and the like. The person-per-room measure was the measure that provided the highest correlation between density and juvenile delinquency, higher death and fertility rates, and more public assistance. High density can produce a host of problems, but human beings do not stand passively by in situations that demand a long-term commitment to high density. Instead, we try various methods to cope with or offset potentially harmful effects.

Coping with High Density. Milgram believes that city dwellers are exposed to an overload of information, people, things, problems, and the like.[13] As a result, these city dwellers engage in behavior that is designed to reduce this overload, which sometimes causes outsiders to see them as distant and emotionally detached from others. Some of these methods for coping in populated cities include: (1) spending less time with each input—for example, having shorter conversations with people; (2) disregarding low-priority inputs—for example, ignoring the drunk on the sidewalk or not talking to people one sees on a commuter train every day; (3) shifting the responsibility for some transactions to others—for example, relieving bus drivers of the responsibility for making change; (4) blocking inputs—for example, using doormen to guard apartment buildings; and so on.

We now shift our attention from spatial relationships in overpopulated conditions to the relationships involved in a two-person conversation.

CONVERSATIONAL DISTANCE

You have probably had the experience (perhaps not conscious) of backing up or moving forward when speaking to another person. Sometimes this movement is caused by a need to find a comfortable conversational distance. In different situations, when discussing different topics, these "comfortable" distances vary. Is there any consistency to the distances chosen? Is there a specific distance that most people select when talking to others?

Anthropologist Edward T. Hall's astute observations regarding human spatial behavior were published in a book called *The Silent Language*.[14] This book, probably as much as any other single work, is responsible for a surge of scholarly interest in trying to answer these and related questions. Hall identified several types of space, but our concern here is with what he called "informal" or "personal space." Informal space is carried with each individual and expands and contracts under varying circumstances, depending on the type of encounter, the relationship of the communicating persons, their personalities, and many other factors. Hall further classified informal space into four subcategories: intimate, casual-personal, social-consultative, and public. According to Hall, intimate distances range from actual physical contact to about eighteen inches; casual-personal extends from one and a half feet to four feet; social-consultative (for impersonal business) ranges from four to twelve feet; and public distance covers the area from twelve feet to the limits of visibility or hearing. Hall is quick to note that these distances are based on his observations of a particular sample of adults from business and professional occupations, primarily middle class, and native to the northeastern United States and that generalization to various ethnic and racial groups in this country should be made with considerable caution.

Argyle and Dean have theorized that distance is based on the balance of approach and avoidance forces.[15] Burgoon and Jones say that the expected distance in a given conversation is a function of the social norms combined with idiosyncratic patterns of the interactants.[16] What are some of these norms and idiosyncratic patterns? What factors modify the distances we choose?

Age and Sex. Willis studied standing speaking distance of 775 people in a variety of contexts and recorded speaking distance at the beginning of the interaction.[17] Among his conclusions were that speakers stood closer to women than men, and peers stood closer than did persons older than the listener. The first conclusion seems to be in line with other studies that suggest that mixed sex pairs interact at closer distances than all-female pairs, who choose closer distances than all-male pairs. Conversational space for males, then, may be greater than for females, but this will probably be highly variable as other factors in the situation are known. Age differences have not been carefully studied, but it seems reasonable to assume that we would interact closer to people in our own general age range. The exceptions are the very old and the very young who, for various reasons, often elicit interaction at closer quarters. Most of these generalizations about age and sex do not consider cultural or ethnic backgrounds.

Cultural and Ethnic Background. Volumes of folklore and isolated personal observations suggest that spatial relationships in other cultures with different needs and norms may produce very different distances for interacting. Watson and Graves found substantial and consistent differences between pairs of Arab students and pairs of United States students in a conversational setting.[18] These differences included such things as: (1) Arabs confronted one another more directly; (2) Arabs moved closer together; (3) Arabs used more touch behavior; and (4) Arabs were apt to look each other squarely in the eye—an event that occurred less frequently with students from the United States. Watson and Graves also found a tendency toward subcultural homogeneity among Arabs from four different nations and among Americans from four regions of the United States. These results are tempered by the statistical tests used to measure the differences and by the small number of pairs used—sixteen pairs of subjects for each culture. In a much more extensive treatment of cross-cultural proxemics, Watson reports numerous observations on individuals representing "contact" and "noncontact" cultures.[19] Contact refers to interactants who face one another more directly, interact closer to one another, touch one another more, look one another in the eye more, and speak in a louder voice. Contact groups in Watson's study were Arabs, Latin Americans, and Southern Europeans. Noncontact groups were Asians, Indians and Pakistanis, Northern

Europeans, and North Americans. Forston and Larson, however, found that Latin American students did not necessarily exhibit the traditional space differences of sitting closer than North Americans; in fact, their tendency was to sit further apart.[20] Shuter's systematic field observations suggest that we are too imprecise when we talk about broad cultural groups.[21] He found, for instance, that there were significant differences within the so-called Latin American cultural group. Costa Ricans interacted more closely than did Panamanians or Colombians.

The findings relevant to black Americans, white Americans, and Mexican-Americans are generally so haphazard that only a maze of contradictions remains. There is no consistent spatial pattern for comparing black interactants with white interactants, but a couple of studies show that black-white pairs maintain greater distances than white-white or black-black dyads. A developmental study that examined black and white children in the first, third, and fifth grades suggested that subcultural proxemic differences may exist when a child enters school, but by the fifth grade these differences are minimized through maturation and acculturation.[22] Scherer believes that any differences between blacks, whites, and Mexican-Americans are socioeconomic differences and not differences that are attributable to ethnic background.[23] This study found that middle-class children maintained greater conversational distance than lower-class children, but that there were no differences between middle-class blacks and whites or between lower-class blacks and whites.

Topic or Subject Matter. Erickson wanted to find out if proxemic shifts (forward or backward) were associated with any other events in a conversation.[24] By coding co-occurring behavior, he determined that proxemic shifts may mark important segments of the encounter, for example, beginnings, endings, and topic changes.

Earlier we noted that Sommer, in his efforts to examine the limits of conversational distance, tried to use "impersonal" topics—topics that would not obviously influence the distances chosen. Leipold's work demonstrates how the anticipated treatment of the same general topic can influence conversational distance.[25] Students entered a room and were given either stress comments ("Your grade is poor, and you have not done your best"), praise comments ("You are doing very well and Mr. Leipold wants to talk with you further"), or neutral comments ("Mr. Leipold is interested in your feelings about the introductory course"). Students in the stress condition sat furthest from the experimenter and those who were given praise sat closest. Little asked subjects in several different countries to position dolls relative to one another for a variety of social situations and for pleasant, neutral, and unpleasant topics.[26] Pleasant topics clearly produced the closest placement of the figures, but neutral and unpleasant topic situations were not significantly different. Although we are not able to obtain information about specific topics, it is worth noting that close distances may decrease the amount of talking—regardless of the topic.[27]

Setting for the Interaction.   The social setting makes a great deal of difference in how far we stand from others in conversation. A crowded cocktail party demands a different distance than a comfortable evening in the living room with your spouse. Lighting, temperature, noise, and available space will affect your interaction distance. Some authors have hypothesized that as room size increases, people tend to sit closer together. If you perceive the setting as a formal and/or unfamiliar one, we would predict greater distances from unknown others and closer distances to those you know. Little had people arrange actresses in certain settings to determine the interpersonal distances that were perceived as necessary in various situations.[28] Each student was a director and was to place the interactants in a street-corner setting, an office waiting room, the lobby of a public building, and a campus location. The maximum placement distance was in the office, whereas the closest placement was in the street scene.

Physical Characteristics.   The size of your interaction partner (height and weight) may call for changes in interaction distance—to avoid overpowering or being overpowered or simply to achieve a better angle of gaze. A series of studies conducted by Kleck showed that persons interacting with stigmatized individuals (a left-leg amputation was simulated with a special wheelchair) chose greater initial speaking distances than with nonstigmatized, or "normal," persons, but that this distance decreased as the length of the interaction increased.[29] Perceived epileptics elicited similar reactions.

Attitudinal and Emotional Orientation.   Kleck's work also included situations in which the subject was told that the other person was "warm and friendly" or "unfriendly." Not surprisingly, the subjects chose greater distances when interacting with a person who was perceived to be unfriendly. Similarly, when they were told to enter into a conversation with another person and to behave in a friendly way, the subjects chose closer distances than when they were told to "let him know you aren't friendly." This friendly-unfriendly relationship to distance even seems to manifest itself with preschool children.[30] The number of unfriendly acts was directly related to the distance maintained by the recipient of such acts during free-play situations. The distance could be reduced by putting a prized toy near the aggressive child. In some instances our anger will cause us to withdraw from others, but seeking retaliation may reduce distance.[31] Changes in our emotional state can sometimes make vast differences in how close or far away we want to be from others—

for example, states of depression or fatigue as opposed to states of extreme excitement or joy.

An unpublished study mentioned by Patterson reveals that we may make a whole host of interpersonal judgments about another person based on distance.[32] Subjects were told to interview others and to secretly rate them on traits of friendliness, aggressiveness, dominance, extroversion, and intelligence. The interviewees were actually confederates who approached the interviewers at different distances and gave standard answers to the questions asked. The mean ratings for all the traits at four different distances were tabulated and revealed that the most distant position yielded significantly lower (less favorable) ratings. So, barring any contradictory information, closer people are often seen as warmer, liking one another more, and being more empathic and understanding.

When we seek to win the approval of another person, there will be a reduction in conversational distance as compared to instances when we are deliberately trying to avoid approval. Rosenfeld's female subjects seeking approval maintained a mean distance of fifty-seven inches, whereas those who were trying to avoid approval maintained a mean distance of ninety-four inches. When the distance was held constant at five feet, the approval seekers compensated by smiling more and engaging in gestural activity.[33] Mehrabian concluded his review of attitude-distance research by saying:

> . . . the findings from a large number of studies corroborate one another and indicate that communicator-addressee distance is correlated with the degree of negative attitude communicated to and inferred by the addressee. In addition, studies carried out by sociologists and anthropologists indicate that distances which are too close, that is, inappropriate for a given interpersonal situation, can elicit negative attitudes when the communicator—addressee relationship is not an intimate one.[34]

Characteristics of the Interpersonal Relationship. Willis also found that strangers seemed to begin conversations further away than did acquaintances; women stood closer to friends than did men, but further away from "just friends" (the author suggests this may be the result of a more cautious approach used by some women in making friends), and parents were found to be as distant from their adolescent children as strangers.[35] The range of distance measured in Willis' study was from 17.75 inches (close friends speaking to women) to 28 inches (whites speaking to blacks). Little, in a cross-cultural study, found that friends were perceived as interacting closer together than acquaintances, and that acquaintances interacted closer than strangers.[36]

In our culture, status is associated with greater space or distance. Generally those with higher status have more and better space and greater freedom to move about. Theodore White, in *The Making of the*

President 1960, tells of an instance in which John Kennedy's status was emphasized by the distance his fellow campaign workers maintained from him on a particular occasion, about thirty feet. Hall recounts a problem of status and distance in the military.

> The Army, in its need to get technical about matters that are usually handled informally, made a mistake in the regulations on distance required for reporting to a superior officer.... Instructions for reporting to a superior officer were that the junior officer was to proceed up to a point three paces in front of the officer's desk, stop, salute, and state his name, his rank, and his business.... The normal speaking distance for business matters, where impersonality is involved at the beginning of the conversation, is five and a half to eight feet. The distance required by the Army regulations borders on the edge of what we would call "far." It evokes an automatic response to shout. This detracts from the respect which is supposed to be shown to the superior officer. There are, of course, many subjects which it is almost impossible to talk about at this distance....[37]

Burns reports an experiment in which subjects consistently identified a man's status according to spatial relationships.[38] Short films depicted a man at a desk sorting through a card index. He stopped to answer the phone. Then the film switched to another man who stopped, knocked on the office door, entered, and approached the man seated at the desk. The second man pulled out some papers, and the two men discussed them. Two actors switched roles throughout the films. The audiences were asked to rate the relative status of the two men. The caller was consistently rated subordinate if he stopped just inside the door and conversed from that distance with the man at the desk. The time between the knock and when the man at the desk rose was also related to status—the longer it took the man to respond to the knock, the higher his status was judged. Mehrabian cites two studies that suggest "that the distance between two communicators is positively correlated with their status discrepancy."[39]

Personality Characteristics.   Much has been written about the influence of introversion and extroversion on spatial relationships. It is difficult to draw any firm conclusions, however. Some have found that introverts tend to stand further away than extroverts, particularly in intimate situations. Some have found that extroverts allow others to approach them more closely. Others have found no differences in the distances that persons with these personality characteristics maintain when approaching others. Other studies suggest that anxiety-prone individuals will maintain greater distances. However, closer distances are seen when people have a high self-concept, have high affiliative needs, are low on authoritarianism, and are "self-directed." People with various personality abnormalities can probably be counted on to show greater nonnormative spatial behavior—both too far away and too close.

In addition to studying human spatial behavior in overcrowded situations and in conversation, some researchers have examined such questions in the context of meetings or small groups—particularly with regard to seating patterns.

SEATING BEHAVIOR AND SPATIAL ARRANGEMENTS IN SMALL GROUPS

This body of work is known as small-group ecology. The results of these studies show that our seating behavior is not generally accidental or random. There are explanations for much of our seating behavior—whether we are fully conscious of them or not. The particular position we chose in relation to the other person or persons varies with the task at hand, the degree of relationship between the interactants, the personalities of the two parties, and the amount and kind of available space. Summaries of the findings about seating behavior and spatial positioning can be listed under the categories of leadership, dominance, task, sex and acquaintance, motivation, and introversion-extroversion.

Leadership. It seems to be a cultural norm that leaders are expected to be found at the head or end of the table. At a family gathering we gen-

erally find the head of the household sitting at the head of the table. Elected group leaders generally put themselves in the head positions at rectangular tables, and the other group members try to position themselves so that they can see the leader. Strodtbeck and Hook set up some experimental jury deliberations that revealed that a man sitting at the head position was chosen significantly more often as the leader—particularly if he was perceived as a person from a high economic class.[40] If the choice was between two people at each end, the one perceived as being of higher economic status was chosen.

Howells and Becker add further support to the idea that one's position in a group is an important factor in leadership emergence.[41] They reasoned that spatial position determines the flow of communication which, in turn, determines leadership emergence. Five-person decision-making groups in which three people sat on one side of a rectangular table and two sat on the other side were examined. Since previous work suggested that communication usually flows across the table rather than around it, the researchers believed that the side with two people would be able to influence the most people (or at least talk more) and would, therefore, emerge more often as group leaders. This hypothesis was confirmed.

Dominance. The end positions also seem to carry with them a status or dominance factor. Russo found that people rating various seating arrangements on an "equality" dimension stated that if one person was at the head of the table and one on the side, this was a more unequal situation in terms of status than if they were side by side or both on the ends.[42] In an analysis of talking frequency in small groups, Hare and Bales noted people in positions 1, 3, and 5 (at left) were frequent talkers.[43] Subsequent studies revealed that these people were likely to be dominant personalities, whereas those who avoided the central or focal positions (by choosing seats 2 and 4) were more anxious and actually stated that they wanted to stay out of the discussion.

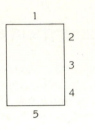

Although further study is necessary, some preliminary work suggests that deliberately placing nondominant persons in focal positions and dominant persons in nonfocal positions will not radically change the frequency of their communications. In groups composed only of nondominant individuals, the results may be much different. Positions 1, 3, and 5 were also considered to be positions of leadership, but leadership of a different type—depending on the position. The two end positions (1 and 5) attracted the task-oriented leader, whereas the middle position was determined to be for more of a socioemotional leader—one concerned about group relationships, getting everyone to participate, and so on. Lott and Sommer wanted to find out how others located themselves vis-à-vis higher- and lower-status people.[44] Generally, the results suggest that people (in this case, students) will sit further away from both higher-status (professor) and lower-status (flunking freshman) persons than from peers.

Task. Sommer's observations of seating behavior in student cafeterias and libraries led him to study how students would sit in different task situations.[45] Persons were asked to imagine themselves sitting at a table with a friend of the same sex in each of the following four situations:

Conversation: Sitting and chatting for a few minutes before class.
Cooperation: Sitting and studying together for the same exam.
Co-action: Sitting studying for different exams.
Competition: Competing in order to see who will be the first to solve a series of puzzles.

Two types of tables were shown to each subject. One table was round and one was rectangular. Each had six chairs. The results of this study are presented in Table 4.1 for rectangular tables and in Table 4.2 for circular tables.

TABLE 4.1
Seating Preferences at Rectangular Tables

(151 RESPONSES)						
Conversation	42%	46%	11%	0%	1%	0%
Cooperation	19	25	51	0	5	0
Co-action	3	32	7	13	43	3
Competition	7	41	8	18	20	5

Conversations before class primarily involved corner or "short" opposite seating at rectangular tables and side-by-side seating at round tables. Cooperation seems to elicit a preponderance of side-by-side choices.

Co-action, studying for different exams or reading at the same table as another, necessitated plenty of room between the participants and the most distant seating positions were generally selected. Most persons wanted to compete in an opposite seating arrangement. Those who wanted to establish a closer opposite relationship apparently felt that this would afford them an opportunity not only to see how the other person is progressing but would also allow them to use various gestures, body movements, and eye contact to "upset" their opponents. The more distant opposite position would, on the other hand, prevent "spying."

A related line of inquiry involved an attempt to determine the impact of discussion topics on seating arrangements. College women discussed topics ranging from very personal to very impersonal. The apparent lack of impact caused Sommer to conclude:

> It seems apparent that it is the nature of the relationship between the individuals rather than the topic itself that characterizes a discussion as

TABLE 4.2
Seating Preferences at Round Tables

(116 RESPONSES)			
Conversation	63%	17%	20%
Cooperation	83	7	10
Co-action	13	36	51
Competition	12	25	63

personal or impersonal. Two lovers discussing the weather can have an intimate conversation, but a zoology professor discussing sex in a lecture hall containing 300 students would be having an impersonal session regardless of topic.[46]

Sex and Acquaintance.   As the previous quote suggests, the nature of the relationship may make a difference in spatial orientation and, hence, in seating selection. Another questionnaire supplemented by some actual observations of persons interacting in a restaurant and several bars was conducted by Cook.[47] Subjects in the questionnaire study were asked to select seating arrangements when: (1) sitting with a casual friend of the same sex, (2) sitting with a casual friend of the opposite sex, and (3) sitting with a boyfriend or girlfriend.

The predominant seating pattern, as stated by questionnaire respondents using a bar as a referent, was corner seating for same-sex friends and casual friends of the opposite sex. Intimate friends appear to desire side-by-side seating. In a restaurant, all variations of sex and acquaintance seem to select opposite seating, with more side-by-side seating occurring between intimate friends. There may be some very practical reasons for opposite seating in restaurants. For instance, others will not have to sit opposite you, which might create some uncomfortable situations with respect to eye contact and overheard conversation. In addition, you won't poke the other person with your elbow while you're eating. The actual observations of seating in a restaurant seem to validate the questionnaire responses. Most people do select opposite seating in restaurants. However, the observations of people sitting in bars do not agree with the questionnaire study of seating preferences in bars. Although questionnaire preferences favored corner seating, actual observations showed a marked preference for side-by-side seating. Cook suggests that this may have been the result of the fact that the bars were equipped with many seats located against the wall. Supposedly this allowed persons to sit side by side, not have their back to anyone, and have a good view of the other patrons. Thus, paper-and-pencil preferences were overruled by environmental factors. From this study we must conclude that sex and acquaintance with the other person do have an effect on one's actual and preferred seating positions. This is also consistent with a great deal of work that suggests we will try to reduce the distance between those we feel have attitudes similar to ours. And similarly, we seem more frequently to develop positive relationships with those whom we find in close proximity to us—at home or at work.

Motivation.   The idea that one may regulate intimacy with another through either increasing eye gaze or decreasing distance has been mentioned. Of course, one may do both. What we did not know prior to a further study by Cook was what conditions prompt the use of distance and what conditions prompt the use of eye gaze.[48] Again respondents made seating selections based on different types (positive and negative) and different levels (high, medium, and low) of motivation. For example, high-positive motivation was "sitting with your boy or girl friend" and low-negative motivation was "sitting with someone you do not like very much and do not wish to talk to." Cook found that as motivation increased, persons wanted to sit closer or have more eye gaze. When the motivation was affiliative the choice was to sit closer, and when the motivation was competitive, the choice was one that would allow more eye gaze. It seems, then, that the choice of eye gaze or proximity depends on the motives of the interacting pair. It is quite permissible to sit close to another when there is high affiliative motivation, but when there are high levels of nonaffiliative motivation, such proximity is not as permissible, so eye gaze is used.

Introversion-Extroversion. The possible influence of introversion and extroversion on conversational distance has been discussed. Cook found some relation between this personality variable and seating preference.[49] Extroverts chose to sit opposite (either across the table or down the length of it) and disregard positions which would put them at an angle. Many extroverts also chose positions that would put them in close physical proximity to the other person. Introverts generally chose positions that would keep them more at a distance, both visually and physicially.

The following example seems like a most appropriate way to conclude this chapter. It incorporates elements of territoriality and seating arrangements that are influenced by culture, attitudes, leadership perceptions, and the type of task undertaken. We are referring to the discussions of the size and shape of the negotiation table at the Paris peace talks in 1968, where it took eight months merely to reach an agreement on the shape of the table! The diagrams in Figure 4.1 mark the chronology of the seating proposals.

"The United States (U.S.) and South Vietnam (S.V.) wanted a seating arrangement in which only two sides were identified. They did not want to recognize the National Liberation Front (NLF) as an equal party in the negotiations. North Vietnam (N.V.) and the NLF wanted equal status given to all parties, represented by a four-sided table. The final arrangement was such that both parties could claim "victory." The round table minus the dividing lines allowed North Vietnam and the NLF to claim all four delegations were equal. The existence of the two secretarial tables (interpreted as dividers), the lack of identifying symbols on the table, and an AA, BB speaking rotation permitted the United States and South Vietnam to claim victory for the two-sided approach. Considering the lives lost during the eight months needed to arrive at the seating arrangement, we must certainly conclude that proximity and territoriality are far from trivial concerns in some human encounters."[50]

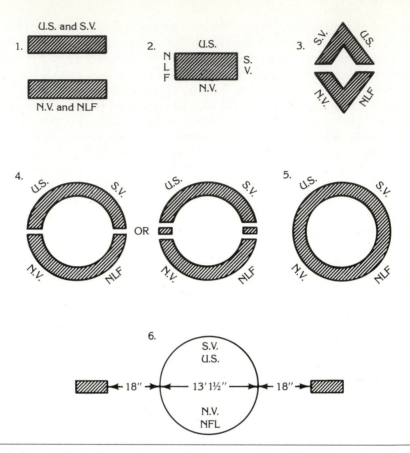

FIGURE 4.1

Proposals for a table to be used at the Paris peace talks, 1968, Drawn from J. C. McCroskey, C. E. Larson, and M. L. Knapp, *An Introduction to Interpersonal Communication* (Englewood Cliffs, N.J.: Prentice-Hall, 1971), p. 98.

SUMMARY

It is clear that our perceptions and use of space contribute extensively to various communication outcomes we seek. We know that some of our spatial behavior is related to a need to stake out and maintain territory. Our territorial behavior can be helpful in regulating social interaction and controlling density; it can also be the source of human conflict when territory is disputed or encroached upon. Although we often think that people vigorously defend their territory, the type of defense is highly dependent on who the intruder is, why the intrusion is taking place, what type of territory is being encroached upon, what type of encroachment is used (violation, invasion, or contamination), how long the encroachment takes, and where it occurs. We often try to prevent people from moving into our territory by marking it as "ours." This can be done by our own physical presence or the presence of a friend who agrees to watch our territory. Territorial invasion can also be prevented by using various kinds of markers (fences, coats, and the like) or a special kind of language. When someone does invade another's territory, we sometimes find the "owner's" physiological arousal increased. In addition, various defense maneuvers are seen—for example, flight, hostile looks, turning or leaning away, blocking advances with objects or hands and arms, or even verbal defenses. People don't like others to invade their territory, but we also find that they are often reluctant to invade the territory of others, often apologizing when it cannot be prevented.

We examined density and crowding from both animal and human perspectives. Animal studies found numerous undesirable effects from overpopulation. High-density human situations, however, are not always disruptive. Sometimes we want the company of many people. The best predictor of individually stressful and socially undesirable outcomes seems to be the number of people per room rather than other density measures. When we do feel the stress of a crowded situation, we seek ways to cope with it. We also distinguished between density (number of people per unit of space) and crowding (a feeling state brought on by the environment, personal factors, or social factors).

Our examination of spatial behavior in conversations revealed many ways of conceptualizing and measuring this behavior. As a result, firm conclusions are difficult to make. We do know that each of us seeks a comfortable conversational distance—a distance that will vary depending on age, sex, cultural and ethnic background, setting, attitudes, emotions, topics, physical characteristics, personality, and our relationship with the other person.

Finally, we discussed seating arrangements in small groups. Distances and seats chosen do not seem to be accidental. Leaders and dominant personalities tend to choose specific seats, and seating will vary with the topic at hand, the nature of the relationship between the parties, and certain personality variables.

NOTES

1. S. M. Lyman and M. B. Scott, "Territoriality: A Neglected Sociological Dimension," *Social Problems* 15 (1967): 235–249.
2. F. D. Becker, "Study of Spatial Markers," *Journal of Personality and Social Psychology* 26 (1973): 439–445.
3. G. McBride, M. G. King, and J. W. James, "Social Proximity Effects of Galvanic Skin Responses in Adult Humans," *Journal of Psychology* 61 (1965): 153–157; also see S. J. Finando, "The Effects of Distance Norm Violation on Heart Rate and Length of Verbal Response" (Ph.D. diss., Florida State University, 1973).

4. M. L. Patterson, "An Arousal Model of Interpersonal Intimacy," *Psychological Review* 83 (1976): 235–245.

5. R. Sommer, *Personal Space* (Englewood Cliffs, N.J.: Prentice-Hall, 1969), pp. 35, 46–48, 64.

6. Ibid., pp. 35–36.

7. D. P. Barach, "Human Ethology: Personal Space Reiterated," *Environment and Behavior* 5 (1973): 67–73.

8. E. S. Knowles, "Boundaries Around Group Interaction: The Effect of Group Size and Member Status on Boundary Permeability," *Journal of Personality and Social Psychology* 26 (1973): 327–332.

9. J. J. Christian and D. E. Davis, "Social and Endocrine Factors are Integrated in the Regulation of Mammalian Populations," *Science* 146 (1964): 1550–1560.

10. J. B. Calhoun, "Population Density and Social Pathology," *Scientific American* 206 (1962): 139–148.

11. W. Rohe and A. H. Patterson, "The Effects of Varied Levels of Resources and Density on Behavior in a Day Care Center," paper presented at Environmental Design and Research Association, Milwaukee, Wis., 1974. Cited in I. Altman, *The Environment and Social Behavior*, (Belmont, California: Wadsworth, 1975), pp. 157, 165, and 182.

12. O. R. Galle, W. R. Gove, and J. M. McPherson, "Population Density and Pathology: What Are the Relationships for Man?" *Science* 176 (1972): 23–30.

13. S. Milgram, "The Experience of Living in Cities," *Science* 167 (1970): 1461–1468.

14. Edward T. Hall, *The Silent Language* (New York: Doubleday & Co. 1959).

15. M. Argyle and J. Dean, "Eye Contact, Distance and Affiliation," *Sociometry* 28 (1965): 289–304.

16. J. K. Burgoon and S. B. Jones, "Toward a Theory of Personal Space Expectations and Their Violations," *Human Communication Research* 2 (1976): 131–146.

17. F. N. Willis, "Initial Speaking Distance as a Function of the Speaker's Relationship," *Psychonomic Science* 5 (1966): 221–222.

18. O. M. Watson and T. D. Graves, "Quantitative Research in Proxemic Behavior," *American Anthropologist* 68 (1966): 971–985.

19. O. M. Watson, *Proxemic Behavior: A Cross-Cultural Study* (The Hague: Mouton, 1970).

20. R. F. Forston and C. U. Larson, "The Dynamics of Space: An Experimental Study in Proxemic Behavior Among Latin Americans and North Americans," *Journal of Communication* 18 (1968): 109–116.

21. R. Shuter, "Proxemics and Tactility in Latin America," *Journal of Communication* 26 (1976): 46–52.

22. S. E. Jones and J. R. Aiello, "Proxemic Behavior of Black and White First, Third, and Fifth Grade Children," *Journal of Personality and Social Psychology* 25 (1973): 21–27.

23. S. E. Scherer, "Proxemic Behavior of Primary School Children as a Function of Their Socioeconomic Class and Subculture," *Journal of Personality and Social Psychology* 29 (1974) 800–805.

24. F. Erickson, "One Function of Proxemic Shifts in Face-to-Face Interac-

tion," in A. Kendon, R. M. Harris, and M. R. Key (eds.), *Organization of Behavior in Face-to-Face Interactions* (Chicago: Aldine, 1975), pp. 175–187.

25. W. E. Leipold, "Psychological Distance in a Dyadic Interview" (Ph.D. diss., University of North Dakota, 1963).

26. K. B. Little, "Cultural Variations in Social Schemata," *Journal of Personality and Social Psychology* 10 (1968): 1–7.

27. R. Schulz and J. Barefoot, "Non-verbal Responses and Affiliative Conflict Theory," *British Journal of Social and Clinical Psychology* 13 (1974): 237–243.

28. K. B. Little, "Personal Space," *Journal of Experimental Social Psychology* 1 (1965): 237–247.

29. R. Kleck, "Physical Stigma and Task Oriented Interaction," *Human Relations* 22 (1969): 51–60.

30. M. G. King, "Interpersonal Relations in Preschool Children and Average Approach Distance," *Journal of Genetic Psychology* 108 (1966): 109–116.

31. M. Meisels and M. Dosey, "Personal Space, Anger Arousal, and Psychological Defense," *Journal of Personality* 39 (1971): 333–334.

32. M. Patterson, "Spatial Factors in Social Interaction," *Human Relations* 21 (1968): 351–361.

33. H. Rosenfeld, "Effect of Approval-Seeking Induction on Interpersonal Proximity," *Psychological Reports* 17 (1965): 120–122. Also H. Rosenfeld, "Instrumental and Affiliative Functions of Facial and Gestural Expressions," *Journal of Personality and Social Psychology* 4 (1966): 65–72.

34. A. Mehrabian, "Significance of Posture and Position in the Communication of Attitude and Status Relationships," *Psychological Bulletin* 71 (1969): 363.

35. Willis, "Initial Speaking Distance as a Function of the Speaker's Relationship."

36. K. B. Little, "Cultural Variations in Social Schemata," *Journal of Personality and Social Psychology* 10 (1968): 5.

37. Hall, *The Silent Language*, p. 163.

38. T. Burns, "Nonverbal Communication," *Discovery* (October, 1964): 31–35.

39. A. Mehrabian, "Significance of Posture and Position." p. 363.

40. F. Strodtbeck and L. Hook, "The Social Dimensions of a Twelve Man Jury Table," *Sociometry* 24 (1961): 297–415. Also see B. M. Bass and S. Klubeck, "Effects of Seating Arrangement on Leaderless Group Discussions," *Journal of Abnormal and Social Psychology* 47 (1952): 724–726.

41. L. T. Howells and S. W. Becker, "Seating Arrangement and Leadership Emergence," *Journal of Abnormal and Social Psychology* 64 (1962): 148–150.

42. N. Russo, "Connotation of Seating Arrangement," *Cornell Journal of Social Relations* 2 (1967): 37–44.

43. A. Hare and R. Bales, "Seating Position and Small Group Interaction," *Sociometry* 26 (1963): 480–486.

44. B. S. Lott and R. Sommer, "Seating Arrangement and Status," *Journal of Personality and Social Psychology* 7 (1967): 90–95.

45. R. Sommer, "Further Studies of Small Group Ecology," *Sociometry* 28 (1965): 337–348.

46. Sommer, *Personal Space*, p. 65.

47. M. Cook, "Experiments on Orientation and Proxemics," *Human Relations* 23 (1970): 61–76.
48. Ibid.
49. Ibid.
50. J. C. McCroskey, C. E. Larson, and M. L. Knapp, *An Introduction to Interpersonal Communication* (Englewood Cliffs, N.J.: Prentice-Hall, 1971), p. 98.

ADDITIONAL READINGS

Altman, I. *The Environment and Social Behavior*. Belmont, Calif. Wadsworth, 1975.

Ardrey, R. *The Territorial Imperative*. New York: Atheneum Press, 1966.

Calhoun, J. B. "Population Density and Social Pathology." *Scientific American* 206 (1962): 139–148.

Esser, A. H. (ed.). *Environment and Behavior: The Use of Space by Animals and Men*. New York: Plenum, 1971.

Evans, G. W. and R. B. Howard. "Personal Space." *Psychological Bulletin* 80 (1973): 334–344.

Freedman, J. L. *Crowding and Behavior*. New York: Viking, Press, 1975.

Hall, E. T. *The Silent Language*. Garden City, N.Y.: Doubleday & Co., 1959.

Scheflen, A. E. and N. Ashcraft. *Human Territories: How We Behave in Space-Time*. Englewood Cliffs, N.J.: Prentice-Hall, 1976.

Sommer, R. *Personal Space*. Englewood Cliffs, N.J.: Prentice-Hall, 1969.

———. "Small Group Ecology." *Psychological Bulletin* 67 (1967): 145–152.

Watson, M. "Symbolic and Expressive Uses of Space: An Introduction to Proxemic Behavior," Module No. 20. Reading, Mass.: Addison-Wesley, 1972.

THE EFFECTS OF PHYSICAL APPEARANCE AND DRESS

By a man's finger-nails, by his coat-sleeve, by his boots, by his trouser-knees, by the callosities on his forefinger and thumb, by his expression, by his shirt-cuffs—by each of these things a man's calling is plainly revealed. That all united should fail to enlighten the competent inquirer in any case is almost inconceivable. SHERLOCK HOLMES

Picture the following scene: Mr. and Mrs. American awake and prepare to start the day. Mrs. American takes off her nighttime bra and replaces it with a "slightly padded uplift" bra. After removing her chin strap, she further pulls herself together with her girdle. Then she begins to "put on her face," which involves the use of an eyebrow pencil, mascara, lipstick, rouge, eyeliner, and false eyelashes. Then she removes the hair under her arms and on her legs and places a hairpiece on her head. False fingernails, nail polish, and tinted contact lenses are then applied followed by the deodorant, perfume, and endless decisions concerning clothes. Mr. American shaves the hair on his face, puts a toupee on his head, and carefully attaches his newly purchased sideburns. He removes his false teeth from a solution used to whiten them, gargles with a breath sweetener, selects his after-shave lotion, puts on his elevator shoes, and begins making his clothing decisions. Although this hypothetical example represents an extreme, people do go to great lengths to make themselves attractive. Why? Does it make any difference to our interpersonal contacts?

OUR BODY: ITS GENERAL ATTRACTIVENESS

Although it is not uncommon to hear people muse about how inner beauty is the only thing that really counts, research suggests that outer beauty, or physical attractiveness, plays an influential role in determining responses for a broad range of interpersonal encounters.

Studies of the persuasion process also show attractiveness to be important. Mills and Aronson found that an attractive female could modify attitudes of male students more than an unattractive woman could.[1] One woman was made up to look different under two conditions. In the unattractive condition she was rated repulsive by independent observers; she wore loose-fitting clothing, her hair was messy, makeup was conspicuously absent, a trace of a mustache was etched on her upper lip, and her complexion was oily and unwholesome looking. The experimenter suggested to a group of students that they would more quickly complete some measuring instruments if a volunteer would read the questions aloud and indicate what they meant. The "volunteer" was either the attractive or unattractive woman. Although this study used a male audience, females are certainly not exempt from responding favorably to speaker attractiveness.[2] In Widgery's study, females attributed higher credibility ratings to attractive sources than males did. And Widgery and Webster offer some evidence that attractive persons, regardless of their sex, will be rated high on the character dimension of credibility scales.[3] Although more work needs to be done, attractiveness does seem to be an influential factor in the perception of initial credibility and is thus an influential factor in one's ultimate persuasiveness.

A number of studies in which people were asked to act as jurors in cases involving attractive and unattractive defendants show, as expected, that unattractive defendants are more likely to be judged guilty and more likely to receive longer sentences.[4] Obviously, a defendant's attractiveness is rarely assessed in isolation in the courtroom, and other factors will interact with attractiveness—for example, the extent to which the defendant expresses repentance, the degree of commitment that jurors have toward impartiality, the extent to which jurors "discuss" the case, the perceived similarity of jurors and defendant, the defendant's verbalizations, and the nature of the crime being examined—that is, the extent to which attractiveness was a part of the crime, as in a swindle.

The evidence from this culture overwhelmingly supports the notion that initially we respond much more favorably to those whom we perceive as physically attractive than those who are seen as less attractive or ugly. Summarizing numerous studies in this area, it is not at all unusual to find physically attractive persons outstripping unattractive ones on a wide range of socially desirable evaluations, such as success, personality, popularity, sociability, sexuality, persuasiveness, and often happiness. Attractive women are more likely to be helped and are less likely to be the objects of aggressive acts.[5] These judgments that are linked to a person's attractiveness begin early in life (preschool, kindergarten)—apparently reflecting similar attitudes and evaluations made by teachers and parents. Not only do teachers seem to interact less (and less positively) with the so-called unattractive elementary school child but the child's peers also react unfavorably. There are many occasions in a child's life when adults ask, "Who dunnit?" If an unattractive child is available, the chances are stronger that he or she will be pointed out as the culprit.[6] As the unattractive child grows older, he or she probably will not be discriminated against as long as his or her task performance is impressive, but as soon as performance declines, the less attractive person will receive more sanctions than the attractive one.

Physical attractiveness also seems to be an extremely important factor in courtship and marriage decisions. Numerous studies provide testimony from unmarried men and women that physical attractiveness is a critical factor in mate selections. One early study asked students if they would marry a person who ranked low in such qualities as economic status, good looks, disposition, family religion, health, education, intelligence, or age.[7] Men most frequently rejected women who were deficient in good looks, disposition, morals, and health, whereas women did not seem to worry as much about marrying a man who was deficient in good looks. Table 5.1, based on the responses of 28,000 readers of *Psychology Today*, shows a continued emphasis on female attractiveness, by both men and women. The percentages indicate the number of respondents who said attractiveness was "essential" or "very important" to the ideal.[8]

It was just such a disproportionate concern for physical attractiveness that prompted Susan Sontag to argue against the social convention that aging enhances a man but progressively destroys a woman.[9] She points out that women are taught from childhood to care in a "pathologically exaggerated way" about their appearance. Men, she says, need only have a clean face, but a woman's face is a "canvas upon which she paints a revised, corrected portrait of herself." "Ruggedly attractive men" is a familiar concept, but is there a similar form of attractiveness for women who do not conform to the ideal? In many quarters masculinity means, among other things, not caring for one's looks; femininity,

TABLE 5.1
Attractiveness and the Ideal Man and Woman

	MALE RESPONDENTS	FEMALE RESPONDENTS
Ideal man	26%	29%
Ideal woman	47%	32%

on the other hand, means caring a great deal. We've heard a lot about discrimination against women, but when men apply for jobs that have traditionally been held by women they often feel discriminated against. Could it be that a secretary, for instance, is perceived by the male employers as a "decoration" as well as a worker? A man may be able to type competently, but will his male supervisors like to look at him all day?

On the other hand, gender seemed to make little difference in a study in which persons were asked to evaluate strangers of the same or opposite sex—strangers who had previously been rated as either physically attractive or unattractive.[10] Interpersonal attraction was found to be greatest toward the physically attractive strangers—regardless of sex. In this phase of the study, subjects had no other information about the stranger; through subsequent study, the same researchers found that physical attractiveness was still an important determinant of attraction when subjects had additional information about the strangers—for example, information on several of the strangers' attitudes. These traits do not seem limited to the United States. A study conducted in India found that men wanted wives who were more physically beautiful than themselves, and women wanted husbands who were equal to them in physical beauty.[11]

In light of this general preference for a physically attractive partner, we might suspect that actual dating patterns would reflect these preferences. Such a hypothesis would certainly be confirmed by a series of "computer dance" studies at the universities of Texas, Illinois, and Minnesota, where physical attractiveness superseded a host of other variables in determining a liking for one's partner and a desire to date in the future. For example, Walster and her colleagues randomly paired 752 college students for a freshman dance.[12] A great deal of information was gathered from each student, including self-reports about popularity, religious preference, height, race, expectations for the date, self-esteem, high school academic percentile rank, scholastic aptitude score, and personality test scores. In addition, each student was rated by several judges for attractiveness. It was found that physical attractiveness was by far the most important determinant of how much a date would be liked by his or her partner. It appears that physical attractiveness was just as important an asset for a man as for a woman, since it was a reliable predictor for both groups. Brislin and Lewis replicated this study with fifty-eight unacquainted men and women and again found a strong correlation (.89) between "desire to date again" and "physical attractiveness."[13] In addition, this study asked each person whether he or she would like to date anyone else at the dance. Of the thirteen other people named, all had previously, and independently, been rated as very attractive.

It seems that in many situations everyone prefers the most attractive date possible regardless of his or her own attractiveness and regardless of the possibility of being rejected by the most attractive date. There are obvious exceptions. Some gigolos argue that if they approach a woman somewhat less attractive—particularly in the company of some who are very attractive—their chances of succeeding are greatly increased. Some attractive persons have more dating opportunities than they desire; others, however, are almost untouched in the mainstream of dating behavior. Why? Walster and her colleagues proposed what they call the "matching hypothesis." Since this hypothesis was presented, other studies have confirmed its validity—including a study of middle-aged married couples. Essentially, the matching hypothesis argues that each person may be attracted to only the best looking partners, but reality sets in when actual dates are made. You may face an unwanted rejection if you select only the best looking person available, so the tendency is to select a person who is similar to yourself with respect to physical attractiveness. Hence, the procedure seems to be to try to maximize the attractiveness of your choice while simultaneously minimizing the possibilities of rejection. If you have high self-esteem, you might seek out highly attractive partners in spite of a considerable gap between your looks and theirs.[14] Self-esteem, in this case, will affect the perception of and possible reaction to rejection.

Sometimes we observe couples who seem to be "mismatched" with regard to their physical attractiveness. One study suggests that evaluations of males may change dramatically if they are viewed as "married" to someone very different in general physical attractiveness.[15] Unattractive men who were seen with attractive women were judged, among other things, as making more money, as being more successful in their occupation, and as being more intelligent than attractive men with attractive partners. The judges must have reasoned that for an unattractive man to marry an attractive woman, he must have had to offset this imbalance in physical appearance by succeeding in other areas, such as making money. Handsome men, however, don't seem to be able to significantly increase the ratings of unattractive women.

Although some people would like to believe that "everything is beautiful in its own way"—as a 1970 pop song put it—it should also be recognized that some people are beautiful in much the same way to large segments of the population. The stereotypes of American beauty promoted by *Playboy* and the Miss America Pageant, among numerous others, seem to be very influential in setting cultural norms of beauty. Their recognition of this influence caused many women to condemn *Playboy*'s portrayal of ideal womanhood and prompted some black leaders to organize a Miss Black America Pageant. It is not surprising to find that in one case over four thousand judges, differing in age, sex, occupation, and geographical location, exhibited high levels of agreement concerning prettiness in young women's faces.[16] Physical attractiveness seems to play an important role in persuading and/or manipulating others—whether in courtship, a classroom, or a public speaking situation.

101

Attractiveness is certainly very influential on first impressions and expectations for an encounter.

It would not be right to leave this section on attractiveness without at least noting that there are some important qualifications to the dictum that "what is beautiful is good." For instance, attractive people are not consistently rated as more intelligent or more trustworthy, and unattractive couples have been judged by others to be more happily married than physically attractive couples. Handsome men do not seem to score any better on tests measuring happiness, self-esteem, and psychological well-being. Although attractive women seem to score slightly better on such measures than unattractive ones, this does not seem to be a lasting result. For example, middle-aged women who had been identified as attractive college students seemed to be less happy, less satisfied with their lives, and less well adjusted than their "plain" counterparts.[17]

Methodological issues may also provide comfort to those who perceive themselves as something short of attractive. Most, although not all, studies of physical attractiveness use photographs that, prior to the study, are judged by a panel of "experts" to fall into the "beautiful" or "ugly" category. Hence, in most cases, we are not reporting results from live, moving, talking human beings in a particular environment and we are not generally dealing with subtle differences in physical attractiveness that lie between the extremes of beautiful and ugly. Furthermore, we must remember that one's appearance may be relative to the context in which it is judged—for example, you may perceive a popular singer on stage or on television as "sexy," but the same person in your living room may seem much less glamorous. Some maintain that neither very attractive nor very unattractive women are the most likely to succeed in business in today's society; that is, extreme attractiveness may actually be a barrier to a woman's rapid and high-level achievement in this environment. And finally, one's degree of attractiveness will, in most communication situations, interact with other factors that may offset or change perceptions of appearance—for example, the content of one's verbal messages.

Now that we have examined the global concept of attractiveness, we can ask: What specific aspects of another person's appearance do we respond to? Does it make any difference how we perceive our own body and appearance? The answers to these questions make up the focus for the remainder of this chapter.

OUR BODY: ITS SHAPE, COLOR, SMELL, AND HAIR

Body Shape, In order to add a personal dimension to some of the theory and research in this section, a short SELF-DESCRIPTION TEST is provided. By taking this test, you can gather some data on yourself that can be compared with that of others who have taken it.[18]

Instructions: Fill in each blank with a word from the suggested list following each statement. For any blank, three of which appear in each statement, select any word from the list of twelve immediately below the statement. An exact word that fits you may not be in the list, but you are to select the words that seem to fit most closely the way you are.

1. I feel most of the time_____, _____, and _____.

calm	relaxed	complacent
anxious	confident	reticent
cheerful	tense	energetic
contented	impetuous	self-conscious

2. When I study or work, I seem to be_____, _____, and _____.

efficient	sluggish	precise
enthusiastic	competitive	determined
reflective	leisurely	thoughtful
placid	meticulous	cooperative

3. Socially, I am_____, _____, and _____.

outgoing	considerate	argumentative
affable	awkward	shy
tolerant	affected	talkative
gentle-tempered	soft-tempered	hot-tempered

4. I am rather _____, _____, and _____.

active	forgiving	sympathetic
warm	courageous	serious
domineering	suspicious	softhearted
introspective	cool	enterprising

5. Other people consider me rather_____, _____, and _____.

generous	optimistic	sensitive
adventurous	affectionate	kind
withdrawn	reckless	cautious
dominant	detached	dependent

6. Underline one word out of the three in each of the following lines that most closely describes the way you are:
   (a) assertive, relaxed, tense
   (b) hot-tempered, cool, warm
   (c) withdrawn, sociable, active
   (d) confident, tactful, kind
   (e) dependent, dominant, detached
   (f) enterprising, affable, anxious

This test has been given to numerous individuals participating in studies concerned with the relationship between certain personality and temperament characteristics and certain body types or builds. These studies are generally concerned with a person's physical similarity to three extreme varieties of human physique, which are shown in Figure 5.1.

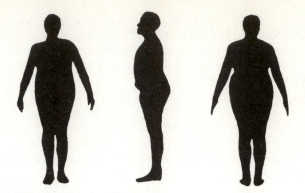

(a) The endomorph: soft, round, fat

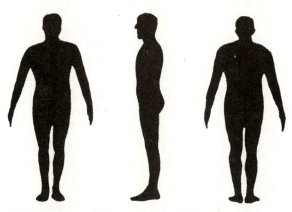

(b) The mesomorph: bony, muscular, athletic

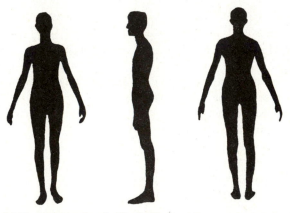

(c) The ectomorph: tall, thin, fragile

FIGURE 5.1

Since most of us do not fit these extremes exactly, a system has been developed for specifying body type based on the assumption that we may have some features of all three types. Sheldon's work helps to explain this system.[19] A person's physical characteristics are rated on a scale from 1 to 7—7 representing the highest correspondence with one of the three extreme body types. An individual's "somatype" is represented by three numbers—the first referring to the degree of endomorphy, the second referring to the degree of mesomorphy, and the third to the degree of ectomorphy. A grossly fat person would be 7/1/1; a broad shouldered, athletic person would be 1/7/1; and a very skinny person would be a 1/1/7. It is reported that Jackie Gleason was roughly 6/4/1, Muhammad Ali 2/7/1, and Abraham Lincoln 1/5/6. There has been a considerable amount of scientific criticism of Sheldon's work. His work has, however, been the basis for many studies investigating the same general question, and in spite of critical errors in Sheldon's methodology, many of the later studies—using more precise measurements and research designs—have confirmed many of his early conclusions.

Now to the test you took earlier. Cortes and Gatti used this test to measure temperament and found a very high correspondence between temperament and physique. In other words, on the basis of this work we would expect to have a pretty good idea of your body build by the answers you gave on the SELF-DESCRIPTION TEST. To calculate your score on the test, simply add up the number of adjectives you chose from each of the endomorph, mesomorph, and ectomorph categories listed in Table 5.2

If you chose six adjectives from the endomorph category, twelve from the mesomorph, and three from the ectomorph lists, your temperament score would be 6/12/3. If we assume a high correlation with body features we would assume that you are primarily mesomorphic with a leaning toward endomorphism. (Your author is 5/11/5). This test and the body-personality research allow us to make some predictions based on probabilities, but in individual cases there may be exceptions. Nor can we assume from this work that the body causes temperament traits. The high correspondence between certain temperament traits and body builds may also be the result of life experiences, environmental factors, self-concept, and a host of other variables.

The obvious question at this point is: "What does all this have to do with human communication?" Simply this: If a case can be made that there are clearly defined and generally accepted physique-temperament stereotypes, we can reason that they will have a lot to do with the way you are perceived and responded to by others, and with the personality traits expected of you by others. Wells and Siegel uncovered some data supporting the existence of such stereotypes.[20] One-hundred twenty adult subjects were shown silhouette drawings of the endomorph, ectomorph, and mesomorph and were asked to rate them on a

TABLE 5.2

ENDOMORPHIC	MESOMORPHIC	ECTOMORPHIC
dependent	dominant	detached
calm	cheerful	tense
relaxed	confident	anxious
complacent	energetic	reticent
contented	impetuous	self-conscious
sluggish	efficient	meticulous
placid	enthusiastic	reflective
leisurely	competitive	precise
cooperative	determined	thoughtful
affable	outgoing	considerate
tolerant	argumentative	shy
affected	talkative	awkward
warm	active	cool
forgiving	domineering	suspicious
sympathetic	courageous	introspective
softhearted	enterprising	serious
generous	adventurous	cautious
affectionate	reckless	tactful
kind	assertive	sensitive
sociable	optimistic	withdrawn
soft-tempered	hot-tempered	gentle-tempered

set of twenty-four bipolar adjective scales such as lazy-energetic, fat-thin, intelligent-unintelligent, dependent-self-reliant; and so on. The investigators deliberately chose people who had not been to college under the assumption that these people would not be contaminated with information from previous studies that might structure their answers. Their results show that (1) the endomorph was rated as fatter, older, shorter (silhouettes were the same height), more old-fashioned, less strong physically, less good-looking, more talkative, more warmhearted and sympathetic, more good-natured and agreeable, more dependent on others, and more trusting of others; (2) the mesomorph was rated as stronger, more masculine, better looking, more adventurous, younger, taller, more mature in behavior, and more self-reliant; (3) the ectomorph was rated thinner, younger, more ambitious, taller, more suspicious of others, more tense and nervous, less masculine, more stubborn and inclined to be difficult, more pessimistic, and quieter. Several reports suggest that the relationship between body build and temperament also holds for younger children.[21] For example, thin ectomorphic boys and girls were rated more anxious, more conscientious, and more meticulous than children with other body builds. The reactions to endomorphs or obese individuals are encountered frequently. They are discriminated against when seeking life insurance, adopting children, obtaining jobs, and even getting in to college.[22] One author suggests that obesity is stamped with a stigma of moral turpitude.[23]

We have been trained for so long to believe that stereotypes are harmful distortions of the truth, we often fail to consider another equally plausible explanation—that a particular stereotype may be the result of a distillation of ages of social experience. In other words, a stereotype may be more accurate than we wish to admit—there may be some reason for the stereotype other than prejudicial whims. Clearly, the evidence shows that we do associate certain personality and temperament traits with certain body builds. These expectations may or may not be accurate, but they do exist; they are a part of the psychological mortar in interpersonal communication. We must recognize these stereotypes as potential stimuli for communication responses, so that we can deal with them more effectively.

Another dimension of body build that may influence interpersonal responses is height. In American society there seems to be a preference for the taller man. Tall women, however, are often labeled "ungainly." Short businesswomen, in fact, may have an advantage in not acquiring whatever "threatening" overtones may attend increased height. This argument, however, assumes a uniformity of perceived "intimidation" by height for both males and females—an assumption that seems tenuous at best. The ideal male lover is not short, dark, and handsome; rather male romantic leads are usually tall. The taller of the two national presidential candidates seems to have been a consistent winner since 1900—with five-foot-nine-inch Jimmy Carter a notable exception. Policemen and firemen are, in some areas, required to be at least five feet, eight inches tall. A survey at the University of Pittsburgh has shown that shorter men are often shortchanged on job opportunities and salaries. Pittsburgh graduates who were six feet, two inches to six feet, four inches tall received average starting salaries that were 12.4 percent higher than those of men who were under six feet. Further support for discrimination against the shorter man comes from a study of 140 corporate recruiters who were asked to make a choice between two men just by reading their applications for employment. The applications were exactly the same except that one listed a height of six feet, one inch and the other was listed as five feet, five inches. Only about 1 percent of the recruiters favored the short man. There are even cases on record in which short men who did not measure up to the arbitrary height requirements set for policemen actually bludgeoned their heads in the hope that the swelling would make up the needed inches! Shorter children are encouraged to "drink your milk so you'll grow up and be healthy and strong"; attention is focused on shortness or tallness when children are asked to line up by height for various reasons in school. Tallness is often associated with power, but an interesting reversal occurs when the same behavior is labeled "competitive" in a taller man and a "Napoleonic complex" in a shorter one.

Does a tall person have a natural advantage in persuading people? Some preliminary evidence indicates that a man does not.[24] Photographs

107

were taken of the same man from two different angles—one designed to make him look short, the other to make him look tall. These pictures, plus a tape-recorded persuasive speech, were the stimuli for various student groups. Attitude measures indicated there was no statistically significant difference between the "tall" and "short" speakers. It is more likely that tallness interacts with other factors such as general body size, girth, facial features, and numerous other variables. In your own experience, you can probably recall some tall individuals who seemed almost frighteningly "overpowering" whereas others of the same height did not have this quality. Another investigator looked at height from the standpoint of the receiver rather than that of the communicator or sender.[25] Will receivers perceive differences in height of people they think to be different in status? Again, only tentative conclusions can be drawn from some early work. A single individual was introduced to five similar groups of students. Each time he was introduced as a person with a different status—for example, student, lecturer, Ph.D., full professor. Students were then told that they needed numerical data for their statistics lesson, and were asked to estimate the height of the person who had been introduced to them. The results of this study seem to suggest there is some perceptual distortion of height—the higher the ascribed status, the higher are the judgments of height.

Thus far we have been discussing our perceptions of others. An equally important dimension of interpersonal communication is what we think of ourselves—our self-image. The self-image is the root system from which all of our overt communication behavior grows and blossoms. Our overt communication behavior is only an extension of the accumulated experiences that have gone into making up our understanding of self. In short, what you are, or think you are, organizes what you say and do. An important part of your self-image is your body image—perhaps the first part formed in very young children. Jourard and Secord found that males were most satisfied with their bodies when they were somewhat larger than normal, and females were most satisfied when their bodies were smaller than normal—but when their busts were larger than average.[26] Sex researchers have frequently noted emotional problems in males resulting from perceived incongruence between their genital size and the supposed masculine ideal perpetuated by our literary and oral heritage. As we develop, we learn the cultural ideal of what the body should be like, and this results in varying degrees of satisfaction with the body, particularly during adolescence.[27]

Body Color. In many respects, skin color has been the most potent body stimulus for determining interpersonal responses in this culture. There is no need to review the abuses heaped upon black persons in the United States on the basis of skin color alone. The words of a white man whose skin pigmentation was changed, and who experienced the dramatic and unforgettable life of a black man in the United States, is a sufficient reminder:

> When all the talk, all the propaganda has been cut away, the criterion is nothing but the color of skin. My experience proved that. They judged me by no other quality. My skin was dark. That was sufficient reason for them to deny me those rights and freedoms without which life loses its significance and becomes a matter of little more than animal survival.
>
> I searched for some other answer and found none. I had spent a day without food and water and for no other reason than that my skin was black. I was sitting on a tub in the swamp for no other reason.[28]

Such abuses frequently cause detrimental self-images for blacks—the effects of which only serve to confirm the self-fulfilling prophecy for the abusers. Brody reports tragic cases of young black boys who had great anxiety and guilt complexes that stemmed from their desire to be white.[29] He also reports deliberate, though unwitting indoctrination about color status by the mothers of these black children. The slogan "Black is beautiful" and the Miss Black America Pageant are two of many attempts to cope with this identity problem. The whole concept of skin color has been further complicated by an attempt to label all Negroes as blacks. Those who do not see themselves as "black" but some lighter shade, may have additional identity crises to face. Although there is little doubt that blacks are at an immediate disadvantage in communicating with prejudiced persons, another interesting phenomenon has developed in recent years, in which a reverse effect may take place. The black person is still judged only by his or her skin color, but the judgment is indiscriminately positive instead of negative. Some explain this phenomenon as an overreaction caused by widespread guilt feelings among some whites. Most blacks, however, would probably argue that this effect is not very widespread even today.

Numerous other judgments we make about others are based largely on body color. Expressions such as red-neck and lily-white are used to identify persons who are uncontrollably angry or who appear unusually white. A pale color may indicate a person is ill, and a healthy person is one whose skin is tanned. A rosy flush may indicate embarrassment.

Body Smell. Although vision and hearing are the most important sensors for social situations in Western societies, the sense of smell may also influence responses. The scientific study of the human olfactory system is in its infancy, but we know that other animals obtain a great deal of information from their sense of smell—for example, the presence of an enemy, territorial markers, the location of members of the same species or herd, sexual stimulation, and emotional states. Dogs are well known for their ability to sense fear, hate, or friendship in human beings and to track them with only the scent from the human's clothing. The difficulty that dogs seem to have in distinguishing between the smells of identical twins prompted Davis to suggest that we each have an "olfactory signature."[30]

Generally, North Americans do not rely on their sense of smell for interpersonal cues unless perspiration odor, breath, or some other smell is unusually strong. Some believe that this olfactory repression reflects an antisensual North American bias. It is ironic that each year North American men and women spend hundreds of thousands (if not millions) of dollars on deodorant sprays and soaps, mouthwashes, breath mints, perfumes, after-shave lotions, and other artificial scents. The so-called natural scent seems to have a low priority at this point in our cultural development, but we are not at all reluctant to buy a commercial product that will purportedly make us smell "natural and sexy." Meerloo's comments seem to strike a similar note:

> There is a good explanation for all of my olfactory nostalgia. After all, smell is related to our first loving contacts in the world. The newborn infant lives first in a world of pure smells, although the world soon teaches him to forego his nostril pleasures. For him, mother was love at first smell. When he is older, he cannot sniff and smell keenly anymore because smelling has become taboo. Thanks to the enforced toilet taboos, our innate perceptions of smell degenerates into chemical irritation by soaps and antiseptics. While sexual odors are taboo, man borrows these odors from flowers and plants. The sexual organs of plant and animal—musk, civet, and the rose—bring him what he has suppressed in his own life. Nevertheless, something of the instinctual passion for smells remains in man. It cannot be totally suppressed by the most pristine sanitary habits or by chlorophyll-minded merchants. Modern culture has made people feel ashamed of body odor. Whole industries thrive on that artificially induced self-consciousness. They create diseases such as halitosis just to make people feel inferior. Many a girl has become neurotic because she has completely suppressed the role and delights of perspiration.[31]

Our reactions to odors may be consciously or unconsciously processed, but the message can be quite strong. For me there is a distinct smell associated with high schools, so that each time I enter one it triggers a chain of memories from my own history. Environmental odors are only one source. Human odors are primarily emitted through the sweat glands, but excrement, saliva, tears, and breath provide other sources of odors. Another source of odor is the manipulation of flatulent air—generally adding a negative or insulting aura to an interpersonal encounter in this culture. Anticipation of expelling flatus may lead to rapid termination of an interpersonal contact, although under certain conditions, emission of flatulent air may be used deliberately to draw attention to oneself.

Not all cultures are as reticent about odors in everyday human interaction, as Hall notes:

> Olfaction occupies a prominent place in the Arab life. Not only is it one of the distance-setting mechanisms, but it is a vital part of a complex system

of behavior. Arabs consistently breathe on people when they talk. However, this habit is more than a matter of different manners. To the Arab good smells are pleasing and a way of being involved with each other. To smell one's friend is not only nice but desirable, for to deny him your breath is to act ashamed. Americans, on the other hand, trained as they are not to breathe in people's faces, automatically communicate shame in trying to be polite.[32]

Body Hair. As previously mentioned, skin color has been an extremely influential cue in many human encounters in American society since its inception. During the late 1960s, body hair also took on major significance in structuring interpersonal responses. Males who allowed the hair on their head to grow over their ears and foreheads and sometimes to their shoulders found that they frequently attracted abuses similar to those leveled at black-skinned individuals. Cases of discrimination against long-haired men in housing, school attendance, jobs, and commercial establishments, to mention a few, were numerous. A professor who was concerned about the contribution of long hair to the generation gap took his own shorn locks and those of thirty other men, stuffed the hair in a pillow, and sent the pillow to then Vice President Agnew. The professor said, "Stereotypes based on the way people look are so strongly ingrained that effective communication is impossible. Feelings about hair are as strong as on almost any subject." This observation would seem to be confirmed by the placement officer at Stanford University who stated that long-haired young men graduating from college in 1971 would likely find themselves lacking in job opportunities: "The length of a male's hair is directly proportionate to the job opportunities he can find. . . . In other words, the longer the hair, the fewer the jobs."[33] It is reported that Nader's Raiders must not have long hair because it may prohibit their access to enterprises that they are investigating.

In late 1971, the U.S. Army dropped an advertising campaign using the slogan "We care more about how you think than how you cut your hair" apparently because too many servicemen believed it. The Army, the original sponsor of this advertisement, later stated that it does not condone long hair and that the youth featured in the advertising campaign did not meet regulations set forth by the Army. Visitors to Taiwan in the early 1970s were greeted with cards saying, "Welcome to the Republic of China. No long hair or long beards, please." The mania against long hair may even be fatal: United Press International ran a story in April 1970, which reported that a father had shot his son to death in a row over long hair and a "negative attitude toward society." The label longhair no longer refers exclusively to the revered and accomplished musicians and writers of the past; now it is also a label for young (and old) "undesirables."

The preceding accounts of the impact of one's hair refer to the 1960s and early 1970s. Since then, I've accumulated enough additional accounts to convince me that "the hair issue" has more than maintained the momentum it achieved in the 1960s.

Equally undesirable reactions would probably result if people went to the other extreme by shaving all the hair off their heads—as an anti-hair group called the Skinheads actually did. In 1974 an organization called Bald-Headed Men of America was formed to "cultivate a sense of pride and eliminate the vanity associated with the loss of one's hair." The motivation for negative responses to these extreme hairstyles by some members of our culture is an interesting question, but not our major concern here. The fact that body hair, in and of itself, elicits feelings either of appreciation or repugnance is the important point. Other body hair also seems to be important in judgments of attractiveness—illustrated by the comment, "I like him, but he's so hairy." For years, *Playboy* magazine, a primary reference work for many men on the nude female figure, neatly "brushed out," or did not display, pubic hair on its models. Even magazines depicting human figures in nudist colonies were so well known for such alterations of pubic hair that many of them now advertise their magazines as "unretouched." It is reported that the Chacobo Indians of the Amazon rain forest carefully trim and groom their head hair, but feel that other body hair is not attractive and methodically eliminate eyebrows by completely plucking them. Some European women allow natural hair to grow under their arms, on their legs, and on their upper lip. Most North American women are taught to regularly shave leg and underarm hair and remove facial hair with wax or some other depilatory. The lack of eyebrows on the Mona Lisa is some evidence that it may at one time have been desirable for women to pluck the eyebrows for beauty's sake.

Finally Freedman's work, though far from a conclusive treatise, offers some interesting hypotheses on the beard.[34] In 1969 he asked a group of undergraduate students how they felt about beardedness. None of the men in the group wore a beard. The majority of both men and women used adjectives of youthfulness to describe unbearded men. Of the men, 22 percent described the personalities of bearded men as independent, and 20 percent described them as extroverted. Women were envisioning an idealized husband, says Freedman, when they described bearded men as masculine, sophisticated, and mature—which accounted for 55 percent of the adjectives they used. Further interviews with women suggested that a beard heightens sexual magnetism—it makes a man more masculine to a woman, and she feels more feminine toward him. Freedman goes on to say that people will stand closer to beardless men, whereas bearded men report that they are less tense with unbearded male strangers than with other bearded men. In another study, photographs were taken of eight men who were fully bearded, only with a goatee, only with a mustache, or clean-shaven.[35] These photographs were shown to 128 students who judged the men at various stages in the process. The more hair the man had, the more he was judged to be masculine, mature, good-looking, self-confident, dominant, courageous, liberal, nonconformist, and industrious. Whether these findings extend beyond the campus environment is still open to question.

We have not covered many other body-related cues, such as freckles, moles, acne, and so-called beauty marks, all of which may be very important in a given situation. The numerous individuals who have had "nose jobs" must have felt a great communicative potential for the nose. However, our responses to body shape, color, smell, and hair seem to be the major factors involved, aside from dress and other artifacts, such as cosmetics, eyeglasses, jewelry, and the like.

OUR BODY: CLOTHES AND OTHER ARTIFACTS

Examine the clothing types shown in Figure 5.2 (see page 115). What are your first impressions?

On the following list you will find twenty characteristics that may be associated with one or more of these clothing types. Check the spaces that you think apply to specific clothing types and compare your impressions with those of your friends, family, or associates.

MALES				FEMALES				
1	2	3	4	1	2	3	4	
___	___	___	___	___	___	___	___	1. Has smoked marijuana.
___	___	___	___	___	___	___	___	2. Has "hippie" friends.
___	___	___	___	___	___	___	___	3. Is a fraternity or sorority member.
___	___	___	___	___	___	___	___	4. Is a Democrat.
___	___	___	___	___	___	___	___	5. Is involved in athletics
___	___	___	___	___	___	___	___	6. Is married.
___	___	___	___	___	___	___	___	7. Is generous.
___	___	___	___	___	___	___	___	8. Drives a sports car.
___	___	___	___	___	___	___	___	9. Is a Republican.
___	___	___	___	___	___	___	___	10. Is vocationally oriented.
___	___	___	___	___	___	___	___	11. Is active politically.
___	___	___	___	___	___	___	___	12. Is dependable.
___	___	___	___	___	___	___	___	13. Was against the war in Vietnam.
___	___	___	___	___	___	___	___	14. Lives with parents.
___	___	___	___	___	___	___	___	15. Has long hair.
___	___	___	___	___	___	___	___	16. Has many friends.
___	___	___	___	___	___	___	___	17. Is intelligent.
___	___	___	___	___	___	___	___	18. Is religious.
___	___	___	___	___	___	___	___	19. Is open-minded.
___	___	___	___	___	___	___	___	20. Is older.

Did you find any similarities in your responses and those of your peers? Were there any major differences between your responses and the responses of people with distinctly different backgrounds? Later in this chapter we focus on the particular impressions that are communicated by clothes, but first we need to answer an even more basic question, "Do clothes communicate?" Anecdotal evidence on this question is plentiful. For instance, a newspaper article based on a story from the Associated Press reported that the Lutheran Church felt that the attire worn by clergymen in the pulpit was responsible for some churchgoers' switching denominations. Many tailors, manufacturers, and sellers of clothes claim to be "wardrobe engineers"—engineering your outward appearance in order to increase your sales, assert your authority, or help you win more cases in court. In the early 1970s, the Associated Press reported that an eighth-grade girl in Clifton, Arizona, was sent home from her graduation ceremony because she did not have on the right style of dress. After admitting that the girl's dress met the "pastel" requirement, the head of the local school board said, however, that the dress had flowers on it and "we couldn't have everybody different. She was defying authority."

You may have had the experience in a restaurant of responding only to the uniform of the waiter or waitress and later, when you were ready to leave, not knowing who waited on your table. It is reasonable to assume that, in most instances, our perception of others is influenced partly by clothes and partly by other factors. In order to determine whether our judgments of others are ever made on the basis of clothing alone, it is necessary to measure the effects of changing the type of clothing while keeping everything else the same. Experiments by Hoult were designed on this basis.[36] First, forty-six students rated thirteen male students of similar background on such things as "best-looking," "most likely to succeed," "most intelligent," "most like to date or double date with," "best personality," and "most like to have as class president." The four men with the highest ratings were told to "dress down," whereas the four with the lowest ratings were told to "dress up." Others were told to dress the same. Two weeks later, when ratings were again obtained, Hoult found no evidence that the clothes had been influential in changing the ratings—even though independent ratings of the clothes showed that they did, indeed, indicate "dressing up" or "dressing down" from the previous outfits. A high correlation between the social closeness of the raters and models and the social ratings prompted Hoult to conduct another study using models who were complete strangers to the raters. In this study, he used photographs of male strangers who were rated by 254 students from two colleges. Having obtained independent ratings of clothes and the models' heads, Hoult was able to place high-ranked outfits on models with low-ranked heads. Lower-ranked clothing was placed on models with higher-ranked heads. Hoult

Males

Females

FIGURE 5.2

found that higher-ranked clothing was associated with an increase in rank, whereas lower-ranked clothing was associated with loss of rank. Clothing, then, did seem to be a significant factor affecting the judgments that students made about these strangers.

Although Hoult's work is helpful in demonstrating the communicative value of clothes, an equally important conclusion can be derived from the failure of his first experiment. This first experiment demonstrates one of the conditions under which clothing may not be a highly influential factor in interpersonal perception of others—when the observer is well acquainted with the person being observed. Changes in the clothing of a family member or close friend may indicate a temporary change of mood, but it is likely that we will not perceive any basic

115

changes in values, attitudes, or personality traits unless the clothing change becomes permanent for that individual. In addition to social closeness to the person being observed, other factors may modify responses to clothes, such as the psychological-social orientation and background of the observer and the particular task or situation within which the observation is made. We should also remember that any given item of clothing can convey several different meanings. For instance, the tie a person selects to wear may reflect "sophistication" or "high status," but the way the tie is worn—that is, tightly knotted, loosened, thrown over one's shoulder, and so on—may provide additional information about the wearer and evoke different reactions.

To understand the relationship between clothes and communication, we should be familiar with the various functions clothes may fulfill: decoration, protection (both physical and psychological), sexual attraction, self-assertion, self-denial, concealment, group identification, and display of status or role.[37] Since there are some widely accepted cultural rules for combining certain colors and styles of dress, clothes may also function to inform the observer of one's knowledge of such rules. With such a variety of functions, it is interesting to ponder the effects a trend toward unisexism in dress would have. Perhaps the type of incident in which one customer in a store mistakenly asks another customer (dressed in coat and tie) for assistance would occur more frequently. Some clothing may serve more than one function—a woman's bra is, in one sense, used for concealment but in another sense it may also fulfill the sexual attraction function. An interesting study by Lefkowitz, Blake, and Mouton shows not only how clothes fulfill a particular function but how they affect the behavior of others.[38] They found that pedestrians violated the instructions given by a traffic signal light more often when another person violated it ahead of them. More important, there were significantly more violations when the original violator was dressed to represent a high-status person. Additional studies of this type find that a variety of requests (making change, accepting leaflets, giving detailed street directions, returning a dime left in a telephone booth, and so on) are more easily granted if one is dressed to fit the situation or is dressed in what would be considered higher-status clothing. Bickman, for example, had four men stop 153 adults on the streets of Brooklyn and make various requests.[39] The men's clothing varied and included civilian (sports jacket and tie), milkman (uniform, white pants, milk bottles), and guard (uniform, badge, insignia, no gun). The men asked the pedestrians either to pick up a bag, to put a dime in a parking meter for someone else, or to stand on the opposite side of a bus stop sign. In each case, the guard uniform received the greater compliance. In fact, 83 percent of those who were asked to put a dime in the parking meter obeyed even after the person in the guard uniform had left the scene. Lawyers have long known that their client's manner of dress may have an impact on the judgments made by the judge and/or jury. Some defendants have even been encouraged to put on a simulated wedding ring to offset any prejudice against single persons.

To make a list of the things that are invariably communicated by clothes would be impossible; such a list would vary with the demands of each particular situation and would also change with time. If the fashion industry could devise such a list, it would need to spend far less on advertising that was designed to persuade women that a particular cosmetic or dress actually does communicate "beauty." Some of the potential personal attributes that may be communicated by dress include sex, age, nationality, relation to opposite sex (a function, sometimes, of matched sweaters), socioeconomic status, identification with a specific group, occupational or official status, mood, personality, attitudes, interests, and values. Clothes also set our expectations for the behavior of the wearer—especially if it is a uniform of some type. The accuracy of such judgments varies considerably—the more concrete items such as age, sex, nationality, and socioeconomic status being signaled with greater accuracy than more abstract qualities such as attitudes, values, and personality. Personality judgments are probably dependent on the traits being judged. Observers may depend more on clothes for judging such things as efficiency or aggressiveness and more on facial characteristics for judging friendliness or shyness. For some personality judgments, clothes probably play a minimal role. Another factor that influences the accuracy of such judgments is the similarity of the observer to the person being observed with respect to the traits being rated. If you belong to the same group or have characteristics similar to those of the person being observed, your accuracy in judging those characteristics may increase.

We have previously discussed the effect of one's self-image on his or her communication behavior. Extending this same idea, we now consider the possible effects of clothes on the wearer. Some authors believe that clothes help satisfy a personal image of one's ideal self. Gibbins, in his work with fifteen- and sixteen-year-old girls, found a definite relationship between dresses which were liked and ratings of ideal self.[40] In another discovery, a potential link was found between clothing and self-concept. High school boys who had much higher "achievement scores" but who wore clothing deemed "unacceptable" by their peers were found to have lower grade point averages than those who wore "acceptable" clothing. This latter group also found themselves in less conflict and in more school activities. Clothes, then, may encourage or discourage certain patterns of communication. A new outfit may promote feelings of gaiety and happiness; you may feel less efficient in shoes that hurt you; self-consciousness may result from wearing an "inappropriate" outfit, a common feeling for adolescents trying to understand their own self-image.

Aiken wanted to determine whether the selection of certain types of clothing was related to certain personality traits.[41] He prepared a clothing opinionnaire to test five factors on a female population: (1) *Interest in dress*. Personality traits related to this factor included: "conventional," "conscientious," "compliant before authority," "stereotyped in thinking," "persistent," "suspicious," "insecure," and "tense"—that is, uncomplicated and socially conscientious, with indications of adjustment problems. (2) *Economy in dress*. Personality measures related to this factor included "responsible," "conscientious," "alert," "efficient," "precise," "intelligent," and "controlled." Another study using Aiken's opinionnaire found that material status and increasing age contributed heavily to economy orientation. (3) *Decoration in dress*. Personality measures related to this factor included "conscientious," "conventional," "stereotyped," "nonintellectual," "sympathetic," "sociable," and "submissive"—that is, uncomplicated and socially conscientious. (4) *Conformity in dress*. Personality variables associated with this factor included a large number of conformity variables: "restraint," "socially conscientious," "moral," "sociable," "traditional," "submissive," "emphasis on economic, social and religious values," and "minimized aesthetic values." (5) *Comfort in dress*. Personality measures related to this factor included "self-controlled," "socially cooperative," "sociable," "thorough," and "deferent to authority,"—that is, controlled extrovert.

Each person adorns him or herself with a number of other objects and cosmetics, such as badges, tattoos, masks, other jewelry, and the like. We have termed these *artifacts*. Any discussion of clothing must take these artifacts into consideration because they are also potential communicative stimuli. A ring worn on a particular finger, a pin worn in a particular way, and a man's ring worn around the neck of a woman all signify a close relationship with a member of the opposite sex. There is a dearth of research on such artifacts. Thornton found that people who wore eyeglasses were rated higher in intelligence and industriousness by college students in 1944.[42] Argyle and McHenry, twenty-seven years later, found the same effect when evaluators saw those wearing eyeglasses for only fifteen seconds.[43] McKeachie had female interviewees rated by male interviewers after a ten-minute interview.[44] Females behaved similarly but varied with respect to whether or not they wore lipstick. With lipstick, they were rated more frivolous than serious, more placid than worrying, less talkative, more conscientious, and less interested in the opposite sex. Although studies such as these make efforts to keep everything constant except the eyeglasses or lipstick or any other factor, the generalizations that may be made are limited to the shade of lipstick, the type of eyeglasses, and many other factors. Cosmetics and other artifacts interact with other clothing, facial, verbal, and body features,[45] but under some yet unspecified conditions, they may be the primary source of information communicated about a particular person.

SUMMARY

The exact role of appearance and dress in the total system of nonverbal communication is still unknown. We do know, however, that appearance and dress are part of the total nonverbal stimuli that influence interpersonal responses—and under some conditions they are the primary determiners of such responses. Physical attractiveness may be influential in determining whether you are sought out; it may have a bearing on whether you are able to persuade or manipulate others; it is often an important factor in the selection of dates and marriage partners; it may determine whether a defendant is deemed guilty or innocent; it may even have an effect on whether the prisoner is able to decrease the antisocial behavior responsible for his or her imprisonment; it may be a major factor contributing to how others judge your personality, your sexuality, your popularity, your success, and often your happiness. Fortunately for some and unfortunately for others, such judgments begin early in life. Not all children are "beautiful." There are indications that teachers not only make attractiveness judgments about young children but treat the unattractive ones with fewer and less positive communications. A sizable proportion of the American public still thinks of the ideal man or woman in terms of physical attractiveness.

In spite of the overwhelming evidence that physical attractiveness is a highly desirable quality in interpersonal situations, other factors temper these general findings. For instance, all positive findings for attractiveness are based on probabilities—not certainty. There are many reasons why some unattractive persons will not be evaluated unfavorably—for example, the persons they are seen with, the environment in which they are judged, other communicative behavior they engage in, and/or the time of life at which they are evaluated. In addition, many of the attractiveness studies have used photographs rather than live, interacting human beings.

In addition to the importance of general physical attractiveness in influencing the responses of others, we have some information on stereotyped responses to specific features—for example, general body build, skin color, odor, hair, and clothes. These specific features may have a profound influence on your self-image and hence on your patterns of communication with others. Future work in this area will have to approach such basic questions as: Under what conditions do physical appearance and dress make a critical difference in the total communication event? What is the relative impact of physical appearance and dress when combined with other verbal and nonverbal cues? Are there any specific features of physical appearance that consistently act as primary sources of information for the perceiver? If not, which features act as primary sources of information under certain circumstances? Is there any validity to the various stereotypes associated with physical appearance and dress? What effect does your self-image with respect to your own appearance and dress have on your interpersonal communication behavior?

NOTES

1. J. Mills and E. Aronson, "Opinion Change as a Function of the Communicator's Attractiveness and Desire to Influence," *Journal of Personality and Social Psychology* 1 (1965): 73–77.
2. J. Horai, N. Naccari, and E. Faloultah, "The Effects of Expertise and Physical Attractiveness upon Opinion Agreement and Liking," *Sociometry* 37 (1974): 601–6. Also R. N. Widgery, "Sex of Receiver and Physical Attractiveness of Source as Determinants of Initial Credibility Perception," *Western Speech* 38 (1974): 13–17.
3. R. N. Widgery and B. Webster, "The Effects of Physical Attractiveness upon Perceived Initial Credibility," *Michigan Speech Journal* 4 (1969): 9–15.
4. For summaries of this literature, see R. A. Kulka and J. B. Kessler, "Is Justice Really Blind?—The Influence of Litigant Physical Attractiveness on Juridical Judgments," *Journal of Applied Social Psychology* (in press). See also E. K. Solender and E. Solender, "Minimizing the Effect of the Unattractive Client on the Jury: A Study of the Interaction of Physical Appearance with Assertions and Self-Experience References," *Human Rights* 5 (1976): 201–214; and M. G. Efran, "The Effect of Physical Appearance on the Judgment of Guilt, Interpersonal Attraction and Severity of Recommended Punishment in a Simulated Jury Task," *Journal of Experimental Research in Personality* 8 (1974): 45–54.
5. E. Berscheid and E. H. Walster, "Physical Attractiveness," in L. Berkowitz (ed.), *Advances in Experimental Social Psychology*, vol. 7 (New York: Academic Press, 1974), 158–215.
6. Articles that summarize some of these studies with children include R. Algozzine, "What Teachers Perceive—Children Receive?" *Communication Quarterly* 24 (1976): 41–47; E. Berscheid and E. Walster, "Beauty and the Best," *Psychology Today* 5 (1972): 42–46; G. Wilson and D. Nias, "Beauty Can't Be Beat," *Psychology Today* 10 (1976): 96–98, 103; and M. M. Clifford and E. Walster, "The Effect of Physical Attractiveness on Teacher Expectation," *Sociology of Education* 46 (1973): 248–258.
7. R. E. Baber, *Marriage and Family* (New York: McGraw-Hill, 1939).

8. C. Tavris, "Men and Women Report Their Views on Masculinity," *Psychology Today* 10 (1977): 34–42, 82. Another study (of one thousand people at a "computer dance") also found women weighting physical attractiveness less than men. Cf. R. H. Coombs and W. F. Kenkel, "Sex Differences in Dating Aspirations and Satisfactions with Computer-Selected Partners," *Journal of Marriage and the Family* 28 (1966): 62–66.

9. S. Sontag, "The Double Standard of Aging," *Saturday Review,* September 23, 1972, 29–38.

10. D. Byrne, O. London, and K. Reeves, "The Effects of Physical Attractiveness, Sex, and Attitude Similarity on Interpersonal Attraction," *Journal of Personality* 36 (1968): 259–272.

11. B. N. Singh, "A Study of Certain Personal Qualities as Preferred by College Students in Their Marital Partners," *Journal of Psychological Researches* 8 (1964): 37–48.

12. E. Walster, V. Aronson, D. Abrahams, and L. Rohmann, "Importance of Physical Attractiveness in Dating Behavior," *Journal of Personality and Social Psychology* 4 (1966): 508–516.

13. R. W. Brislin and S. A. Lewis, "Dating and Physical Attractiveness: Replication," *Psychological Reports* 22 (1968): 976.

14. E. Berscheid and E. H. Walster, *Interpersonal Attraction* (Reading, Mass.: Addison-Wesley, 1969), p. 113–114.

15. D. Bar-Tal and L. Saxe, "Perceptions of Similarly and Dissimilarly Physically Attractive Couples and Individuals," *Journal of Personality and Social Psychology* 33 (1976): 772–781.

16. A. M. Iliffe, "A Study of Preferences in Feminine Beauty," *British Journal of Psychology* 51 (1960): 267–273.

17. Cited as an unpublished manuscript by the authors and R. Campbell in E. Berscheid and E. H. Walster, "Physical Attractiveness," in L. Berkowitz (ed.), *Advances in Experimental Social Psychology,* vol. 7 (New York: Academic Press, 1974), pp. 200–201.

18. J. B. Cortes and F. M. Gatti, "Physique and Self-Description of Temperament," *Journal of Consulting Psychology* 29 (1965): 434.

19. W. H. Sheldon, *Atlas of Man: A Guide for Somatyping the Adult Male at All Ages* (New York: Harper & Row, 1954); W. H. Sheldon, *The Varieties of Human Physique* (New York: Harper & Row, 1940); W. H. Sheldon, *The Varieties of Temperament* (New York: Harper & Row, 1942).

20. W. Wells and B. Siegel, "Stereotyped Somatypes" *Psychological Reports* 8 (1961): 77–78. Another study, using a written description of body extremes, asked personality questions about the written descriptions and found similar results. Cf. K. T. Strongman, and C. J. Hart, "Stereotyped Reactions to Body Build," *Psychological Reports* 23 (1968): 1175–1178.

21. R. N. Walker, "Body Build and Behavior in Young Children: II. Body Build and Parents' Ratings," *Child Development* 34 (1963): 1–23. See also R. W. Parnell, *Behavior and Physique: An Introduction to Practical and Applied Somatometry* (London: Edward Arnold, 1958).

22. H. Channing and J. Mayer, "Obesity—Its Possible Effect on College Acceptance," *New England Journal of Medicine* 275 (1966): 1172–1174.

23. W. J. Cahnman, "The Stigma of Obesity," *Sociological Quarterly* 9 (1968): 283–299.

24. E. E. Baker and W. C. Redding, "The Effects of Perceived Tallness in Persuasive Speaking: An Experiment," *Journal of Communication* 12 (1962): 51–53.

25. P. R. Wilson, "Perceptual Distortion of Height as a Function of Ascribed Academic Status," *Journal of Social Psychology* 74 (1968): 97–102.

26. S. M. Jourard and P. F. Secord, "Body Cathexis and Personality," *British Journal of Psychology* 46 (1955): 130–138.

27. For an extensive treatment of body image research, see F. C. Shontz, *Perceptual and Cognitive Aspects of Body Experience* (New York: Academic Press, 1969) and W. Gorman, *Body Image and the Image of the Brain* (St. Louis: W. H. Green, 1969).

28. J. H. Griffin, *Black Like Me* (Boston: Houghton Mifflin, 1960), p. 121–122.

29. E. B. Brody, "Color and Identity Conflict in Young Boys," *Psychiatry* 26 (1963): 188–201.

30. F. Davis, *Inside Intuition* (New York: McGraw-Hill, 1971), p. 129.

31. J. A. M. Meerloo, *Unobtrusive Communication: Essays in Psycholinguistics* (Assen, the Netherlands: Van Gorcum, 1964), pp. 168–169.

32. E. T. Hall, *The Hidden Dimension* (Garden City, N.Y.: Doubleday & Co., 1966), pp. 159–160.

33. Executive's Research Council, *Personnel Management Week*, January 25, 1971.

34. D. G. Freedman, "The Survival Value of the Beard," *Psychology Today* 3 (1969): 36–39.

35. R. Pellegrini, "The Virtue of Hairiness," *Psychology Today* 6 (1973): 14.

36. R. Hoult, "Experimental Measurement of Clothing as a Factor in Some Social Ratings of Selected American Men," *American Sociological Review* 19 (1954): 324–328.

37. One author sees the differences in consumption of clothes by black and white men as reflecting a need by some blacks to compensate for inferior social position and as an anthropometric disguise rather than simply the result of economic differences. Cf. J. Schwartz, "Men's Clothing and the Negro," *Phylon* 24 (1963): 224–231.

38. M. Lefkowitz, R. Blake, and J. Mouton, "Status Factors in Pedestrian Violation of Traffic Signals," *Journal of Abnormal and Social Psychology* 51 (1955): 704–706.

39. L. Bickman, "The Social Power of a Uniform," *Journal of Applied Social Psychology* 4 (1974): 47–61. Also, see L. Bickman, "Social Roles and Uniforms: Clothes Make the Person," *Psychology Today* 7 (1974): 48–51.

49. K. Gibbins, "Communication Aspects of Women's Clothes and Their Relation to Fashionability," *British Journal of Social and Clinical Psychology* 8 (1969): 301–312.

41. L. Aiken, "Relationships of Dress to Selected Measures of Personality in Undergraduate Women," *Journal of Social Psychology* 59 (1963): 119–128.

42. G. Thornton, "The Effect of Wearing Glasses upon Judgments of Personality Traits of Persons Seen Briefly," *Journal of Applied Psychology* 28 (1944): 203–207.

43. M. Argyle and R. McHenry, "Do Spectacles Really Affect Judgments of Intelligence?" *British Journal of Social and Clinical Psychology* 10 (1971): 27–29.

44. W. McKeachie, "Lipstick as a Determiner of First Impressions of Personality: An Experiment for the General Psychology Course," *Journal of Social Psychology* 36 (1952): 241–244.

45. P. N. Hamid, "Some Effects of Dress Cues on Observational Accuracy, a Perceptual Estimate, and Impression Formation," *Journal of Social Psychology* 86 (1972): 279–289. This study attempts to show interactions between makeup, glasses, and the sex of the observer.

ADDITIONAL READINGS

Berscheid, E. and E. H. Walster. *Interpersonal Attraction*. Reading, Mass.: Addison-Wesley, 1969.

Bickman, L. "Social Roles and Uniforms: Clothes Make the Person." *Psychology Today* 7 (1974): 48–51.

Molloy, J. T. *Dress For Success*. New York: Warner Books, 1975; and, *Woman's Dress For Success Book*, Chicago: Follett, 1977.

Roach, M. E. and J. B. Eicher (eds.). *Dress, Adornment, and the Social Order*. New York: John Wiley & Sons, 1965.

Rudofsky, B. *The Unfashionable Human Body*. Garden City, N.Y.: Doubleday & Co., 1971.

Ryan, M. S. *Clothing: A Study in Human Behavior*. New York: Holt, Rinehart and Winston, 1966.

Sheldon, W. H. *Atlas of Man: A Guide for Somatyping the Adult Male at All Ages*. New York: Harper and Row, 1954.

Wilson, G. and D. Nias. "Beauty Can't Be Beat." *Psychology Today* 10 (1976): 96–98, 103.

THE EFFECTS OF BODY MOVEMENT AND POSTURE

We respond to gestures with an extreme alertness and, one might almost say, in accordance with an elaborate and secret code that is written nowhere, known by none, and understood by all.
E. SAPIR

If someone asked you, "What does the word *model* mean?" you might very well reply that its meaning depends on the context in which the word is used and the characteristics of the person who is interpreting its meaning. We have all heard the familiar admonition: "Meanings are in people, not in words." If someone asked you how to make the sound of the letter *l* you could legitimately reply that it would depend on the phonemic context. For example, the *l* in *lit* is made differently from the *l* in *law*. If someone asked you what is meant by a clenched fist, or a wink, you could apply the same reasoning that you use with verbal behavior. Most body movements do not have precise social meanings. To say that a woman's crossed legs indicate that she is sexually closing out those around her is just as dangerous as the assumption that the word *fast* always means to keep from eating. Common meanings of words, as found in a variety of contexts, are studied, and individual differences are compared to these common usage patterns. Similarly, body movements can be studied within a range of contexts to determine their usual meaning. This chapter outlines meanings that people may attribute to various gestures and body movements, but new meanings for these movements may arise as situations and people change. First we examine some of the behavioral categories mentioned in Chapter 1—emblems, illustrators, regulators, and adaptors. Although facial expressions are also a part of this taxonomy, a full discussion of this behavior is deferred to Chapter 8.

EMBLEMS

Emblems are those nonverbal acts that have a specific verbal translation which is known by most members of a communicating group. Until now, few researchers have systematically investigated emblems. In Chapter 2 we reported a study of emblem usage by children.[1] Efron recorded a glossary of emblems for immigrant Italians and Jews in 1941.[2] Saitz and Cervenka have also developed a list of American and Colombian emblems.[3] In this list some of the similarities between emblem usage in these two different cultures were nodding the head for agreement, shaking one's fist for anger, clapping for approval, raising one's hand for attention, yawning for boredom, waving a hand during leave-taking, rubbing hands to indicate coldness, and making the "thumbs down" gesture for disapproval.

Johnson, Ekman, and Friesen conducted a study of emblems used in the United States.[4] These authors do not claim to have identified a complete list of emblems for the United States, but their study is the most comprehensive effort available at the time of this writing. Those emblems which were decoded correctly (with encoder's meaning) by every person asked are as follows: (1) Interpersonal Directions or Commands—sit down beside me; be silent or hush; come here; I can't hear you; wait—hold it; I warn you; get lost; be calm; follow me; time to go or what time is it; stop; (2) Own Physical State—I'm hot or hard work or a close shave; it's cold or I'm cold; how could I be so dumb? (3) Insults—fuck you or up yours or screw you; the hell with you or rejection; he's crazy or he's stupid; shame on you; (4) Replies—Ok; or no I disagree; I don't know; yes or I agree or I like it; absolutely no or no way; I dislike it or no way; I promise or cross my heart (5) Own Affect—I'm angry; something stinks; (6) Physical Appearance of Person—woman or nice figure; (7) Unclassified—you; me; hitchhiking; counting. Do you and your friends agree on how to perform these emblems?

ILLUSTRATORS AND OTHER BODY MOVEMENTS LINKED WITH HUMAN SPEECH

Illustrators are those nonverbal acts that are intimately linked to spoken discourse. A few studies focusing specifically on illustrators were reviewed in Chapter 1. Our major concern in this chapter is with a number of attempts to carefully scrutinize the patterns of movement co-occurring with various patterns of speech—that is, speech-body movement synchrony. Generally, this research has not separated gestures that are intentionally used to illustrate verbal behavior from other body movements. The findings, however, have obvious implications for studying illustrators and other movement categories. This research amply illustrates that movements are not produced randomly during the stream of speech; speech behavior and movement behavior are inextricably linked—they are part and parcel of the same system.

Condon's analysis of interaction films shown in slow motion is one cornerstone of this body of information.[5] Condon and others believe that normal human beings manifest a pattern of synchronous speech-body acts. This means that a change in one behavior (a body part, for instance) will coincide or be coordinated with the onset or change in another behavior (phonological segment or some other body part). Our head and eyes often mark spoken "sentences," a shift in posture may forecast a new topic or change in viewpoint, and speaker gazes may coincide with grammatical pauses. Condon argues that a similar synchrony exists between two interactants. In some cases, this interactional synchrony may be imitative or a mirror image of the other's behavior. This is probably most evident at the beginning and end of utterances. Other researchers have shown how we tend to match the other person's utterance duration, loudness, precision of articulation, conversational latency, silence duration, and speech rate.[6] Sometimes our feedback in the form of facial expressions or head movements will also appear at specific junctures in the speech of the other person. Flora Davis described her reaction to one of Condon's films in this way:

> The third film clip Condon showed me was an example of heightened synchrony. A man and a woman—employer and job applicant—sat facing each other in a sequence that at normal speed seemed to merely involve rather a lot of shifting around, as the man first uncrossed and then recrossed his legs and the woman stirred in her chair. But when the film was run through a few frames at a time, their synchrony became clear. In the same frame, the two began to lean toward each other. They stopped at the same split second, both raised their heads, and then they swept backwards together into their chairs, stopping in the same frame. It was very much like the elaborate courtship dances of some birds, or—in Condon's favorite analogy—they were like puppets moved by the same set of strings. Condon told me that this kind of heightened synchrony happens often between male and female. During courtship, it's one of the ways in which vast statements can be made between a man and a woman without a word being said.[7]

The implications of this research on speech-body movement synchrony may be far-reaching. Condon suggests that people suffering from various pathologies will manifest "out of sync" behavior; synchrony may assist in the identification of the quality of an ongoing relationship—for example, determining listening behavior, rapport, or the degree of intimate interpersonal knowledge of the other person. Synchrony may even be a precursor of language learning. Condon and Sander found twelve-hour-old babies whose head, hands, elbows, hips, and leg movements tended to correspond to the rhythms of human speech.[8] When the babies were exposed to disconnected speech or to plain tapping sounds, the rhythmic pattern was not observed. If this finding is validated by other researchers, it may mean that an infant has participated in, and laid the groundwork for, various linguistic forms and structures long before formal language learning begins.

The work of Dittmann and his co-workers represents another approach to understanding the interrelationships between speech and body movements.[9] This research is based on the idea that some movements are so closely tied to the speech-encoding process that they are virtually motor manifestations of that process. You can probably recall instances when you were trying to communicate an exciting idea, an idea that was difficult to conceptualize, or an idea that you felt was very important. In such cases you can get a "general feel" for the connections between the flow of your thoughts and the flow of your body movements. Dittmann's work provides us with some specific data regarding the timing and location of body movements in the speech stream. He finds that movements tend to occur early in an encoding unit or following pauses in speech. He also provides further evidence of interactional synchrony. Listener responses in the form of vocalizations ("mm-hmm," "I see," and other comments), head nods, and movements of hands and feet tend to occur at the ends of rhythmical units of the talker's speech—that is, at pauses within phonemic clauses, but mainly at junctures between these clauses. There also seems to be a tendency for vocally stressed words to be accompanied by movements.

REGULATORS

Regulators are nonverbal acts that maintain and regulate the back and forth nature of speaking and listening between two or more interactants. Regulators also play a prominent role in initiating and terminating conversations.

Greetings and Good-byes. Greetings perform a regulatory function by signaling the beginning of interaction. Greetings also convey information about the relationship between the two communicators, which helps structure the ensuing dialogue. Verbal and nonverbal behavior during greetings may signal status differences (subordinate/supervisor) and the degree of intimacy (acquaintance/lover). An emotionally charged greeting may reflect one's desired involvement with the other person or it may reflect a long absence of contact. Goffman proposed an "attenuation rule" that states that the expansiveness of a greeting with a particular person will gradually subside as you are continually brought into contact with that person in a short period of time—for example, a co-worker at an office.[10] Kendon and Ferber found that the following six stages characterized greetings that were initiated from a distance:[11]

1. Sighting, Orientation, and Initiation of the Approach.
2. The Distant Salutation. This is the "official ratification" that a greeting sequence has been initiated and who the participants are. A wave, smile, or call may be used in recognition. Two types of head movements were noted at this point. One, the head toss, is a fairly rapid back and forward tilting motion. Some people tended to lower their head, hold it for a while, then slowly raise it.
3. The Head Dip. This movement has been noted by researchers in other contexts as a marker for transitions between activities or shifts in psychological orientation. Interestingly, this movement was not observed by Kendon and Ferber if the greeter did not continue to approach his or her partner.
4. Approach. As the greeting parties continued to move toward each other, several behaviors were observed. Gazing behavior probably helped signal that the participants were cleared for talking. An aversion of this gaze was seen just prior to the close salutation stage, however. Grooming behavior and one or both arms moved in front of the body were also observed at this point.
5. Final Approach. Now the participants are less then ten feet from each other. Mutual gazing, smiling, and a positioning of the head not seen in the sequence thus far can be seen. The palms of the hands may be turned toward the other person.
6. Close Salutation. As the participants negotiate a standing position, we hear the more stereotyped, ritualistic verbalizations that are so characteristic of the greeting ceremony; for example, "Hi, Steve!" "How ya doin"?, and so on. If the situation calls for body contact (handshakes, embraces, and the like), it will occur at this time.

Our study of greeting behavior has confirmed some of the observations of Kendon and Ferber.[12] The specific nature of greetings will vary according to the relationship between the communicators, the setting, and the attendant verbal behavior. Our major concern here is with the nonverbal behavior. The greetings we observed were frequently initiated by a vertical or sideways motion of the head accompanied by eye gaze. Smiles, regardless of the degree of acquaintantship, were also common. Perhaps the smiles serve the function of setting a positive, friendly initial mood. The eye gaze signals that the communication channels are open and that an obligation to communicate exists. Other eye-related greeting behaviors included winks and eyebrow flashes (discussed in Chapter 2). The hands are often active in the greeting process with salutes, waves, handshakes,[13] hand slaps, and various emblematic gestures such as the peace sign, the raised fist, or the "thumbs up" gesture. Hands may also be engaged in grooming—for example, running fingers through your hair. Touching may take the form of embraces, kisses, or hitting on the hands or arm. The mouth may smile or assume an oval shape, suggesting a possible readiness for talk.

Our analysis of everyday leave-taking situations prompted us to conclude that the rhetoric of saying good-bye serves three functions.[14] The primary regulatory function is signaling the end of the interaction—that is, immediate physical and/or vocal contact will soon be terminated. Again, specific nonverbal manifestations of these functions will vary with the relationship between the communicators, the preceding dialogue, body position (standing/sitting), the anticipated time of separation, and other factors. Decreasing eye gaze and positioning one's body toward the nearest exit were the two most frequent nonverbal behaviors observed in our study and seem to adequately signal impending absence. Leave-taking rituals also sometimes serve to summarize the substance of the discourse. This is usually done verbally, but a good-night kiss may sufficiently capture the evening's pleasantries to qualify as a summarizer. Finally, departures tend to signal supportiveness, which tends to offset any negativity that might arise from encounter termination signals while simultaneously setting a positive mood for the next encounter—that is, our conversation has terminated but our relationship has not. Nonverbal supportiveness may be found in a smile, a handshake, a touch, head-nodding, and forward body lean. Since signaling supportiveness seems so important we often use the more direct verbal signals—for example, "Thanks for your time. I'm glad we got a chance to talk."

Head-nodding and forward lean serve several functions at the same time. Rapid head-nodding toward the end of a conversation serves to reinforce the speaker for what he or she is saying, but it is a rather empty reinforcement since it also signals a desire to terminate the conversation. After all, if there is no apparent disagreement or lack of understanding, the speaker will feel no need to expand on his or her remarks. And, although people may sometimes accompany their feelings of liking by leaning toward another person, it is also necessary to lean forward in order to stand up prior to exiting. So, like words, movements have multiple meanings and serve several functions.

Other nonverbal leave-taking gestures included looking at one's watch; placing hands on thighs for leverage in getting up—which also signals the other person that the catapult is imminent; gathering one's possessions together in an orderly fashion; and accenting the departure ritual by nonvocal sounds, such as slapping your thighs as you rise, stomping the floor with your feet as you rise, or tapping a desk or wall with your knuckles or palm. Finally, we noticed that nearly all the nonverbal variables we studied tended to increase in frequency during the last minute of interaction—with a peak occurring during the fifteen seconds just prior to standing. This increasing activity in at least ten body areas just prior to termination may suggest why we are so frustrated when our partings "fail"—that is, when our partner calls us back with "Oh, just one more thing . . . ." It means we have to go through the entire process of leave-taking again.

Turn-Taking in Conversations. Conversations begin and they are eventually terminated. Between these two points, however, it is necessary to exchange speaking and listening roles, that is, to take turns. Without much awareness for what we are doing, we use body movements, vocalizations, and some verbal behavior that often seems to accomplish this turn-taking with surprising efficiency. The act of smoothly exchanging speaking and listening turns is an extension of our discussion of interaction synchrony. And, since a number of the turn-taking cues are visual, it is understandable that we might have a harder time synchronizing our exchanges during telephone and intercom conversations.

Turn-taking behavior is not just an interesting curiosity of human behavior. We seem to make important judgments about others on the basis of how the turns are allocated and how smoothly exchanges are accomplished. Effective turn-taking may elicit the perception that you and your partner "really hit it off well" or that your partner is a very competent communicator; ineffective turn-taking may prompt evaluations of "rude" (too many interruptions), or "dominating" (not enough turn-yielding), or "frustrating" (unable to make an important point).

The turn-taking behaviors have generally been derived from analyses of adult white, middle- and upper-socioeconomic-class interactants, and some of these behaviors and behavior sequences may not apply to other groups. LaFrance and Mayo found that black interactants gazed more while speaking, whereas Caucasians gazed more while listening.[15] Other groups may develop speaking patterns with more unfilled pauses that may communicate turn-yielding to those unfamiliar with the group norm. Children who are learning turn-taking rules engage in behaviors we rarely see in adults, such as tugging at their parents' clothing and raising their hands to request a speaking turn.

Speakers engage in two turn-taking behaviors (1) turn-yielding and (2) turn-maintaining; listeners also initiate two types of turn-taking behaviors: (1) turn-requesting and (2) turn-denying. The behaviors associated with these acts are derived from careful analyses of both audio and visual elements enacted at junctures at which the interactants exchange or maintain the speaking turn.[16] It should be noted, however, that a familiarity with the rules of interaction is also an important part of effective turn-taking—for example, before any specific turn-taking behaviors are observed, most people enter conversations with the knowledge that speaking roles will generally alternate in an a b a b a b sequence, and that when one person "finishes" an utterance, the other person is generally obligated to "take the conversational ball."

1. *Turn-Yielding.* To "yield" literally means that you are giving up your turn and you expect the other person to start talking. Figure 6.1 shows how the termination of one's utterance can be communicated with kinesic markers that rise or fall with the speaker's pitch level. Questions are clearly an indication that a speaker yields his or her turn and

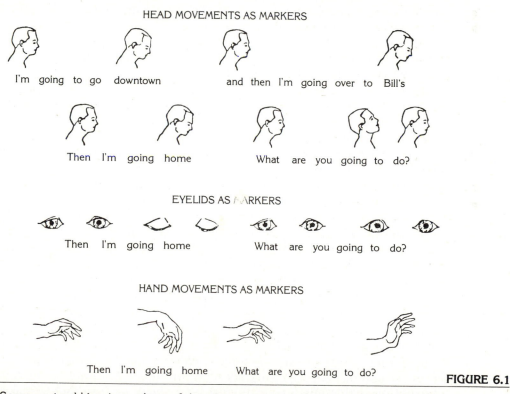

HEAD MOVEMENTS AS MARKERS

I'm going to go downtown   and then I'm going over to Bill's

Then I'm going home   What are you going to do?

EYELIDS AS MARKERS

Then I'm going home   What are you going to do?

HAND MOVEMENTS AS MARKERS

Then I'm going home   What are you going to do?

FIGURE 6.1

Some postural-kinesic markers of American syntactic sentences. From A. E. Scheflen,"The Significance of Posture in Communication Systems," *Psychiatry* 27 (1964): 321. Used by permission of the author and publisher.

expects the partner to respond. If the speaker plans to answer a rhetorical question, we will probably see some turn-maintaining cues, but if the listener is eager to get into the conversation he or she may attempt to answer even the rhetorical question. We can also indicate the end of our utterance vocally by a decreased loudness, a slowed tempo, a drawl on the last syllable, or an utterance "trailer" such as "you know," "or something," or "but, uh." Naturally an extended unfilled pause is also used to signal turn-yielding. More often than not, however, the silence becomes awkward, and the speaker adds a trailer onto the utterance. Body movements, which have been accompanying the speech, may also be terminated—for example, illustrative gestures come to rest and body tenseness becomes relaxed. Gazing at the other person will also help to signal the end of your utterance. If the listener does not perceive these yielding cues (and gives no turn-denying cues), the speaker may try to convey more explicit cues, such as touching the other person, raising and holding the eyebrows in expectation, or saying something like "Well?"

2. *Turn-Maintaining.* If, for some reason, the speaker does not want to yield a speaking turn, several behaviors are likely to be seen. The voice loudness will probably increase as turn-requesting signals are perceived in the listener. Gestures will probably not come to rest at the end of verbal utterances, creating a gestural equivalent to the filled pause. Filled pauses will probably be increased and the frequency and duration of silent pauses will be decreased. This minimizes the opportunities for the other person to start speaking without interrupting or speaking simultaneously. Sometimes we see a light touching of the other person by the speaker, which seems to say, "Hold on a little bit longer. I want to make a few more points and then you can talk." This touching is sometimes accompanied by a patting motion as if to soothe the impatient auditor. In some respects, this act of touching has the effect of the speaker putting his or her hand over the mouth of the auditor—an act that interpersonal etiquette would not allow in this society.

3. *Turn-Requesting.* When we do not have the floor and we want to talk, we may exhibit one or more of the following behaviors. An upraised index finger almost seems to symbolize an instrument for creating a conversational "hole" in the speaker's stream of words, but it also approximates a familiar formal turn-requesting signal learned in school—a raised hand. Sometimes this upraised index finger is accompanied by an audible inspiration of breath and a straightening and tightening of posture, signaling the imminence of talk. In some cases, certain self-adaptors classified as "preening" behavior may also signal preparation for a new role. The very act of simultaneous talking (extended interruption) will convey your request for a speaking turn, but to make sure that your request is granted, you may have to speak louder than your partner, begin gesturing, and look away as if the turn was now

yours. When the speaker and listener are well synchronized, the listener will anticipate the speaker's juncture for yielding and will prepare accordingly—getting the rhythm before the other person has stopped talking, much like a musician tapping a foot preceding his or her solo performance. If the requestor's rhythm does not fit the speakers, we might observe some stutter starts, for example, "I . . . I . . . I . . . wa . . ." Sometimes the turn-requesting mechanism will consist of efforts to speed up the speaker, realizing that the sooner the speaker has his or her say, the sooner you'll get yours. This same behavior was noted in our leave-taking study when people were anxious to terminate the conversation. The most common method for encouraging the other person to finish quickly is the use of rapid head nods, often accompanied by verbalizations of pseudoagreement, such as "yeah," "mm-hmm," and the like. The requester hopes the speaker will perceive that these comments are given much too often and do not logically follow ideas expressed to be genuine signs of reinforcement.

4. *Turn-Denying.* There are instances when we receive turn-yielding cues from the speaker, but we do not want to talk. At such times we will probably maintain a relaxed listening pose, maintain silence, or gaze intently at something in the surrounding environment. More often, we exhibit behavior that shows our continuing involvement in the content of the speaker's words, but denies that we are seeking a turn. This might take the form of smiling, nodding, or shaking the head; completing a sentence started by the speaker; briefly restating what the speaker just said; briefly requesting clarification of the speaker's remarks; or showing approval by appropriately placed "mm-hmms," "yeah," or other noises such as the "clicking" sound that suggests, "You shouldn't have said that."

ADAPTORS

Adaptors, as the term implies, are behavioral adaptations we make in response to certain learning situations—for example, learning to perform some bodily or instrumental action, learning to manage our emotions, learning to satisfy our needs, or learning to get along with other people. These behaviors (or some residue of them) seem to appear in situations that the person feels approximate the conditions of the early learning experiences. Generally we are not aware of performing these behaviors, but frequent feedback may heighten our sensitivity—for example, when someone says to us, "Stop picking your nose!" Although the research on adaptors is not extensive, there seems to be some consensus that adaptors are generally associated with negative feelings—for oneself or another person. There are also some useful classifications of different types of adaptors. These classifications include both the probable referent for the behavior (self, other, object) and the type of behavior (scratch, rub). Some attempts are being made to link various adaptors to specific emotional or mood states. Most of the research has focused on self-adaptors.

Ekman's and Friesen's examination of psychiatric patients and normal individuals finds that self-adaptors increase as a person's psychological discomfort and anxiety increase.[17] If, however, the anxiety level is too high, a person may "freeze" and engage in little movement at all. The finding that self-adaptors were also associated with guilt feelings in the patients studied illuminates one aspect of the deception research that is reviewed later in this chapter. Specifically, Ekman and Friesen discovered that picking and scratching self-adaptors are related to a person's hostility and suspiciousness. Theoretically, this picking and scratching is a manifestation of aggression against oneself or aggression felt for another person that is projected upon oneself. Other speculations and hypotheses about self-adaptors include the possibility that rubbing may be designed to give self-assurance, that covering one's eyes is associated with shame, and that self-grooming may show a concern for one's self-presentation.

Freedman and his colleagues have combined self and object adaptors into one category called "body-focused movements."[18] Freedman says that there may be a close link between body-touching and preoccupation with oneself, reduction of communicative intent, withdrawal from interaction, and a possible impoverishment of symbolic activity.

Since our discussion of adaptors has proposed a number of relationships between various body movements and affective or mood states, we conclude this section with Ekman's ideas regarding the type of emotional information carried by different body parts.[19] On the basis of his research, Ekman suggests that the head-face area carries information about the emotion being experienced (anger, joy, and the like), whereas the body cues primarily communicate information about the intensity of the emotional experience. Although some affect information may be communicated through bodily cues, it is probably infrequent and difficult for observers to perceive. More specifically, Ekman says that facial expressions and body acts (movements of some duration) communicate specific emotional states, whereas body positions (nonmoving positions of some duration) and head orientations (tilts, leanings) usually communicate gross affective states, but not specific emotions.

COMMUNICATING ATTITUDES, STATUS, AND DECEPTION THROUGH GESTURES, POSTURES, AND OTHER BODY MOVEMENTS

Some of the investigations of body movements and posture have examined various communication outcomes rather than specific types of nonverbal behavior. Several specific types of behavior combine with each other to communicate a particular impression. We are concerned here with the following outcomes or communicative goals: (1) attitudes of liking/disliking; (2) status and power; and (3) deception.

Most of the body movements we are discussing are learned and vary from culture to culture. For example, Efron found that the sharp contrasts in gestural styles of Eastern European Jews and southern Italians gradually disappeared and were assimilated into the gestural norms of the new culture when these people emigrated to the United States.[20] Thus, unless otherwise specified, our discussion of body movements should be considered culture specific—that is, primarily derived from and generalizable to adult, Caucasian, middle- and upper-socioeconomic-class people in the United States.

Attitudes.   Body movements and attitudes have been studied in the context of liking or disliking toward another person. Mehrabian's work is one baseline from which to draw generalizations in this area.[21] Broadly summarized, Mehrabian's research demonstrates that liking is distinguished from disliking by more forward lean, a closer proximity, more eye gaze, more openness of arms and body, more direct body orientation, more touching, more postural relaxation, and more positive facial and vocal expressions.

The use of an arms-akimbo (hands on hips) position by a standing communicator was also indicative of communicator attitude according to Mehrabian. This position was used with greater frequency while interacting with disliked persons than with liked persons.

Other investigators have explored similar liking/disliking behaviors under the labels of warm/cold. Reece and Whitman identified the body language components that lead to one's being perceived as a "warm" person.[22] Warmth indicators included a shift of posture toward the other person, a smile, direct eye contact, and hands remaining still. A "cold" person looked around the room, slumped, drummed fingers, and did not smile. The warmth cues, coupled with the verbal reinforcer "mm-hmm," was effective for increasing verbal output (a particular kind of output) from the other person. The verbal reinforcer alone was not sufficient.

Clore and his colleagues collected a large number of verbal statements that described nonverbal liking and disliking.[23] These behaviors were limited to a female's actions toward a male. The large number of behavioral descriptions were narrowed down by asking people to rate the extent to which the behavior accurately conveyed liking or disliking. Table 6.1 lists (in order) the behaviors that were rated highest and lowest. An actress then portrayed these behaviors in an interaction with a male, and the interaction was videotaped. To no one's surprise, viewers of the videotape felt that the warm behaviors would elicit greater liking from the male addressee. The interesting aspect of these studies is what happened when the viewers were exposed to a combined tape in which

TABLE 6.1
Behaviors Rated As Warm and Cold

WARM BEHAVIORS	COLD BEHAVIORS
Looks into his eyes	Gives a cold stare
Touches his hand	Sneers
Moves toward him	Gives a fake yawn
Smiles frequently	Frowns
Works her eyes from his head to his toes	Moves away from him
Has a happy face	Looks at the ceiling
Smiles with mouth open	Picks her teeth
Grins	Shakes her head negatively
Sits directly facing him	Cleans her fingernails
Nods head affirmatively	Looks away
Puckers her lips	Pouts
Licks her lips	Chain-smokes
Raises her eyebrows	Cracks her fingers
Has eyes wide open	Looks around the room
Uses expressive hand gestures while speaking	Picks her hands
Gives fast glances	Plays with the split ends of her hair
Stretches	Smells her hair

Adapted from G. L. Clore, N. H. Wiggins, and S. Itkin, "Judging Attraction from Nonverbal Behavior: The Gain Phenomenon," *Journal of Consulting and Clinical Psychology* 43(1975):491-497. Copyright 1975 by the American Psychological Association. Reprinted by permission.

the actress' behavior was initially warm and then turned cold, or when her behavior was initially cold, and then turned warm. The reactions to these videotapes were compared with responses to videotapes that showed totally warm or totally cold portrayals by the actress. People judged that the man on the videotape would be more attracted to the woman who was cold at first and warm later than he would to the woman who was warm for the entire interaction. Further, people felt that the woman whose behavior turned from warm to cold was less attractive to the man than the woman who was cold during the entire interaction.

One contribution by Scheflen to the literature on interpersonal attitudes of liking and disliking is related to his observations on courtship patterns in the United States.[24] He made sound films of numerous therapeutic encounters, business meetings, and conferences. His content analysis of these films led him to conclude that consistent and patterned quasi-courtship behaviors were exhibited in these settings. Scheflen then developed a set of classifications for such behaviors. *Courtship readiness* defines a category of behaviors characterized by constant manifestations of high muscle tone, reduced eye bagginess and jowl sag, lessening of slouch and shoulder hunching, and decreasing belly sag. *Preening behavior* is exemplified by such things as stroking the hair, rearrangement of makeup, glancing in the mirror, rearranging clothes in a sketchy fashion, leaving buttons open, adjusting suit coats, tugging at socks, and readjusting tie knots. *Positional cues* were reflected in seating arrangements that suggested, "We're not open to interaction with any-one else." Arms, legs, and torsos were arranged so as to inhibit others from entering the conversation. *Actions of appeal* or invitation included glancing flirtatiously, gaze-holding, rolling the pelvis, crossing the legs to expose a thigh, exhibiting the wrist or palm, protruding the breasts, and others.

Others have discussed Scheflen's positional cues in terms of who is excluded and who is included. The positioning of the torsos and legs in Figure 6.2 clearly suggests, "We're not open to others" in (a), and "I'm with you—not him" in (b).

Rosenfeld designed an experiment in which female undergraduate students were trying either to win or avoid approval from other female students.[25] Smiles, head-nodding, and a generally higher level of gestural activity characterized the approval seekers. Rosenfeld, like Ekman, believed that the larger amount of gestural activity gave information about the intensity of the affective state—approval seeking inducing more intense emotion. Although smiles and head nods have other meanings in other contexts, they seem to be nonverbal concomitants of approval-seeking behavior.

Some believe that people who have very similar attitudes will share a common interaction posture, whereas noncongruent postures may reflect attitudinal or relationship distance. There may, of course, be a number of other reasons for congruent or noncongruent postures—for example, relaxation postures. Therapists have reported the use of posture matching to promote greater client-therapist rapport, and one study of counselor behavior did find that empathic responses were communicated primarily by nonverbal behaviors.[26] Nonverbal signals used in this study included forward lean, direct body orientation, and eye gaze, and maintaining a distance of seventy-two inches.

It should be clear by now that we do communicate interpersonal attitudes of liking and disliking through our body movements. Davis reports that in the trial of the Chicago Seven, defense attorney William

(a)   (b)

FIGURE 6.2

Kunstler objected that Judge Julius Hoffman effectively communicated his attitude for all to see—leaning forward in an attentive position during the prosecutor's summation and leaning so far back that he almost seemed to be asleep during the concluding arguments of the defense.[27]

Status.   Mehrabian's work also provides us with some information concerning the role of status in kinesic communication. For instance, in standing positions, shoulder orientation was found to be more direct with a high-status addressee than with a low-status addressee, regardless of the speaker's attitude toward the addressee. The arms-akimbo position is more likely when you are talking to a person you see as having a lower status than your own. Mehrabian also found that his subjects would raise their heads more when speaking to a high-status person— especially male subjects speaking to high-status males. Observational evidence seems to confirm that those assuming inferior roles more often lower their heads, whereas those assuming superior roles more frequently keep their heads raised. Leg and hand relaxation was found to be greater for standing communicators communicating with lower-status addressees. Also, sideways lean was greater when communicating with lower-status persons than with high-status persons. Goffman's observations of staff meetings in a psychiatric hospital confirm this finding.[28] Goffman noted that the high-status individuals (psychiatrists) sat in relaxed postures, putting their feet on the table and lying slumped in their seats, whereas lower-status people more often sat formally, straight in their chairs.

To summarize Mehrabian's research on nonverbal indicators of status/power, we could say that high-status persons are associated with less eye gaze, postural relaxation, greater voice loudness, more frequent use of arms-akimbo, dress ornamentation with power symbols, greater territorial access, more expansive movements and postures, and greater height; and more distance. All of these characteristics are in the context of comparisons to lower-status behavior, whereas the higher-status person will sometimes exhibit constant eye gaze (for example, to intimidate). Similarly, a lower-status person is often seen as "keeping distance" between him or herself and the higher-status person, but this may be partly a result of the need for the higher-status person to maintain a large territory or to emphasize his or her prominence.

Henley reviewed literature pertaining to the verbal and nonverbal behavior of men and women and compared it to behavioral indicators of status and power.[29] The comparisons of the nonverbal behaviors are summarized in Table 6.2.

Deception.   Freud once said, "He that has eyes to see and ears to hear may convince himself that no mortal can keep a secret. If his lips are silent, he chatters with his fingertips; betrayal oozes out of him at every

TABLE 6.2
Henley's Summary of Status and Power Gestures

BEHAVIOR	BETWEEN STATUS EQUALS		BETWEEN STATUS NONEQUALS		BETWEEN MEN AND WOMEN	
	Intimate	Nonintimate	Used by Superior	Used by Subordinate	Used by Men	Used by Women
Posture	Relaxed	Tense (less relaxed)	Relaxed	Tense	Relaxed	Tense
Personal space	Closeness	Distance	Closeness (optional)	Distance	Closeness	Distance
Touching	Touch	Don't touch	Touch (optional)	Don't touch	Touch	Don't touch
Eye gaze	Establish	Avoid	Stare, ignore	Avert eyes, watch	Stare, ignore	Avert eyes, watch
Demeanor	Informal	Circumspect	Informal	Circumspect	Informal	Circumspect
Emotional Expression	Show	Hide	Hide	Show	Hide	Show
Facial Expression	Smile*	Don't smile*	Don't smile	Smile	Don't smile	Smile

*Behavior not known.

From Nancy M. Henley, *Body Politics: Power, Sex, and Nonverbal Communication*, © 1977, p. 181. Adapted by permission of Prentice-Hall, Inc. Englewood Cliffs, New Jersey.

pore."[30] An increasing number of researchers are exploring the specific nature of Freud's hypothesis—asking what particular nonverbal cues give a person away when he or she is trying to deceive someone. Unsystematic observations of deception such as the liar's "shifty eyes" are plentiful. The famous trial lawyer Louis Nizer suggests that jurors may associate deception with witnesses who (1) scissor their legs when asked certain questions, (2) look at the ceiling (as if for help), or (3) pass their hands over their mouths before answering questions in a certain area, as if so say, "I wish I didn't have to say what I am about to say."[31]

Scholarly investigations have found a variety of nonverbal behaviors associated with liars as compared to truthful communicators. According to these studies, liars will have a higher pitch,[32] less gaze duration and longer adaptor duration,[33] fewer illustrators (less enthusiastic), more hand-shrug emblems (uncertainty, more adaptors—particularly face play adaptors,[34] and less nodding, more speech errors, slower speaking rate, and less immediate positions relative to their partners.[35] The findings of these studies have not always been consistent, and researchers have used many methods of creating a deception situation to study. Furthermore, we don't know which, if any, of the cues just listed are used by observers when attempting to detect deception. We do know, however, that most studies show that untrained human observers can detect deceptive communications by strangers at about chance level—about 50 percent of the time.

Ekman and Friesen developed a theoretical framework regarding the manifestation of nonverbal signals relating to deception.[36] Attention was given particularly to the face, hands, and feet/legs since Ekman and Friesen believed that posture was so easy to simulate it would not be a major source of leakage (revealing specific hidden information) or deception clues (revealing that a deception is taking place, without indicating specific information). Considering sending capacity, internal feedback, and external feedback, the face ranks highest on all three dimensions; hands are next; and feet/legs rank last. The availability of leakage and deception clues reverses this pattern—the feet/legs being a good source of leakage and deception clues; the hands next, and the face being the poorest source. It is reasoned that you will not expend much effort inhibiting or dissimulating with areas of the body that are largely ignored by others. Equally important, you cannot inhibit or dissimulate actions in areas of the body about which you have learned to disregard internal feedback, or about which you receive little external feedback.

Leakage and deception clues in the face generally come from microfacial movements (rarely observed in everyday conversation) and imperfectly performed simulations—the smile drawn out too long and the frown that is too severe.[37] Hands are easier to inhibit than the face because you can hide them from view without the hiding itself becoming a deception clue. Your hands, however, may be digging into your cheek, tearing at your fingernails, or protectively holding your knees while your face is smiling and pleasant. Leakage cues in the legs or feet might include aggressive foot kicks, flirtatious leg displays, autoerotic or soothing leg squeezing, or abortive, restless flight movements. Deception clues might be tense leg positions, frequent shifts of leg posture, or restless or repetitive leg and foot acts. Obviously, a failure to perform nonverbal acts that ordinarily accompany verbal acts is a sign that something is wrong.

Subsequent experimentation has confirmed the idea that most people pay attention to their facial behavior when attempting to deceive another, but observers who were unfamiliar with the communicators could not isolate deceivers by examining body cues only—unless they were also exposed to the person's behavior under honest message-sending conditions.[38]

If you fail at deception because of nonverbal leakage or deception clues, it may be because of a conscious wish to be caught, secondary guilt, or shame or anxiety about engaging in deception or possibly about being discovered. You may also fail because you cannot monitor and disguise forms of behavior for which you have no feedback and have learned that most people will not attend to—forgetting that the slightest hint of deception will cause intense monitoring of these traditionally neglected areas.

At this point, let us reiterate an important point. The nonverbal behaviors associated with the areas surveyed in this chapter must be kept in a contextual perspective—that is, although a given configuration of nonverbal cues may seem to convey the feeling of interpersonal warmth, the same configuration may take on a completely different meaning in a context in which the warmth behaviors are neutralized, added to, or canceled out by other factors.

SUMMARY

This chapter dealt with the heart of human nonverbal study—the human body and the movement it makes during interpersonal contacts. Dozens of studies have been reviewed, summarized, and categorized. Any time we subdivide and categorize a complex set of behaviors, we should remember that behaviors are not, in actuality, seen alone—they work together and form clusters of cues. We should also remember that the meaning of these behaviors will ultimately be found in a specific context by the specific people in that context. This is not to say that a particular behavior may not be weighted more heavily than another in any given situation; it is simply a reminder to avoid oversimplification in analyzing nonverbal behavior.

What does the information in this chapter teach us? We know that in looking at body language, we are looking at a system that has some parallels to spoken language. Current evidence suggests that kinesics is not a communication system with exactly the same structure as spoken language. Larger and smaller body movements do, however, seem to have a distinct relationship to correspondingly large and small speech units. Movements do not seem to be produced randomly—they are inextricably linked to human speech. From birth there seems to be an effort to synchronize speech and body movements, and adults have manifested body self-synchrony and interactional synchrony. People whose body movements and speech are out of synchrony may have some pathology; two people who are out of synchrony may not know each other well, or there may be an absence of listening behavior. Some of these body movements that accompany speech are made prior to the speech unit, some are made during, and some are made after. Dittmann's work showed that vocalizations, head nods, and movements of the hands and feet of listeners tended to occur at the end of rhythmical units of the talker's speech—that is, pauses within phonemic clauses, but mainly at the junctures between these clauses.

We also presented a list of common emblems used in the United States. Regulators were discussed in the contexts of greetings and good-byes, and conversational turn-taking. Head movements and eye behavior were seen to be central in initiating and terminating dialogue. Some of the body behaviors seemed to serve several functions and carry the potential for several different meanings—within the greeting and departure rituals. The methods we use to exchange speaking turns were analyzed as an extension of the concept of interactional synchrony. We noted how the speaker can yield or maintain his or her speaking turn through nonverbal behavior and how the listener can nonverbally request or deny a speaking turn. The research on adaptors generally suggested that they were linked to negative feelings, anxiety, discomfort, covert hostility, preoccupation with self, and low involvement in the communicative event.

The last part of the chapter considered how clusters of nonverbal behavior can help communicate several common and important ideas. Attitudes of liking and disliking were examined under several related labels: interpersonal warmth or coldness, approval seeking, quasi-court-ship behavior, and open and closed positioning. We outlined a number of nonverbal behaviors that seem to be related to perceptions of status and power. Henley's analysis revealed that many of the behaviors associated with status and power were not used by or encouraged in women, but they were in men. We concluded the chapter with a discussion of several nonverbal behaviors that were linked to deceivers, and of Ekman's and Friesen's theoretical framework for studying deception.

NOTES

1. L. Kuman and M. Lazar, "Gestural Communication in Preschool Children," *Perceptual and Motor Skills* 38 (1974): 708–710.

2. D. Efron, *Gesture and Environment* (New York: King's Crown Press, 1941).

3. R. Saitz and E. Cervenka, *Columbian and North American Gestures* (The Hague: Mouton Press, 1973).

4. H. G. Johnson, P. Ekman, and W. V. Friesen, "Communicative Body Movements: American Emblems," *Semiotica* 15 (1975): 335–353.

5. W. S. Condon and W. D. Ogston, "Soundfilm Analysis of Normal and Pathological Behavior Patterns," *Journal of Nervous and Mental Disease* 143 (1966): 338–347. Also W. S. Condon and W. D. Ogston, "A Segmentation of Behavior," *Journal of Psychiatric Research* 5 (1967): 221–235.

6. Some specific references to this work can be found in Chapter 10. Also see J. T. Webb, "Interview Synchrony: An Investigation of Two Speech Rate Measures," in A. W. Siegman and B. Pope (eds.), *Studies in Dyadic Communication* (Elmsford, N.Y.: Pergamon Press, 1972).

7. F. Davis, *Inside Intuition* (New York: McGraw-Hill, 1971), p. 103.

8. W. S. Condon and L. W. Sander, "Neonate Movement Is Synchronized with Adult Speech: Interactional Participation and Language Acquisition," *Science*, January 11, 1974, 99–101.

9. A. T. Dittmann and L. G. Llewellyn, "The Phonemic Clause as a Unit of Speech Decoding," *Journal of Personality and Social Psychology* 6 (1967): 341–349; A. T. Dittmann and L. G. Llewellyn, "Relationship Between Vocalization and Head Nods as Listener Responses," *Journal of Personality and Social Psychology* 9 (1968): 79–84; A. T. Dittmann and L. G. Llewellyn, "Body Movement and Speech Rhythm in Social Conversation," *Journal of Personality and Social Psychology* 11 (1969): 98–106; and A. T. Dittmann, "The Body Movement—Speech Rhythm Relationship as a Cue to Speech Encoding," in A. W. Siegman and B. Pope (eds.), *Studies in Dyadic Communication* (Elmsford, N.Y.: Pergamon Press, 1972).

10. E. Goffman, *Relations in Public* (New York: Basic Books, 1971), pp. 84–85.

11. A. Kendon and A. Ferber, "A Description of Some Human Greetings," in R. P. Michael and J. H. Cook (eds.), *Comparative Ecology and Behaviour of Primates* (London: Academic Press, 1973).

12. P. D. Krivonos and M. L. Knapp, "Initiating Communication: What Do You Say When You Say Hello?" *Central States Speech Journal* 26 (1975): 115–125.

13. For an interesting discussion of the handshake, see D. Schiffrin, "Handwork as Ceremony: The Case of the Handshake," *Semiotica* 12 (1974): 189–202.

14. M. L. Knapp, R. P. Hart, G. W. Friedrich, and G. M. Shulman, "The Rhetoric of Goodbye: Verbal and Nonverbal Correlates of Human Leave-Taking," *Speech Monographs* 40 (1973): 182–198.

15. M. LaFrance and C. Mayo, "Racial Differences in Gaze Behavior During Conversations: Two Systematic Observational Studies," *Journal of Personality and Social Psychology* 33 (1976): 547–552.

16. The turn-taking behaviors listed here were derived from many sources.

For an examination of the foremost researcher in this area, see S. Duncan, Jr., "Interaction Units During Speaking Turns in Dyadic, Face-To-Face Conversations," in A. Kendon, R. M. Harris, and M. R. Key (eds.), *Organization of Behavior in Face-To-Face Interaction* (Chicago: Aldine, 1975). Also see S. Duncan, Jr., and D. W. Fiske, *Face-To-Face Interaction: Research, Methods, and Theory* (Hillsdale, N.J.: Lawrence Erlbaum Associates, 1977). For a summary of a number of studies, see J. M. Wiemann and M. L. Knapp, "Turn-Taking in Conversations," *Journal of Communication* 25 (1975): 75–92. The vocal elements of turn-taking are treated more extensively in Chapter 10.

17. P. Ekman and W. V. Friesen, "Hand Movements," *Journal of Communication* 22 (1972): 353–374.

18. A. Freedman, T. Blass, A. Rifkin, and F. Quitkin, "Body Movements and the Verbal Encoding of Aggressive Affect," *Journal of Personality and Social Psychology* 26 (1973): 72–85; N. Freedman, "The Analysis of Movement Behavior During the Clinical Interview," in A. W. Siegman and B. Pope, *Studies in Dyadic Communication* (Elmsford, N.Y.: Pergamon Press, 1972); N. Freedman and S. P. Hoffman, "Kinetic Behavior in Altered Clinical States: Approach to Objective Analysis of Motor Behavior During Clinical Interviews," *Perceptual and Motor Skills* 24 (1967): 527–539.

19. P. Ekman, "Differential Communication of Affect by Head and Body Cues," *Journal of Personality and Social Psychology* 2 (1965) 726–735. Also P. Ekman, "Head and Body Cues in the Judgments of Emotion: A Reformulation," *Perceptual and Motor Skills* 24 (1967): 711–724.

20. Efron, *Gesture and Environment*.

21. For a summary of this work through 1972, see A. Mehrabian, *Nonverbal Communication* (Chicago: Aldine, 1972).

22. M. Reece and R. Whitman, "Expressive Movements, Warmth, and Verbal Reinforcement," *Journal of Abnormal and Social Psychology* 64 (1962): 234–236.

23. G. L. Clore, N. H. Wiggins, and S. Itkin, "Gain and Loss in Attraction: Attributions from Nonverbal Behavior," *Journal of Personality and Social Psychology* 31 (1975): 706–712.

24. A. E. Scheflen, "Quasi-Courtship Behavior in Psychotherapy," *Psychiatry* 28 (1965): 245–257.

25. H. Rosenfeld, "Instrumental Affiliative Functions of Facial and Gestural Expressions," *Journal of Personality and Social Psychology* 4 (1966): 65–72.

26. R. F. Hasse and D. T. Tepper, "Nonverbal Components of Empathic Communication," *Journal of Counseling Psychology* 19 (1972): 417–424.

27. Davis, *Inside Intuition*, p. 93.

28. E. Goffman, *Encounters* (Indianapolis, Ind.: Bobbs-Merrill, 1961).

29. N. M. Henley, *Body Politics: Power, Sex, and Nonverbal Communication* (Englewood Cliffs, N.J.: Prentice-Hall, 1977).

30. S. Freud, "Fragment of an Analysis of a Case of Hysteria (1905)," *Collected Papers*, (New York: Basic Books, 1959), vol. 3.

31. L. Nizer, *The Implosion Conspiracy* (Greenwich, Conn.: Fawcett, 1973), p. 16.

32. P. Ekman, W. V. Friesen, and K. R. Scherer, "Body Movement and Voice Pitch in Deceptive Interaction," *Semiotica* 16 (1976): 23–27.

33. M. L. Knapp, R. P. Hart, and H. S. Dennis, "An Exploration of Deception as a Communication Construct," *Human Communication Research* 1 (1974): 15–29.

34. P. Ekman and W. V. Friesen, "Hand Movements."

35. A. Mehrabian, *Nonverbal Communication* (Chicago: Aldine-Atherton, 1972).

36. P. Ekman, and W. V. Friesen, "Nonverbal Leakage and Clues to Deception," *Psychiatry* 32 (1969): 88–106.

37. Ekman and Friesen elaborate on how people try to lie with their face and some sources of leakage that will help observers, such as, facial morphology, timing and location of the expression, and micromomentary expressions. Cf. Chapter 11, "Facial Deceit," in P. Ekman and W. V. Friesen, *Unmasking the Face* (Englewood Cliffs, N.J.: Prentice-Hall, 1975).

38. P. Ekman and W. V. Friesen,"Detecting Deception from the Body or Face," *Journal of Personality and Social Psychology* 29 (1974): 288–298.

ADDITIONAL READINGS

Birdwhistell, R. L. "Background to Kinesics." *ETC* 13 (1955): 10–18.

Davis, F. *Inside Intuition*. New York: McGraw-Hill, 1971.

Efron, D. *Gesture, Race and Culture*. The Hague: Mouton, 1972.

Ekman, P. and W. V. Friesen. "The Repertoire of Nonverbal Behavior: Categories, Origins, Usage, and Coding." *Semiotica* 1 (1969): 49–98.

Hayes, F. "Gestures: A Working Bibliography." *Southern Folklore Quarterly* 21 (1957): 218–317.

Henley, N. *Body Politics: Power, Sex, and Nonverbal Communication*. Englewood Cliffs, N.J.: Prentice-Hall, 1977.

Hewes, G. W. "The Anthropology of Posture." *Scientific American* 196 (1957): 123–132.

Key, M. R. *Paralanguage and Kinesics*. Metuchen, N.J.: Scarecrow Press, 1977.

Mehrabian, A. *Silent Messages*. Belmont, Calif.: Wadsworth, 1972.

Morris, D. *Manwatching: A field Guide to Human Behavior* New York: Harry N. Abrams, 1977.

Scheflen, A. E. and A. Scheflen, *Body Language and the Social Order*. Englewood Cliffs, N.J.: Prentice-Hall, 1972.

THE EFFECTS OF TOUCHING BEHAVIOR

We often talk about the way we talk, and we frequently try to see the way we see, but for some reason we have rarely touched on the way we touch.   D. MORRIS

The setting is in a library, but it could just as easily be the local supermarket, bank, or restaurant. What happens takes about half a second, and even though it is not noticed by the recipients, this act apparently affects their evaluation of their experience in the library. Let's begin at the beginning. Researchers at Purdue University wanted to systematically investigate the effects of a brief, "accidental" touch in a nonintimate context.[1] They had male and female clerks return library cards to some students by placing their hand directly over the other's palm, making physical contact; other students whose cards were also returned were not touched. Outside the library the students were given instruments to measure their feelings toward the library clerk and the library in general. The students who were touched—especially the females—evaluated the clerk and the library significantly more favorably than those who were not touched. This was true for both students who were aware of being touched and those who were not. The clerks may have been doing other things when they touched the students (for example, smiling), even though they were trained to maintain consistent behaviors for all students. So we know that touch was influential, but it may have worked in conjunction with other aspects of the setting, the relationship to the other, experiences with touch, other behaviors, and so on.

Touch is a crucial aspect of most human relationships. It plays a part in giving encouragement, expressing tenderness, showing emotional support, and many other things. The growth of body-awareness and personal-growth workshops testifies that many people in the United States feel a need to rediscover communication through touch. These workshops encourage physical contact as a way of breaking through some psychological barriers. People try to become more aware of themselves, other people, and the world around them through physical experiences rather than through words or sight. It is, as some say, a widespread movement reflecting a yearning for human contact. It may also be a movement to restore some unfilled tactile needs. As Montagu says:

> When affection and involvement are conveyed through touch, it is those meanings as well as the security-giving satisfactions, with which touch will become associated. Inadequate tactile experience will result in a lack of such associations and a consequent inability to relate to others in many fundamental human ways.[2]

Perhaps the most dramatic testimony to the communicative potential of touch comes from the blind. Helen Keller's diary tells of an incident when she was touching her dog: "He was rolling on the grass . . . his fat body revolved, stiffened and solidified into an upright position, and his tongue gave my hand a lick. . . . If he could speak, I believe he would say with me that paradise is attained by touch."

The act of touching is like any other message we communicate—it may elicit negative reactions as well as positive ones depending on the configuration of people and circumstances. We should be very careful about the extent to which we generalize from the material presented thus far. We know that people sometimes get "uptight," anxious, and/or uncomfortable when they are touched; we know that touching that is perceived as inappropriate for the relationship can be met with aggressive reactions—that is, "touching" back in the form of slapping or hitting. Everyday observation would lead us to assume that some people evaluate almost all touching negatively. In some cases this dislike for touching may be related to early experiences they had with touch.

TOUCHING AND HUMAN DEVELOPMENT

Tactile communication is probably the most basic or primitive form of communication. In fact, tactual sensitivity may be the first sensory process to become functional. In fetal life, the child begins to respond to vibrations of the mother's pulsating heartbeat, which impinge on the child's entire body and are magnified by the amniotic fluid. In one sense, our first input about what "life" is going to be like comes from the sense of touch. Newborn infants continue to gain knowledge of themselves and the world around them through tactile explorations. Some of the common touch experiences include the touch of the obstetrician's hands and the hands that change their diapers, feed them, bathe them, rock them, and comfort them. During early childhood, words accompany touch until the child associates the two; then words replace touch entirely. For example, a mother may gently stroke or pat an infant to console him or her. As the child grows older, the mother may stroke and pat the child while murmuring encouraging words. Eventually, the mother may call from another room, "It's all right dear—mummy's here." As words replace touching, an intimate closeness is replaced by distance. Frank, who has hypothesized an important relationship from this sequence, says that symbols without primary tactile validation in childhood may be less clearly and less effectively established as basic codes of communication later in life.[3]

Several efforts have been made to examine parental touching of infants and children. It would seem reasonable to assume that the neonate and infant receive more tactile stimulation than children aged fourteen months to two years. In view of infant needs, this would seem both needed and predictable. However, Clay's results indicate that children begin to receive more touching between fourteen months and two years of age than they do as infants. This study also indicates that girl babies tend to receive more of these physical acts of affection than boy babies.[4] Lewis, however, summarizing several research projects, reports that for the first six months of life, boys receive more physical contact than girls. After six months of age, the girls are not only allowed, but encouraged, to spend more time touching and staying near their parents than boys.[5]

Willis and his colleagues observed children in elementary school and junior high school.[6] From kindergarten through sixth grade the amount of touching the children received steadily declines but still surpasses most reports of adult touching. This same trend occurs in junior high school, showing about half as much touching as in the primary grades. Some other interesting findings emerged from these studies. The most touching occurred between same-sexed dyads. Black children—especially black females—tended to exhibit more touching behavior. Although the touching in the primary grades is more often initiated with the hands, the junior high school students showed much more shoulder-to-shoulder and elbow-to-elbow touching. Junior high school females began to show more aggressive touching and junior high school boys were touched in more places—primarily because of the play fighting so common at that age.

Following childhood, the child in the United States goes through a "latency" period in which tactile communication plays only a small role. Then, during adolescence, tactile experiences with members of the same, and then opposite, sex become increasingly important. The use of touch to communicate emotional and relational messages to the elderly may be crucial—particularly as the reliance on verbal/cognitive messages wanes. Although we seem to give the aged in this country a greater "license" to touch others, it is not clear how much others touch them. No doubt the infirmities of age will require more touching, but it may make a big difference whether this increased touching is just "functional/professional" or expresses affectionate feelings.

Early tactile experiences seem crucial to later mental and emotional adjustment. Youngsters who have little physical contact during infancy may walk and talk later; many schizophrenic children are reported to have been deprived of handling as infants; some instances of difficulties and retardation in reading and speech are also associated with early deprivation of, and confusion in, tactile communication. Montagu cites vast numbers of animal and human studies to support the theory that tactile satisfaction during infancy and childhood is of fundamental importance to subsequent healthy behavioral development of the person. He maintains that we cannot handle a child too much since "there is every reason to believe that, just as the salamander's brain and nervous system develops more fully in response to peripheral stimulation, so does the brain and the nervous system of the human being."[7] Harlow's famous "surrogate mother" experiments offer some supporting evidence from the animal world for the importance of touch to infants. Harlow constructed a monkey mother figure out of wire that could provide milk and protection; then he constructed another one out of sponge rubber and terry cloth that did not provide milk. Since infant monkeys consistently chose the terry cloth mother, Harlow concluded that "contact comfort" was a more important part of the mother-child relationship for monkeys, and that nursing was less important as a food source and more important as a source of reassuring touch.

WHO TOUCHES WHOM, WHERE, AND HOW MUCH?

The amount and kind of contact in adulthood vary considerably with the age, sex, situation, and relationship of the parties involved. There are reports of some married couples who either have so little to say to each other, or who find it so difficult to establish closeness through verbal contact, that physical contact during sexual encounters becomes a primary mode of communication for establishing "closeness." In fact, Masters and Johnson, the famous sex researchers, claim they are trying to help people achieve more effective communication: "We believe that effective sexual intercourse is the ultimate in communication." Many factors in the development of the United States have led to a common expectation that touching will only be conducted in extremely personal and intimate relationships, which makes most touching sensual in nature. For some individuals, the contact involved in a crowded commuter train or theater lobby is very discomforting—particularly if these contacts are with a member of the same sex. There are many explanations for such feelings. Some children grow up learning "not to touch" a multitude of animate and inanimate objects; they are told not to touch their own body and later not to touch the body of their dating partner; care is taken so children do not see their parents "touch" one another intimately; some parents demonstrate a noncontact norm through the use of twin beds; touching is associated with admonitions of "not nice" or "bad" and is punished accordingly; and frequent touching between father and son is thought to be something less than masculine.

Certain situations will have a facilitating or inhibiting effect on touching behavior, as well. Henley's research suggests that people may be more likely to touch when: (1) giving information or advice rather than asking for it; (2) giving an order rather than responding to it; (3) asking a favor rather than agreeing to do one; (4) trying to persuade rather than being persuaded; (5) the conversation is "deep" rather than casual; (6) at a party rather than at work; (7) communicating excitement rather than receiving it from another; and (8) receiving messages of worry from another rather than sending such messages.[8] Heslin and Boss found that 60 percent of the people they observed greeting or saying good-bye to someone at an airport were touching.[9] Extended embraces and greater intimacy of touch was observed more frequently in departures or good-byes than in greetings. The greater the emotional feeling (as reflected in facial expressions) and the closer the perceived relationship, the greater are the chances of increased touching. This study also reconfirmed another important finding, namely, that touching behavior is often initiated by men.

Henley has explored this recurrent finding that men seem to be the touchers and women the touchees in the context of status relationships.[10] Henley asks us to consider whom we would expect to initiate touching behavior in dyads such as the following: teacher-student; police-accused; doctor-patient; master-slave; foreman-worker; and advisor-advisee. Most people tend to see the person of higher status initiating the touching. For a "subordinate" to initiate (or even reciprocate, sometimes) touching is often perceived as being out of line, presumptuous, or an affront. Thus, Henley argues that the predominantly male-initiated touch is just as likely (if not more so) to be an indication of power as a reflection of affection. When women initiate touch with men, it is frequently associated with sexual intent—since, as Henley concludes, "the implication of power is unacceptable."

Jourard counted the frequency of contact between couples in cafes in various cities and reports the following contacts per hour: San Juan, Puerto Rico, 180; Paris, 110, Gainesville, Florida, 2; London, 0.[11] In addition, Jourard wanted to know what parts of the body are touched most often. He administered a questionnaire to students who indicated which of the twenty-four body parts they touched on others or which parts of themselves others had touched. Information was obtained for four other persons: mother, father, same-sex friend, and opposite-sex friend, within the past twelve months. Among other findings, Jourard's study found that females were considerably more accessible to touch by all persons than were males. Opposite-sex friends and mothers did the most touching, whereas many fathers touched not much more than the hands of the subjects.

Jourard's data for Figure 7.1 was gathered in 1963–1964. A replication of this study performed over a decade later revealed about the same results—with one exception.[12] In the later study, both males and females were found to be even more accessible to opposite-sex friends than they were a decade earlier, with increased touching reported for body parts normally considered more intimate, such as chest, stomach,

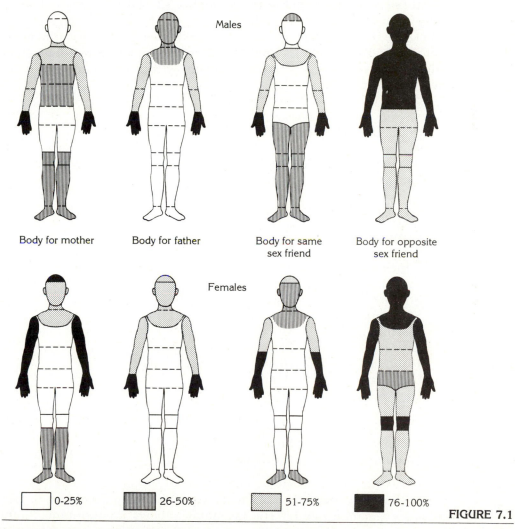

Body for mother	Body for father	Body for same sex friend	Body for opposite sex friend

0-25% 26-50% 51-75% 76-100%

FIGURE 7.1

Areas of the body involved in bodily contact.

hips, and thighs. In the early 1970s, Barnlund constructed a comparative study of Japan and the United States touching patterns.[13] Data was obtained from 120 college students in each culture, 60 female and 60 male. The results of this study, shown in Figure 7.2, indicate that in almost every category, the amount of physical contact reported by Americans is twice that reported by Japanese. In general, Americans seem to be both more accessible to, and more physically expressive toward, others in the areas of touch.

Although our primary interest is in everyday social communication, the study of touch also has important implications for institutionalized persons. Watson found that there was more touching of residents in a home for the elderly if the following conditions were present: (1) the area of touch was far from the genital region, (2) staff and resident were of the same sex, (3) the touch initiator was perceived to have high status, and (4) the resident was relatively free of stigmatizing physical impairments.[14] Watson also points out that severely impaired residents and males (because the staff is largely female) will probably receive relatively little touching.

DIFFERENT TYPES OF TOUCHING BEHAVIOR

Argyle says that the following kinds of bodily contact are most common in Western culture:[15]

TYPE OF TOUCH	BODY AREAS TYPICALLY INVOLVED
Patting	Head, back
Slapping	Face, hand, buttocks
Punching	Face, chest
Pinching	Cheek
Stroking	Hair, face, upper body, knee, genitals
Shaking	Hands, shoulders
Kissing	Mouth, cheek, breasts, hand, foot, genitals
Licking	Face, genitals
Holding	Hand, arm, knee, genitals
Guiding	Hand, arm
Embracing	Shoulder, body
Linking	Arms
Laying-on	Hands
Kicking	Legs, buttocks
Grooming	Hair, face
Tickling	Almost anywhere

Heslin categorized the various types of touching according to the messages communicated.[16] His taxonomy reflects a continuum, from very impersonal touching to very personal touching.

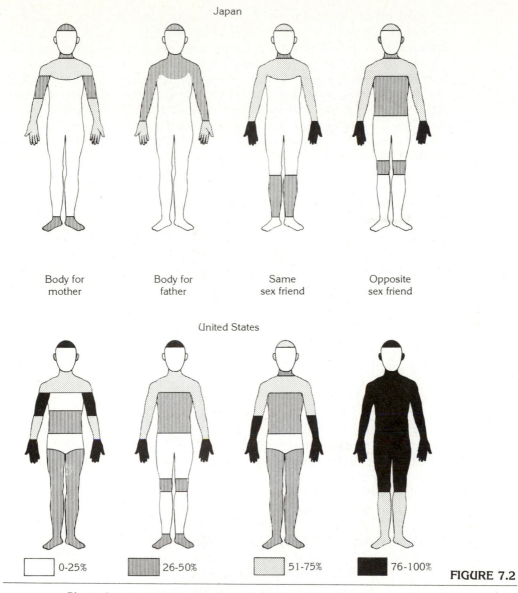

Physical contact patterns in Japan (above) and the United States (below).

1. Functional-Professional. The communicative intent of this impersonal, often "cold" and businesslike touching is to accomplish some task—to perform some service. The other person is considered as an object or nonperson in order to keep any intimate or sexual messages from interfering with the task at hand. Examples of such situations may include a golf pro with his or her student, a tailor with a customer, or a physician with his or her patient.

153

Like other forms of nonverbal behavior, touching may support or contradict information communicated by other systems. A doctor may explain that you need not worry about your pending operation, and his or her touch may add confirmation; but the doctor's touch may also contradict the verbalization if the doctor is nervous or abrupt. Agulera reports an instance in which touch behavior by nurses increased verbal output of the patients and improved patient attitudes toward nurses.[17] The phrase *verbal output* does not necessarily mean a deeper level of self-disclosure; it may just mean more small talk. A positive relationship between the amount of tactile contact and self-disclosure has not been established.[18]

2. Social-Polite. The purpose of this type of touching is to affirm the other person's identity as a member of the same species, operating by essentially the same rules of conduct. Although the other is treated as a "person," there is still very little perceived involvement between the interactants. The handshake is the best example of this type of touching. Although the handshake is thought to be only about 150 years old, it was probably preceded by a handclasp, which goes back in time at least as far as ancient Rome.

3. Friendship-Warmth. This kind of touching behavior begins to recognize more of the other person's uniqueness and expresses a liking for that person. In short, this type of touching is oriented toward the other person as a friend.

4. Love-Intimacy. When you lay your hand on the cheek of a person of the opposite sex or when you fully embrace another person, you are probably expressing an emotional attachment or attraction through touch. The other person is the object of one's feelings of intimacy or love. The various kinds of touching at this point will probably be the least stereotyped and the most adapted to the specific other person.

5. Sexual Arousal. Although sexual arousal is sometimes an integral part of love and intimacy, it may also have characteristics distinct from that category. Here we are primarily looking at touch as an expression of physical attraction only. The other person is, in common parlance, a sex object.

Morris believes that heterosexual couples in Western culture normally go through a sequence of steps—like courtship patterns in other animal species—on the road to sexual intimacy.[19] Notice that each step, aside from the first three, involves some kind of touching: (1) eye to body, (2) eye to eye, (3) voice to voice, (4) hand to hand, (5) arm to shoulder, (6) arm to waist, (7) mouth to mouth, (8) hand to head, (9) hand to body, (10) mouth to breast, (11) hand to genitals, and (12) genitals to genitals and/or mouth to genitals. Morris believes that these steps generally follow the same order, although he admits there are some variations. One form of skipping steps or moving to a level of intimacy beyond what would be expected is found in socially formalized types of bodily contact—for example, a good-night kiss or a hand-to-hand introduction. Although mouth-to-mouth touching in heterosexual pairs may frequently reflect an advancing stage of intimacy, it may also occur in the most nonintimate settings with the most nonintimate meaning attached to it— as, for example, when a host of TV quiz show dutifully "pecks" the female contestants as they are greeted or as they depart.

We also engage in self-touching. This, again from the observations of Morris, may include: (1) shielding actions to reduce input or output— for example, putting your hand over your mouth or over your ears; (2) cleaning actions—bringing the hand up to the head to scratch, rub, pick, wipe, and the like; (3) specialized signals to communicate specific messages—for example, holding a hand under your chin to signal "I'm fed up to here" or thumbing your nose at someone; and (4) self-intimacies— holding your own hands, hugging your legs, masturbating, and so on.[20] Freedman has studied the self-touching of psychiatric patients. He was concerned only with these "body-focused" touches during the patient's speech—and under conditions in which the subject was expected to speak rather than listen.[21] Some of his preliminary studies show that acutely depressed patients may show a preponderance of these body-focused hand movements. Freedman further suggests that there may be a close linkage between body touching and preoccupation with self.

Morris sums up the various kinds of intimate touching, which form the substance of his book, through this example:

> (1) When we are feeling nervous or depressed, a loved one may attempt to reassure us by giving us a comforting hug or a squeeze of the hand. (2) In the absence of a loved one, it may have to be one of the specialist touchers, such as a doctor, who pats our arm and tells us not to worry. (3) If our only company is our pet dog or cat, we may take it in our arms and press our cheek to its furry body to feel the comfort of its warm touch. (4) If we are completely alone and some sinister noise startles us in the night, we may hug the bed-clothes tightly around us to feel secure in their soft embrace. (5) If all else fails, we still have our own bodies, and we can hug, embrace, clasp and touch ourselves in a great variety of ways to help soothe away our fears.[22]

THE MEANINGS OF TOUCHING BEHAVIOR

The meaning of any message will vary according to a multitude of factors—for example, cultural and environmental context, the relationship between the communicators, the intensity and duration of the message, whether it was perceived as intentional or unintentional, and so on. For instance, you could plot the following touch behavior along an intimacy continuum: touch and release (least intimate), touch and hold, touch and stroke. The available data on the meaning of touch is scarce, and the following efforts represent early ground-breaking efforts.

Argyle believes that touch can be decoded as communicating various interpersonal attitudes—for example, it may mean sexual interest, nurturance-dependence (cradling or caressing an infant), affiliation (establishing friendly relations), and aggression (establishing unfriendly relations). Other touching signals may simply be interpreted as managing the interaction itself. These management touches may guide someone without interrupting verbal conversation. They may get somebody's attention by tugging at that person's arm or tapping him or her on the shoulder, indicate or mark the beginning (greeting) or end (goodbye) of a conversation, or fulfill some ritualistic function, such as congratulating a person at graduation or touching a baby's head at a baptism. We can also interpret touching as "accidental" or "meaningless" when it occurs in overcrowded situations or when a passerby brushes against you. Like any other message, the two communicators may not have a similar meaning for the touch—or one person may deliberately try to mislead another. A not unfamiliar example of this form of deception is when one person touches another in a joking context but intends the touch to be a step toward intimacy. The meanings of touch behavior will also vary somewhat with the parts of the body involved in the touch.

Nguyen, Heslin, and Nguyen conducted two studies on the meaning of touch.[23] First, they presented unmarried people with the body parts diagrammed in Figure 7.3. Each person was asked to indicate what it meant to him or her to be touched in each of the eleven areas—that is, patted, squeezed, stroked, or brushed. To focus reactions, subjects were asked to respond only in the context of touching by an opposite-sex friend (and not parents, siblings, or relatives). The method of responding was limited to scales representing various degrees of playfulness, warmth/love, friendship/fellowship, pleasantness, and sexual desire.

Generally, these relatively young married persons tended to react more positively toward touch and tended to associate it with sex more often than did unmarried respondents. Unless the touch was in the genital region, sexual desire was not a common response for the unmarried persons.

The type of touch seemed to be closely linked to one's judgments of playfulness and warmth/love—for example, patting was associated with play, but stroking was associated with warmth/love and sexual desire. On the other hand (no pun intended), friendliness and sexuality seem most closely linked to the location of the touch—for example, hands, no matter how they were touched, were seen as pleasant, warm, and friendly; the genital area was not seen as very "playful" regardless of what kind of touching was being evaluated.

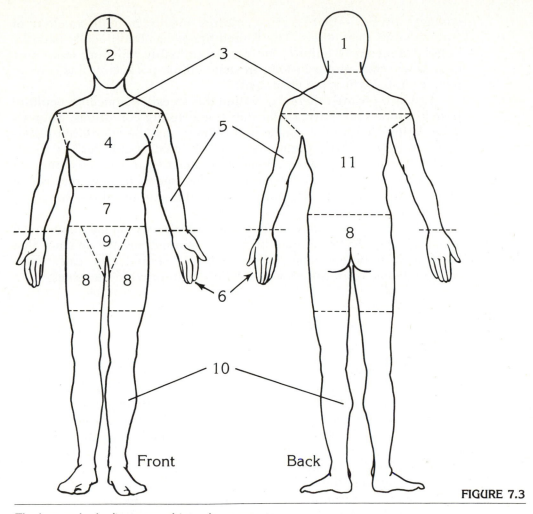

The human body diagrammed into eleven areas.

Although unmarried women did not perceive sexual touching to be as pleasant and as warm as did unmarried men, married women did. Married men attributed less warmth/love and pleasantness to sexual touching than did either single men or married women.

CULTURAL DIFFERENCES IN TOUCHING BEHAVIOR

Anyone who travels has probably observed the vast differences in the amount of touching behavior in some countries when compared with our own. This idea has received much anecdoctal support, and there is probably considerable accuracy in the concept of "contact" versus "non-

157

contact cultures"—that is, some cultures encourage more touching of various kinds than others. The United States has traditionally been labeled a noncontact culture, but we are probably touching more now than at any time in our history. In some ethnic pockets in this country people probably touch a great deal.

Just as there are differences within this so-called noncontact culture based on one's ancestry, social status, and living conditions, Shuter's observations led him to conclude that there may be significant differences in what we have traditionally called "contact cultures" as well.[24] Shuter systematically observed people interacting in natural settings in Costa Rica, Panama, and Colombia. His data seems to show that as one moves southward from Central America, the amount of touching and holding decreases.

Aside from a rich store of anecdotal material, we do not know much about the specifics of cultural differences in touching. We do know that there seem to be enormous differences, for example, two males interacting in some countries may hold hands or intertwine their legs.

SUMMARY

Our first information about ourselves, others, and the environment in which we live probably comes from touching. The act of touching or being touched by another can have a powerful impact on our response to a situation—even if that touch was unintentional or accidental. In some cases, touching is the most effective method for communicating; in others, it can elicit negative or hostile reactions. The meanings we attach to touching behavior vary according to what part of the body is touched, how long the touch lasts, the strength of the touch, the method of the touch (for example, open or closed fist) and the frequency of the touch. Touch also means different things in different environments (institutions, airports, and so on) and with communicators varying in age, sex, and stage of relationship.

Touching behavior can be used to communicate interpersonal attitudes (such as dominance, affection, and the like). Henley believes that the preponderance of male-initiated touch to females represents a consistent reinforcement of perceived status differences. We also use touch to help us manage the interaction, such as to guide another person, to get attention, to accent some verbal or facial message as by squeezing or embracing the other person, and so on. Heslin classified the various types of touching behavior as: (1) functional/professional, (2) social/polite, (3) friendship/warmth, (4) love/intimacy, and (5) sexual arousal.

Although anecdotal reports and a few isolated studies suggest that the United States represents a noncontact culture, there appear to be several indications that this may be changing. At the least, it seems clear that there are sizable variations in the amount of contact within this culture, regardless of what we choose to label the entire culture. There are some indications that children in this culture touch more than adults, but there seems to be a decreasing amount of touch from kindergarten through junior high school. Some research has found that boys and girls get differential early experiences with touch from their parents, but most agree that early experiences with touch are crucial for later adjustment.

NOTES

1. J. D. Fisher, M. Rytting, and R. Heslin, "Hands Touching Hands: Affective and Evaluative Effects of an Interpersonal Touch," *Sociometry* 39 (1976): 416–421.
2. M. F. A. Montagu, *Touching: The Human Significance of the Skin* (New York: Columbia University Press, 1971), p. 292.
3. L. K. Frank, "Tactile Communication." *Genetic Psychology Monographs* 56 (1957): 209–255.
4. V. S. Clay, "The Effect of Culture on Mother-Child Tactile Communication" (Ph.D. diss., Columbia University, 1966).
5. M. Lewis, "Culture and Gender Rules: There is No Unisex in the Nursery," *Psychology Today* 5 (1972): 54–57.
6. F. N. Willis and G. E. Hoffman, "Development of Tactile Patterns in Relation to Age, Sex, and Race," *Development Psychology* 11 (1975): 866. See also F. N. Willis and D. L. Reeves, "Touch Interactions in Junior High Students in Relation to Sex and Race," *Developmental Psychology* 12 (1976): 91–92.
7. Montagu, *Touching*, p. 188.
8. N. M. Henley, *Body Politics: Power, Sex and Nonverbal Communication* (Englewood Cliffs, N.J.: Prentice-Hall, 1977), p. 105.
9. R. Heslin and D. Boss, "Nonverbal Intimacy in Arrival and Departure at an Airport," (Unpublished manuscript, Purdue University, 1976).
10. N. Henley, "The Politics of Touch," in P. Brown (ed.), *Radical Psychology* (New York: Harper & Row, 1973), pp. 421–433. Also see Henley's chapter "Tactual Politics" in her book *Body Politics* (Englewood Cliffs, N.J.: Prentice-Hall, 1977).
11. S. M. Jourard, "An Exploratory Study of Body-Accessibility," *British Journal of Social and Clinical Psychology* 5 (1966): 221–231.
12. L. B. Rosenfeld, S. Kartus, and C. Ray, "Body Accessibility Revisited," *Journal of Communication* 26 (1976):27–30.
13. D. C. Barnlund, "Communicative Styles in Two Cultures: Japan and the United States," in A. Kendon, R. M. Harris, and M. R. Key (eds.), *Organization of Behavior in Face-to-Face Interaction* (The Hague: Mouton, 1975).
14. W. H. Watson, "The Meanings of Touch: Geriatric Nursing," *Journal of Communication* 25 (1975): 104–112.

15. M. Argyle, *Bodily Communication* (New York: International Universities Press, 1975), p. 287. The following alterations were made in the original list: (1) changed bottom to buttocks, (2) added genitals to four categories, and (3) added shoulders to the "shaking" category.

16. R. Heslin, "Steps Toward a Taxonomy of Touching," paper presented to the Midwestern Psychological Association, Chicago, May 1974.

17. D. C. Agulera, "Relationships Between Physical Contact and Verbal Interaction Between Nurses and Patients," *Journal of Psychiatric Nursing* 5 (1967): 5–21.

18. S. M. Jourard and J. E. Rubin, "Self-Disclosure and Touching: A Study of Two Modes of Interpersonal Encounter and Their Inter-Relation," *Journal of Humanistic Psychology* 8 (1968): 39–48.

19. D. Morris, *Intimate Behaviour* (New York: Random House, 1971), pp. 71–101.

20. Ibid., pp. 213–227.

21. N. Freedman, "The Analysis of Movement Behavior During the Clinical Interview," in A. W. Siegman and B. Pope (eds.), *Studies in Dyadic Communication* (New York: Pergamon Press, 1972), pp. 153–175.

22. Morris, *Intimate Behaviour*, p. 214.

23. T. Nguyen, R. Heslin, and M. L. Nguyen, "The Meanings of Touch: Sex Differences," *Journal of Communication* 25 (1975): 92–103; and M. L. Nguyen, R. Heslin, and T. Nguyen, "The Meaning of Touch: Sex and Marital Status Differences," *Representative Research in Social Psychology* 7 (1976): 13–18.

24. R. Shuter, "Proxemics and Tactility in Latin America," *Journal of Communication* 26 (1976): 46–52.

ADDITIONAL READINGS

Frank, L. K. "Tactile Communication." *Genetic Psychology Monographs* 56 (1957): 209–255.

Henley, N. *Body Politics: Power, Sex and Nonverbal Communication.* Englewood Cliffs, N.J.: Prentice-Hall, 1977.

Howard, J. *Please Touch: A Guided Tour of the Human Potential Movement.* New York: McGraw-Hill, 1970.

Levine, S. "Stimulation in Infancy." *Scientific American* 202 (1960): 80–86.

Montagu, M. F. A. *Touching: The Human Significance of the Skin.* New York: Columbia University Press, 1971.

Morris, D. *Intimate Behaviour.* New York: Random House, 1971.

THE EFFECTS OF FACIAL EXPRESSIONS

Your face, my thane, is as a book where men
May read strange matters

SHAKESPEARE, **MacBeth**, *Act I*

The face is rich in communicative potential. It is the primary site for communication of emotional states, it reflects interpersonal attitudes, it provides nonverbal feedback on the comments of others, and some say that next to human speech it is the primary source of information. For these reasons, and because of the visibility of the face, we pay a great deal of attention to the messages we receive from the faces of others. We frequently place considerable reliance on facial cues when we make important interpersonal judgments. This begins when, as infants, we take special interest in the huge face peering over our crib and tending to our needs. Most of the research on facial expressions (and various component parts of the face) has focused on the display and interpretation of emotional states. Although this is the major focus of this chapter, it should at least be mentioned that the face may also be the basis for judging another person's personality and that the face can (and does) provide information other than one's emotional state.

THE FACE AND PERSONALITY JUDGMENTS

The human face comes in many sizes and shapes. There are triangular, square, and round faces; foreheads may be high and wide, high and

161

narrow, low and wide, low and narrow, protruding or sunken; the complexion of a face may be light, dark, coarse, smooth, wrinkled, or blemished; eyes may be balanced, close, far apart, recessed, or bulging; noses can be short, long, flat, crooked, "humpbacked," a "bag," or a "ski slope"; mouths may be large and small with thin and thick lips; ears, too, may be large or small, short or long; and cheeks can bulge or appear sunken. In addition to many features in the face to which we can respond, we also pay a lot of attention to the face. We look to the face as a primary source of information about other people, and we probably make judgments about the personalities of others by their facial characteristics, but at the present time there is almost no reliable, scientific data that provides a full understanding of this process.[1]

In spite of the fact that scientific research doesn't provide us with much help on this question, we can speculate on how perceptions of others are generalized from their facial characteristics. For instance, you may see someone with a face similar to that of someone you know and, without further information, infer similar personality characteristics in the two people. You may make an initial judgment of that person's age, sex, or race from facial information and then infer associated characteristics from these perceptions—for example, this person is young and probably also carefree, energetic, and impatient. And sometimes a particular feature has been stereotypically associated with a particular group of people—for example, a "Jewish" nose.

THE FACE AND INTERACTION MANAGEMENT

Our face is also used to facilitate and inhibit our responses in daily interaction. Component parts of the face are used to (1) open and close channels of communication, (2) complement or qualify verbal and/or nonverbal responses, and (3) replace speech. Behaviors can serve several functions simultaneously—for example, a yawn may replace the spoken message "I'm bored" and serve to shut down the channels of communication at the same time.

Channel Control. When we are desirous of a speaking turn, we sometimes open our mouth in readiness to talk, often accompanied by an inspiration of breath. As we noted in Chapter 2, the eyebrow flash (frequently accompanied by a smile) is found in greeting rituals and signals a desire to interact. Smiles are also found in situations in which there is a desire to close the channels of communication—for example, a smile of appeasement as you back away from a person threatening you with physical harm. Smiling and winking are also used to flirt with others—an invitation that not only opens the channels of communication but suggests the type of communication desired.

Complementing or Qualifying Other Behavior.   In the normal conversational give and take, there are instances when we wish to "underline," magnify, minimize, or support messages. These signals may be given by the speaker or by the listener. A sad verbal message may acquire added emphasis with the eyebrows, which normally accompany the emotional expression of sadness. A smile may temper a message you feel may otherwise be interpreted as extremely negative. Or you may accompany the hand emblem for "A-OK" with a wink, which tends to leave little doubt that you are communicating approval.

Replacing Spoken Messages.   Ekman and Friesen have identified what they call *facial* emblems.[2] Like hand emblems, these displays have a fairly consistent verbal translation. The facial emblems identified thus far are different from the actual emotional expressions in that the sender is trying to talk about an emotion while indicating that he or she is not actually feeling it. These facial emblems will usually occur in contexts that would likely not trigger the actual emotion. They are usually held for a longer or shorter time than the actual expression, and they are usually performed by using only a part of the face. When you drop your jaw and hold your mouth open without displaying other features of the surprise expression, you may be saying that the other person's comment is surprising or that you were dumbfounded by what was said. Widened eyes (without other features of the surprise and fear expressions) may serve the same purpose as a verbal "Wow!" If you want to nonverbally comment on your disgust for a situation, wrinkling your nose, raising your upper lip, or raising one side of your upper lip should get your message across. Sometimes the eyebrows will communicate "I'm puzzled" or "I doubt that." Other facial messages have common verbal translations but are not associated with expressions of emotion—for example, the "You know what I mean" wink; the insult or disapproval associated with sticking your tongue out,[3] or the excessive blinking and lip biting that does not require the verbal statement "I'm anxious (nervous)."

Although the preceding discussion does provide an overview of how the face is used in managing the interaction, it does not sufficiently reflect the complexity a thorough analysis would require. For instance, we did not deal with concomitant gaze behavior and other subtle movements like head tilts, and we talked about smiles as if a smile came in only one variety.

THE FACE AND EXPRESSIONS OF EMOTION

Because of the importance of the face in displaying our emotional states, researchers have frequently subjected the face to empirical study. The central questions of this research have been "What emotions does the face portray?," and "How accurately can we judge facial expressions of emotion?" Recently there has been some interest in the effects of facial displays of emotion on others and on the sender's subsequent behavior. Each of these questions is examined, but first we need to look more closely at the nature of the face itself.

The Face—A Complex Stimulus.   Consider the following situations:

1. An employee feels sure he is doing average work and is told by his supervisor that he is doing excellent work. His immediate reaction is total surprise (probably followed by glee), but how does he react? His face shows mild surprise and he makes some comment to the effect that he thought he was doing pretty good work.
2. A poker player draws his fourth ace in a game with no wild cards. His face would lead the other players to believe he was unmoved.
3. A woman receives a Christmas present, which she is pleasantly surprised and happy to receive. But it is nothing spectacular. Her facial expression and comments, however, lead the giver (who is present) to believe that it was the only thing she ever wanted in her entire life.
4. The wife of a fledgling executive is forced to attend the boss's party and is told explicitly that her behavior will have a profound impact on the promotion of her husband. She is nervous and upset. According to those who describe the party later, however, she was the life of the party—happy and gay, carefree and content.

These four examples illustrate certain display rules we tend to follow. Example 1 illustrates a deintensified affect—strong surprise was made to look like mild surprise; in example 2, the poker player was trying to neutralize an affect—make it appear that there was no emotion at all; the person reacting to the Christmas present tried to make mild surprise appear to be strong surprise—an overintensification of the emotion; the executive's wife was trying to mask an affect of tenseness or despondency with happiness, coolness, and confidence. These display rules are learned, but they are not always at a conscious level of awareness when we use them. We learn that there are culturally prescribed display rules—for example, not laughing at funerals; we also develop personal display rules based on our needs or perhaps the demands of our occupation—for example, politicians or salespersons. We learn that some affect displays are appropriate in some places and not others, for some status and role positions and not others, and for one sex and not another. We may also use different expressions responding to the same event at a different time and with different people.

Another important aspect of our facial expressions is that we do not always portray "pure" or single emotional states in which, for example, all the parts of our face show anger. Instead, the face conveys multiple emotions, which are called *affect blends*. These facial blends of several emotions may appear on the face in a number of different ways: (1) One emotion is shown in one facial area and another is shown in another area—for example, brows are raised as in surprise and lips are pressed as in anger. (2) Two different emotions are shown in one part of the face—for example, one brow is raised as in surprise and the other lowered as in anger. (3) A facial display is produced by muscle action associated with two emotions, but containing specific elements of neither.[4] Figure 8.1 shows two examples of facial blends. The brows/forehead area and the eyes/lids area in one photograph show anger whereas the mouth shows sadness. This might occur, for example, if your supervisor told you that your work performance rated on a system you considered unfair, was "poor." You feel sad about the low evaluation and angry at the supervisor. The other photograph shows a blend of happiness (mouth area) and surprise (eyebrows/forehead, eyes/lids, and a slight

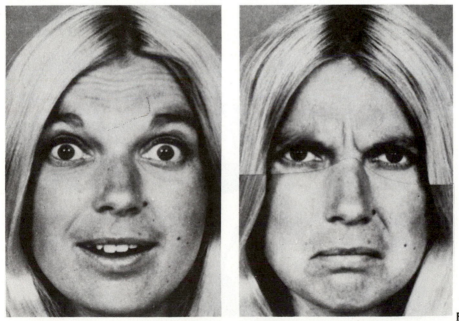

FIGURE 8.1

Facial blends. Figures 8.1 and 8.3 to 8.8 are from P. Ekman and W. V. Friesen, *Unmasking the Face: A Guide to Recognizing Emotions from Facial Clues,* 1975. Reprinted by permission of Prentice-Hall, Inc., Englewood Cliffs, New Jersey.

dropping of the jaw). Such an expression could occur if you thought you were going to get a "poor" rating but you instead received an "excellent."

A final note about the complexity of our face concerns what Haggard and Issacs have called "micromomentary facial expressions."[5] While searching for indications of nonverbal communication between therapist and patient, they ran film at slow motion and noticed that the expression of the patient's face would sometimes change dramatically—from a smile to a grimace to a smile, for example, within a few frames of the film. Further analysis revealed that when they ran their films at four frames per second instead of the normal twenty-four frames, there were two-and-a-half times as many changes of expression. At normal speed, facial expressions that came and went in about one-fifth second escaped notice; expressions that took about two-fifths second were seen as changes, but the kind of change could not be identified; and expressions lasting longer than two-fifths second were usually identified, but not always the same way. It is thought that these micromomentary expressions reveal actual emotional states but are condensed in time because of repressive processes. These expressions are often incompatible with both the apparent expression and the patient's words. One patient, who was saying nice things about a friend, had a seemingly pleasant facial expression; however, slow motion films revealed a wave of anger cross her face. We are now ready to return to one of our original questions: "What emotions does the face portray?"

Pat Oliphant, Copyright © 1974, *The Washington Star*. Reprinted with permission, Los Angeles Times Syndicate.

Primary Affect Displays. Although the face is capable of making hundreds of distinct movements and communicating many emotional states, those that have been uncovered by virtually every researcher since 1940 are surprise, fear, anger, disgust, happiness, and sadness. Other emotional states, such as interest and shame, are also frequently discussed, but the exact facial muscle movements associated with these states are not well known. In addition to information about specific emotions, people also seem to judge facial expressions primarily along the following dimensions: pleasant/unpleasant; active/passive; and intense/controlled. Few researchers have actually measured changes in facial musculature and matched these with various emotional states. For this reason the work of Paul Ekman and his colleagues represents a major advance in the study of facial expressions of emotion. Ekman has developed a coding system for the six emotions that seem to be at the foundation of most expressions—namely, surprise, fear, anger, disgust, happiness, and sadness. (See Figs. 8.4–8.9.) From these expressions, we can derive many emotions that differ only in intensity or are simply blends of these primary emotions. Ekman calls his system the Facial Affect Scoring Technique (FAST).[6] In this system, coding is broken down into three areas of the face: the brows/forehead area; the eyes/lids/bridge of the nose area; and the lower face including the cheek-nose-mouth-chin-jaw. This system recognizes that for each component part of the face, there is an acceptable range of movement or positions which can be enacted and will still communicate the intended emotion. Figure 8.2 shows the FAST items for surprise. Coders are trained to recognize the various components of each emotion from photographic examples and verbal descriptions. After about six hours of training, coders were able to identify emotional expressions with high levels of accuracy. Since twenty-eight different people were used for the stimulus expressions, it is believed that the FAST technique overcomes many of the differences in facial expressions associated with age, sex, physiognomy, and lighting. From this research, we can learn some very specific details about facial movement for different emotional expressions.

For instance, there does not seem to be any one area of the face that best reveals emotions, but for any given emotion, a particular area of the face may carry the most important information for identification. For disgust the nose/cheek/mouth area is crucial; for fear it is the eyes/eyelids; for sadness we would do well to examine the brows/forehead and eyes/eyelids; the important areas for happiness seem to be the cheeks/mouth and brows/forehead areas; and surprise can be seen in any of the three areas of the face.

Now that we have examined the face itself and explored the characteristics of some basic emotional expressions, we return to our question of whether facial expressions of emotion can be accurately judged.

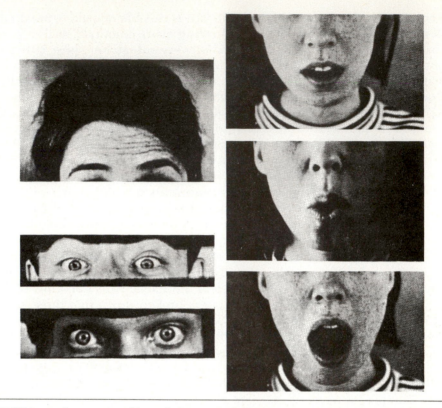

FIGURE 8.2

FAST items for surprise. From P. Ekman, W. V. Friesen, and S. S. Tomkins, "Facial Affect Scoring Technique: A First Validity Study," *Semiotica* 3 (1971): 41.

Judging Facial Expressions of Emotion. An in-depth analysis of all the important studies of facial expression prompted Ekman, Friesen, and Ellsworth to draw the following conclusion: "Contrary to the impression conveyed by previous reviews of the literature that the evidence in the field is contradictory and confusing, our reanalysis showed consistent evidence of accurate judgment of emotion from facial behavior."[7] Ekman and his colleagues rightly acknowledge that this conclusion pertains primarily to posed expressions, but an increasing number of studies of spontaneous expressions also show accurate perceptions. Because of the difficulty involved in measuring responses to facial expressions, and because so much of the literature is concerned with these measurements problems, we discuss measurement more here than we did in previous chapters. The question of how we measure responses to facial expressions is central to any statement about how accurate we are in judging these expressions.

Examine the three faces shown in Figure 8.3, and then consider the

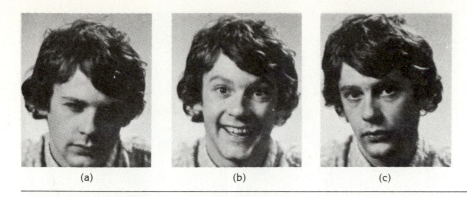

(a)   (b)   (c)   **FIGURE 8.3**

1. In the space provided, write in the emotion being expressed in each of the faces you observed.

   A _____   B _____   C _____

2. From the following choices, select the one emotion that best describes Face A; Face B; and Face C.

A.	Rage_____	B.	Happiness_____	C.	Sadness_____
	Anger_____		Joy_____		Despair_____
	Wrath_____		Delight_____		Solemnity_____
	Indignation_____		Amusement_____		Despondency_____
	Resentment_____		Pleasure_____		Melancholy_____

3. From this list of emotions, select the one that best describes Face A, Face B, and Face C: Happiness, Sadness, Surprise, Fear, Anger.

following methods of responding. Would your responses differ depending on the method used? Is one method easier or harder than another? Is one method likely to elicit greater accuracy?

   This example illustrates one of the many problems involved in testing the accuracy of judgments about facial expressions—the type of response required from the judge. In this case, the accuracy of judging would depend a great deal on which set of instructions the judge received. In the first testing condition, we have a totally open or free response from the judge. This will provide a wide range of responses, and the researcher will be faced with the problem of deciding whether the judge's label corresponds with his or her label for the emotion. Sometimes the researcher elicits a label that, under other testing conditions, may be perceived as a blend, for example, smugness may contain facial features found in both happiness and anger expressions. The labels used by the experimenter and the responder may be different, but both may respond the same way to the actual emotion in real life.

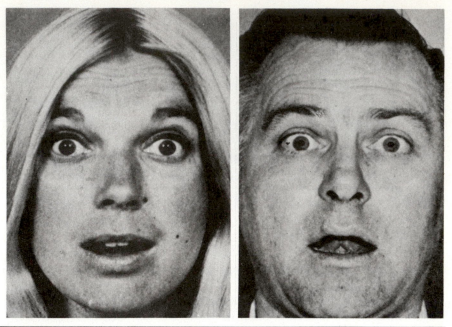

FIGURE 8.4

Surprise.
————The brows are raised, so they are curved and high.
————The skin below the brow is stretched.
————Horizontal wrinkles go across the forehead.
————The eyelids are opened; the upper lid is raised and the lower lid is drawn down; the white of the eye—the sclera—shows above the iris and often below as well.
————The jaw drops open so that the lips and teeth are parted, but there is no tension or stretching of the mouth.

This also raises the problem of the gap between perceiving and naming emotional responses so that others understand. In the second testing condition, the discriminatory task is too difficult—the emotions listed in each category are too much alike. We can predict low accuracy for judges who are given these instructions. In some cases, the labels may all focus on variants of the same emotion and the perceiver sees something completely different, but is prohibited from adding new categories. For example, photograph "C" seems to be perceived by the researcher as a form of sadness, but a judge might see it as neutral. The last set of instructions is just the opposite from the second set—the discriminatory task is very easy. Since the emotion categories are discrete, we can predict high accuracy for the third condition.

Accuracy is also likely to vary based on whether the emotion presented to the judge is "real" rather than simulated or acted. Obviously, acted emotions are based on perceptions of real ones, but they are frequently exaggerated, based on stereotypes, and, hence, easier to iden-

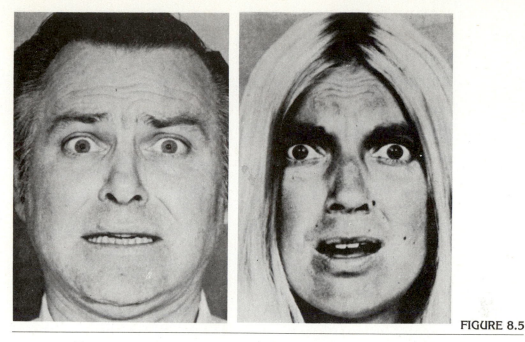

FIGURE 8.5

Fear.
———The brows are raised and drawn together.
———The wrinkles in the forehead are in the center, not across the entire forehead.
———The upper eyelid is raised, exposing sclera, and the lower eyelid is tensed and drawn up.
———The mouth is open and the lips are either tensed slightly and drawn back or stretched and drawn back.

tify. We are also concerned here with the fact that in "real" situations, a person may or may not be trying to communicate a particular state to others, whereas an actor is, by the nature of the experiment, trying his or her best to communicate the emotion he or she is instructed to portray.

Studies have varied with respect to how these emotions are elicited. In some studies a situation is described and the actor is told to react as if he or she were in that situation. Other studies give a list of emotions and the actor is told to portray the emotion, and some use candid photographs of people in real situations. One laboratory study reached an almost comic extreme.[8] A camera was set up in a laboratory ready to catch the subject's expressions at the proper moment. To elicit an expression of pain, the experimenter bent the subject's finger backward forcibly; to produce a startled look, the experimenter fired a pistol behind the subject at an unexpected moment; apprehension was elicited by telling the subject the pistol would be fired again close to his ear on the count of three; at the count of two the photograph was taken; amuse-

171

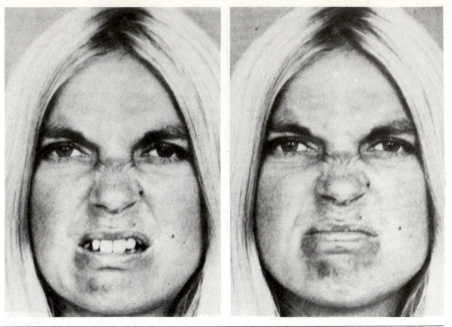

FIGURE 8.6

Disgust.
——————The upper lip is raised.
——————The lower lip is also raised and pushed up to the upper lip, or is lowered and slightly protruding.
——————THe nose is wrinkled.
——————The cheeks are raised.
——————Lines show below the lower lid, and the lid is pushed up but not tense.
——————The brow is lowered, lowering the upper lid.

ment was captured when the experimenter told the subject some jokes; disgust resulted when the subject smelled the odor from a test tube that contained tissues of a dead rat, reposed, and corked for several months; and in an unbelievable manipulation in the name of science, to elicit an expression of grief, a subject was hypnotized and told that several members of his family has been killed in a wreck. "Unfortunately," the camera could not catch the subject's intense grief because he bowed his head and cried—so the experimenter had to settle for an expression of mild grief to be used in the study! Another interesting point from this study brings us back to our discussion of facial control and display rules. Dunlap found that all of his women subjects made facial expressions that approached amusement under what were supposed to be pain conditions. This was not true for the men, nor did it match the women's verbal description of how they felt. It did hurt! This material on how emotions were elicited is reported simply to demonstrate that this factor can make a difference in judging accuracy.

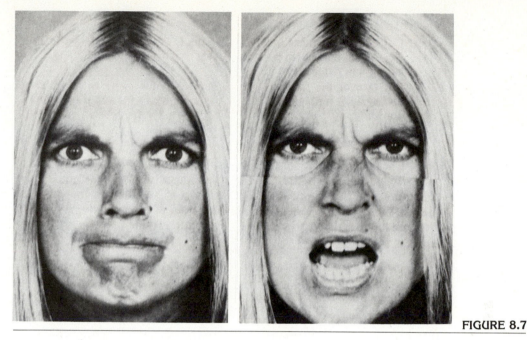

FIGURE 8.7

Anger.
————The brows are lowered and drawn together.
————Vertical lines appear between the brows.
————The lower lid is tensed and may or may not be raised.
————The upper lid is tensed and may or may not be lowered by the action of the brow.
————The eyes have a hard stare and may have a bulging appearance.
————The lips are in either of two basic positions: pressed together, with the corners straight or down; or open, tensed in a squarish shape as if shouting.
————The nostrils may be dilated, but this is not essential to the anger facial expression and may also occur in sadness.
————There is ambiguity unless anger is registered in all three facial areas.

Another variable that confounds interpretation of facial research is the variety of methods by which the facial stimuli have been presented to judges. Are they "live" faces, still photographs, drawings, sketches, videotapes, or films? Some research suggests that greater accuracy is achieved when filmed expressions are used. The length of observation frequently, differs from study to study, and there is always the question of advantages and disadvantages in seeing faces that are larger (on a movie screen) or smaller (small photographs) than those seen in everyday interaction situations. In Chapter 2, we mentioned research by Ekman that found high levels of agreement on posed facial expressions across a variety of literate and preliterate cultures. This led Ekman and his colleagues to propose that posed expressions differ little from spon-

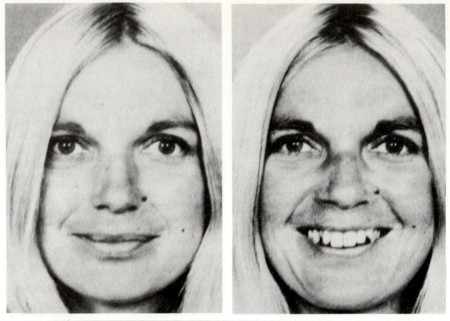

FIGURE 8.8

Happiness.
———Corners of lips are drawn back and up.
———The mouth may or may not be parted, with teeth exposed or not.
———A wrinkle (the naso-labial) runs down from the nose to the outer edge beyond the lip corners.
———The cheeks are raised.
———The lower eyelid shows wrinkles below it, and may be raised but not tense.
———Crow's-feet wrinkles go outward from the outer corners of the eyes (covered by hair in these photographs).

taneous expressions in form. However, there are differences in such things as duration of the expression, the absence of control or manipulation of the expression in posed examples, and the higher frequency of single emotion faces (rather than blends) in posed expressions. One obvious advantage in using filmed expressions is that the judge can easily tell whether a particular feature is part of the person's permanent facial configuration or whether it is only a part of a given emotional expression.

Prior exposure to a face will make a difference in the accuracy of judging emotions. If you are familiar with the face and have seen it express other emotions, you are more likely to correctly identify another emotion you have not seen before. If you are familiar with the person, you again have a better reference point for making judgments. For instance, a person who is frequently smiling and who you see not smiling may seem very sad. With another person, the absence of a smile may

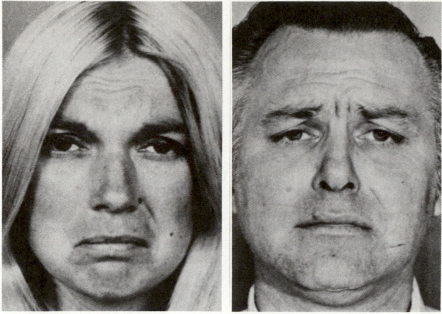

FIGURE 8.9

Sadness.
———The inner corners of the eyebrows are drawn up.
———The skin below the eyebrows is triangulated, with the inner corners up.
———The upper eyelid inner corner is raised.
———The corners of the lips are down or the lip is trembling.

simply be part of a normal, neutral expression. Laughery et al. found that the longer one was exposed to an expression of emotion on a face and the earlier this face appeared in a test series, the greater were the chances of accurate recognition.[9]

Several studies make it clear that additional knowledge concerning the context in which a particular facial expression occurs will affect accuracy in judging the emotion expressed. We can accurately identify facial expressions of emotion without any knowledge of the context in which it occurs, but co-occurring perceptions of the social context, the environment, and other people will surely affect our judgments. Although a number of investigators have pursued the question of whether context or expression dominates perceptions, the issue is far from resolved. Perhaps the most often cited study regarding the influence of context in face judging is one by Munn, in which facial expressions taken from *Life* and *Look* magazines were shown with and without background context.[10] The background information was very helpful in the identification of these facial expressions. Verbal cues describing the situation also seem to increase accuracy. Although Munn's study sampled

175

a limited number of faces, emotions, and contexts, it does bring to our attention another important dimension to consider in studying facial expressions. One of my students, as part of a term project assignment, showed two faces to groups of judges with only the background color varied. The facial expressions were previously identified as "neutral." This student found in her limited study that even changing the background color can change interpretation of the facial expression. Warm, bright colors resulted in more positive or "happy" responses, whereas dark or dull tones produced more negative or "not particularly happy" responses. Cline, who used line drawings to test the effect of having another face as part of the total context, found that the expression on one face influenced interpretation of the other face and vice versa.[11] As an example, when the smiling face in Figure 8.10 was paired with a glum face, it was seen as the dominant face, that of a vicious, gloating, taunting bully. When seen with the frowning face, the smiling face seemed peaceful, friendly, and happy. Cline probably summed up many of the studies of context and facial expression when he made the following observations about his own study: "Certain psychological properties of the drawings appear to inhere in the faces independently of their perceived social matrix, while others are clearly a function of the nature of interaction."[12]

Finally, we must be concerned about the characteristics of the people photographed and the people doing the judging. Although this seems to be an extremely important variable in testing accuracy, consistent and reliable findings are not always available. Some preliminary work by Ekman's research team, which required individuals to imitate certain expressions, uncovered reliable individual differences in the ability to make certain facial movements. The proficiency of the expression "portrayer" may make a vast difference in how accurately others perceive his or her expressions. It is clear that you, as a judge, will probably be influenced by the type and structure of the face you see. Eiland and Richardson report significantly different interpretations of faces differing in age, sex, and race.[13] Several studies by Buck and others

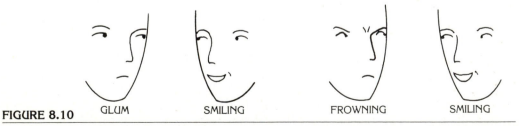

FIGURE 8.10   GLUM   SMILING   FROWNING   SMILING

By permission of Duke University Press.

suggest that females are better senders (portrayers), as well as receivers or decoders.[14] Others, however, have found that the sex of the person presenting the emotion has little influence on observer interpretations.[15] All of these conclusions must remain tentative; differences in the facial properties of emotion portrayers (and the resulting effect) is just beginning to be understood.

If we are seeking the ideal conditions under which a person could be most accurate in judging facial expressions of emotion—and we based our conditions of the research to date—we might suggest something like this: (1) Give the judges some prior experience in judging emotion in faces; train them. (2) Give the judges some exposure to the face they will be judging prior to the experiment, showing it in emotional states other than the one to be judged. (3) Use good actors to portray the emotions and ask them to exaggerate. (4) Use films. (5) Make the judge's discriminatory task easy, use terminology that is familiar, and make the emotions form discrete categories. (6) Make sure the judges can see the entire face; the more of the person they can see, the better. (7) Make sure the judges are not of subnormal intelligence and do not represent extremes in age. (8) Allow the judges to be aware of the context of the expression and what evoked it. (9) Allow the judges plenty of time to observe. (10) Make sure the judges can see the face clearly, preferably on a large screen.

Thus far we have been examining the sending and receiving of messages relevant to one's emotional state. A few researchers have asked questions that go beyond the momentary expression of emotion, that is, does the facial expression of emotion tell us anything about how others will react or what behavior the sender is likely to engage in following a given expression?

Facial Expressions and Subsequent Reactions.   Ekman and his colleagues were interested in learning whether facial expressions displayed while watching televised violence would be related to subsequent aggressiveness.[16] They predicted that facial expressions of emotion showing happiness, pleasantness, and interest would predict more subsequent aggressive behavior than unpleasant, sad, painful, and disinterested expressions. One group of five- and six-year-old children watched a sports program, and others saw a scene from "The Untouchables," which included a killing, a chase, the shooting and death of one villain, and an extended fistfight involving the second villain. The segment from "The Untouchables" was only three-and-one-half minutes long. The children were then put into a situation in which they could help or hurt another child who was supposedly working in the next room. Hurting behavior (making another's task more difficult) was deemed to be a manifestation of aggressiveness. The boys who displayed the pleasant expressions engaged in more aggressive behavior; the girls did not. It remains to be seen whether the portrayal of violence using female role models would evoke similar behavior.

Savitsky and his colleagues were interested in whether facial expressions of emotion on the part of a "victim" would have any effect on the aggressor's behavior.[17] When individuals thought that they were controlling the amount of electric shock that another person (victim) would get, they gave more shocks to victims who responded with expressions of happiness and smiles and fewer to victims who displayed expressions of anger. Expressions of fear and neutrality did not differ from each other nor did they affect shock behavior.

In another study, Savitsky and Sim tried to find out what effect facial expressions had on evaluations of a defendant's account of his crime.[18] Defendants told the story of their crime (petty thefts and vandalism) and varied their emotional expressions. Anger, happiness, sadness, and neutral expressions were used. Sad/distressed and neutral defendants were apparently seen more favorably—that is, their crimes were rated as less severe, they were perceived as less likely to commit another crime, and they were given the least amount of punishment. Angry (and to a lesser degree, happy) defendants were evaluated the most harshly.

SUMMARY

The discussion of the face and its role in human communication in this chapter should leave you with several impressions.

First, the face is a multimessage system, which can communicate information regarding your personality, your interest and responsiveness during interaction, and your emotional states. Although there is little doubt that people do associate certain personality characteristics with certain faces and facial features, the research to date does not tell us much. We know that the face is used as a conversational regulator, opening and closing communication channels, complementing and qualifying other behaviors, and replacing spoken messages.

Facial expressions are very complex entities to deal with. Of all the areas of the body, the face seems to elicit the best external and internal feedback, which makes it easy for us to follow a variety of facial display rules. Not all facial displays represent single emotions; some are "blends" of several emotions. Sometimes we will show some aspects of an emotional display when we are not actually feeling it, as with facial "emblems" that represent commentary on emotions. When we subject the face to microscopic analysis (using slow-motion film), we uncover rapidly changing facial expressions that reflect repressed affective states, called micromomentary facial expressions. They are so fleeting that they are rarely noticed in everyday conversation.

We noted some of the measurement problems involved in the study of facial expressions: the complexity of the decisions that observers are asked to make, simulated as opposed to "real" expressions, the skill of the "portrayer," the method of presenting the face to the observer (films, photographs, and the like), prior exposure to the face, knowledge of the context, and characteristics of the target face and the perceiver. Naturally, all these factors may impinge on our accuracy in identifying facial expressions of emotion, but Ekman's research suggests that we can be accurate in our assessments of emotion from the face if we are given proper training. Ekman's Facial Affect Scoring Technique (FAST) seems to provide us with a useful device for providing that training. Ekman and his colleagues, after studying many people and many emotions in a variety of contexts, have developed what amounts to a facial dictionary for at least six primary facial affects and thirty-three blends. We outlined the components of the six emotions that seem to be uncovered in almost every study of facial expressions to date: anger, sadness, fear, surprise, happiness, and disgust/contempt.

The chapter concluded with reports from a few studies that suggest that the identification of facial expressions of emotion may help us predict subsequent behaviors of the person showing the affect and of people responding to it. Generally, we would predict more immediate aggressiveness from male children who view violent television programs with pleasant affects; we would expect more aggressive reactions from people who see pleasant reactions on the faces of their victims; and we would predict that neutral or sad/distressed looks will be most favorably responded to as judge and jury scrutinize the defendant's expressions.

NOTES

1. Other publications, however, do not hesitate to make grandiose (and unsubstantiated) claims: "The face reveals facts not only about a person's mood, but also about his character, health, personality, sex life, popularity, ability to make money, social status and life expectancy." Cf. B. DeMente, *Face Reading for Fun and Profit* (West Nyack, N.Y.: Parker Publishing, 1968).

2. P. Ekman and W. V. Friesen, *Unmasking the Face* (Englewood Cliffs, N.J.: Prentice-Hall, 1975).

3. W. J. Smith, J. Chase, and A. K. Lieblich, "Tongue Showing: A Facial Display of Humans and Other Primate Species," *Semiotica* 11 (1974): 201–246.

4. P. Ekman, W. V. Friesen, and S. S. Tomkins, "Facial Affect Scoring Technique: A First Validity Study," *Semiotica* 3 (1971): 53.

5. E. A. Haggard and F. S. Issacs, "Micromomentary Facial Expressions as Indicators of Ego Mechanisms in Psychotherapy," in L. A. Gottschalk and A. H. Auerback (eds.), *Methods of Research in Psychotherapy*, (New York: Appleton-Century-Crofts, 1966).

6. Ekman, Friesen, and Tomkins, "Facial Affect Scoring Technique," pp. 37–58. An important extension of this work is the development of a Facial Action Code which measures visibly different movements of the face according to their anatomical bases. See: P. Ekman and W. V. Friesen, "Measuring Facial Movement," *Environment Psychology and Nonverbal Behavior* 1 (1976): 56–75.

7. P. Ekman, W. V. Friesen, and P. Ellsworth, *Emotion in the Human Face: Guidelines for Research and an Integration of Findings* (Elmsford, N.Y.: Pergamon Press, 1972), p. 107.

8. K. Dunlap, "The Role of Eye-Muscles and Mouth-Muscles in the Expression of the Emotions," *Genetic Psychology Monographs* 2 (1927): 199–233.

9. K. R. Laughery, J. F. Alexander, and A. B. Lane, "Recognition of Human Faces: Effects of Target Exposure Time, Target Position, Pose Position, and Type of Photograph," *Journal of Applied Psychology* 55 (1971): 477–483.

10. N. L. Munn, "The Effect of Knowledge of the Situation upon Judgments of Emotion from Facial Expression," *Journal of Abnormal and Social Psychology* 35 (1940): 324–338.

11. M. Cline, "The Influence of Social Context on the Perception of Faces," *Journal of Personality* 25 (1956): 142–158.

12. Ibid., p. 157.

13. R. Eiland and D. Richardson, "The Influence of Race, Sex and Age on Judgments of Emotion Portrayed in Photographs," *Communication Monographs* 43 (1976) 167–175.

14. R. Buck, R. E. Miller, and W. F. Caul, "Sex, Personality, and Physiological Variables in the Communication of Affect via Facial Expression," *Journal of Personality and Social Psychology* 30 (1974): 586–596; M. Zuckerman, J. A. Hall, R. S. DeFrank, and R. Rosenthal, "Encoding and Decoding of Spontaneous and Posed Facial Expressions," *Journal of Personality and Social Psychology* 34 (1977): 966–977.

15. R. Dunhame and J. Herman, "Development of a Female Faces Scale for Measuring Job Satisfaction," *Journal of Applied Psychology* 60 (1975): 629–631.

16. P. Ekman, R. M. Liebert, W. V. Friesen, R. Harrison, C. Zlatchin, E. J. Malstrom, and R. A. Baron, "Facial Expressions of Emotion While Watching Televised Violence as Predictors of Subsequent Aggression," in *Television and Social Behavior*, vol. 5: *Television's Effects: Further Explorations*, report to the Surgeon General's Scientific Advisory Committee on Television and Social Behavior. (Washington, D.C.: U.S. Government Printing Office, 1972).

17. J. C. Savitsky, C. E. Izard, W. E. Kotsch, and L. Christy, "Aggressor's Response to the Victim's Facial Expression of Emotion," *Journal of Research on Personality* 7 (1974): 346–357.

18. J. C. Savitsky and M. E. Sim, "Trading Emotions: Equity Theory of Reward and Punishment," *Journal of Communication* 24 (1974): 140–146.

ADDITIONAL READINGS

Ekman, P. "Facial Signs: Facts, Fantasies, and Possibilities," in T. Sebeok (ed.). *Sight, Sound and Sense.* Bloomington, Ind.: Indiana University Press, 1978, pp. 124–156.

Ekman, P. (ed.). *Darwin and Facial Expression.* New York: Academic Press, 1973.

Ekman, P. and W. V. Friesen. *Unmasking the Face.* Englewood Cliffs, N.J.: Prentice-Hall, 1975.

Ekman, P., W. V. Friesen, and P. Ellsworth. *Emotion in the Human Face.* Elmsford, N.Y.: Pergamon Press, 1972.

Izard, C. E. *The Face of Emotion.* New York: Appleton-Century-Crofts, 1971.

THE EFFECTS OF EYE BEHAVIOR

He speaketh not; and yet there lies
A conversation in his eyes.

HENRY WADSWORTH LONGFELLOW

Throughout history we have been preoccupied with the eye and its effects on human behavior, as evidenced by these phrases: "She could look right through you"; "It was an icy stare"; "He's got shifty eyes"; "She's all eyes"; "Did you see the gleam in his eye?"; "We're seeing eye to eye now"; "He looked like the original Evil Eye"; "His eyes shot daggers across the room"; "She could kill with a glance".

We associate various eye movements with a wide range of human expressions. Downward glances are associated with modesty; wide eyes may be associated with frankness, wonder, naiveté, or terror; raised upper eyelids along with contraction of the orbicularis may mean displeasure; generally immobile facial muscles with a rather constant stare are frequently associated with coldness; and eyes rolled upward may be associated with fatigue or a suggestion that another's behavior is a bit weird.

Our society has established a number of eye-related norms. For example, we don't look too long at strangers in public places, we aren't supposed to look at various body parts except under certain conditions, and so on.

Our fascination with eyes has led to the exploration of almost every conceivable feature of the eyes (size, color, position) and the surround-

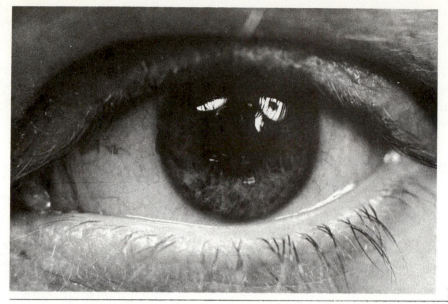

FIGURE 9.1

ing parts (eyebrows, rings, wrinkles). Some believe that excessive blinking of the eyes may be associated with various states of anxiety—as if attempting to cut off reality. Psychiatrists report some patients who blink up to one hundred times per minute, in contrast to normal blinking, needed to lubricate and protect the eyeball, which occurs about six to ten times per minute in adults. There is some evidence that when a person is attentive to objects in the environment or during concentrated thought, his or her blinking rate will decrease. Eye rings are mainly found in other animals, but some speculate that human eyebrows are residual rings—raised during surprise and fear and lowered during threat and anger. Eye patches are the colored eyelids that are sometimes seen in nonhuman primates. These patches are not a part of the natural human communicative repertoire, although women often use eyeliner and eye shadow to achieve a similar effect. Another nonhuman feature that has received scholarly attention is eyespots, which are eye-shaped images located on other body parts. These can be seen in peacock feathers, butterflies, and fish.

One study of eye color attempted to find correlates of eye color and motor performance.[1] Worthy's main thesis is that dark-eyed animals, both human and nonhuman, specialize in behaviors that require sensitivity, speed, and reactive responses, whereas light-eyed animals specialize in behaviors that require hesitation, inhibition, and self-paced responses. His analyses of various sports show that dark-eyed persons

183

are more likely to be running backs in football and effective hitters in baseball, whereas light-eyed persons are more likely to be quarterbacks or offensive linemen in football, effective free throwers in basketball, and proficient pitchers in baseball.

We now turn to the two main subjects of this chapter, the first of which is known by such terms as eye contact, mutual glances, visual interaction, gazing, or line of regard. The other area of discussion concerns pupil dilation and constriction under various social conditions.

GAZE AND MUTUAL GAZE

Gaze refers to an individual's looking behavior, which may or may not be at the other person, whereas mutual gaze refers to a situation in which the two interactants are looking at each other, usually in the region of the face.[2] Eye contact (looking specifically in each other's eyes) does not seem to be reliably distinguished by receivers or observers from gazing at the area surrounding the eyes.[3] Gazing and mutual gazing, however, can be reliably assessed. At a distance of three meters, face-directed gazing can be distinguished; shifting the direction of one's gaze by one centimeter can reliably be detected from a distance of one meter.

We don't look at another person during the entire time we are talking to him or her nor do we avert our gaze 100 percent of the time. What should be considered "normal" gazing patterns will thus vary according to the background and personalities of the participants, the topic, the other person's gazing patterns, objects of mutual interest in the environment, and so on. Keeping such qualifications in mind, we can get a general idea of normal gazing patterns from two studies of focused interaction between two people.[4] See Table 9.1.

TABLE 9.1
Amount of Gazing in Two-Person Conversations

	AVERAGE	RANGE	TALKING	LISTENING
Nielsen	50%*	8–73%	37%	62%
Argyle and Ingham	61%	——	41%	75%

	MUTUAL GAZE	AVERAGE LENGTH OF GAZE	AVERAGE LENGTH OF MUTUAL GAZE
Nielsen	——	——	——
Argyle and Ingham	31%	2.95 sec.	1.18 sec.

*Percentages reflect the amount of time gazing relative to the total interaction time.

Functions of Gaze Behavior

Kendon has identified four functions of gazing: (1) cognitive—subjects tend to look away when having difficulty encoding; (2) monitoring—subjects may look at their interactant to indicate the conclusions of thought units and to check their interactant's attentiveness and reactions; (3) regulatory—responses may be demanded or suppressed by looking; and (4) expressive—the degree of involvement or arousal may be signaled through looking.[5] Our discussion follows a similar pattern: (1) regulating the flow of communication, (2) monitoring feedback, (3) expressing emotions, and (4) communicating the nature of the interpersonal relationship. These functions do not take place independently—that is, visual behavior not only sends information but is one of the primary methods for collecting it; looking at the other person as you finish an utterance may not only tell the other it is his or her turn to speak but is an occasion to monitor feedback regarding the utterance.

Regulating the Flow of Communication Visual contact occurs when we want to signal that the communication channel is open. In some instances, eye gaze can almost establish an obligation to interact. When you seek visual contact with your waiter in a restaurant, you are essentially indicating that the communication channel is open, and that you want to say something to him. You may recall instances when your classroom instructor asked a question of the class and you were sure that you did not know the answer. Establishing eye contact with the instructor was the last thing you wanted to do. You did not wish to signal the instructor that the channel was open. We behave the same way when we see someone coming toward us, and we do not wish to talk to the person. As long as we can avoid eye gaze (in a seemingly natural way), it is a lot easier to avoid having to interact. When you want to disavow social contact, your eye gaze will likely diminish. Thus, we see mutual gazing in greeting sequences and greatly diminished gazing when one wishes to bring an encounter to a halt.

In addition to opening and closing the channel of communication, eye behavior also regulates the flow of communication by providing turn-taking signals. We have already noted that white, adult speakers generally look less often than their listeners, but speakers do seem to glance at grammatical breaks at the end of a thought unit or idea and at the end of the utterance.[6] Although glances at these junctures can signal that the other person can assume the speaking role, we also use these glances to obtain feedback, to see how we are being received, and to see if the other will let us continue. This feedback function is discussed in the next section. The speaker-listener pattern seems to be choreographed as follows: As the speaker comes to the end of an utterance or thought unit, gazing at the listener will continue as the listener assumes the speaking role; the listener will maintain gaze until the speaking role is assumed when he or she will look away. When the speaker does not yield a speaking turn by glancing at the other, the listener will probably delay a response or fail to respond. Further, when a speaker begins an anticipated lengthy response, less gazing is apt to occur and is also often accompanied by an initially lengthy pause. This pattern of adult gazing and looking away during speech seems to have its roots in early childhood development. Observations of the gazing patterns of three-to-four-month-old infants and their parents revealed gross temporal similarities in the looking at and looking away sequence with the vocalizing and pausing sequences in adult conversations.[7]

When two people are jointly watching a third object or person we can again see how this may be the basis for initiating or sustaining an interaction. This process does, however, require monitoring the other person's gaze.

Monitoring Feedback   When people seek feedback concerning the reactions of others, they gaze at the other person. If you find that the other person is looking at you, this is usually interpreted as a sign that the other person is attentive to what you are saying. This notion seems so firmly held that when people were told that their partner looked at them less often than usual—regardless of their actual gaze—the partner was rated as "less attentive."[8] The listener's facial expressions and gazing suggests not only attention but whether the listener is interested in what you're saying (for example, "Good. Continue.").

Both listeners and speakers seem to have a tendency to look away when they are trying to process difficult or complex ideas. This may reflect a shift in attention from external to internal matters. Day found that when we look away during difficult encoding situations it is not in a random pattern.[9] We seem to look away more on reflective questions than on factual ones. Bakan reports studies in which subjects were asked "thought-provoking" questions and their eye movement was measured.[10] It was found that people tend to make about 75 percent of these movements in the same direction. Typical questions asked were: "How many letters are there in the word Washington?" "Multiply twelve by thirteen," and "What is meant by the proverb 'It is better to have a bad peace than a good war?' " Then, after classifying "right movers" and "left movers," other data was collected to further characterize the two groups. Left movers seemed more susceptible to hypnosis, had more alpha brain waves, scored higher on "verbal" parts of the Scholastic Aptitude Test, showed greater fluency in writing, had more vivid imagery, were more likely to major in classical/humanistic areas, were more sociable and more likely to be alcoholic if a male, and reported themselves as more musical and more religious. Right movers appeared more likely to show tension in large postural muscles, tended to have higher "quantitative" scores on the Scholastic Aptitude Test, were more likely to major in science-quantitative areas, had more tics and twitches, spent less time asleep if male, paid more attention to the right side of the body if male, preferred cool colors, and made career choices earlier. Bakan cautions against making too much generalization from these findings because of the integrative nature of the brain. In fact, women were found to be as frequent left movers as right movers, and they were more likely than men to move their eyes in both directions.

Expressing Emotions   Rarely is the eye area tested separately from the entire face in judging emotions. Sometimes, however, a glance at the eye area may provide a good deal of information about the emotion being expressed. In one study of this type, fifty-one faces were used as stimuli for judges.[11] The eyes were better than the brows-forehead or lower face for the accurate perception of fear, but less accurate for a perception of anger and disgust.

The extensive studies of Ekman and his colleagues have given us valuable insights into facial configurations for six common emotions. The following descriptions pertain to the brow and eye area.[12]

Surprise. Brows are raised so they are curved and high. Skin below the brow is stretched. Eyelids are opened; the upper lid is raised, and the lower lid is drawn down; the white of the eye shows above the iris and often below as well.

Fear. Brows are raised and drawn together. The upper eyelid is raised, exposing the white of the eye, and the lower eyelid is tensed and drawn up.

Disgust. Disgust is shown primarily in the lower face and in the lower eyelids. Lines show below the lower lid, and the lid is pushed up but not tense. The brow is lowered, lowering the upper lid.

Anger. The brows are lowered and drawn together. Vertical lines appear between the brows. The lower lid is tensed and may or may not be raised. The upper lid is tense and may or may not be lowered by the action of the brow. The eyes have a hard stare and may have a bulging appearance.

Happiness. Happiness is shown primarily in the lower face and lower eyelids. The lower eyelid shows wrinkles below it, and may be raised but is not tense. Crow's-feet wrinkles go outward from the outer corners of the eyes.

Sadness. The inner corners of the eyebrows are drawn up. The skin below the eyebrow is triangulated, with the inner corner up. The upper eyelid inner corner is raised.

We should also recognize that some expressions of emotion show a lot of changes in the eye area (surprise, fear), whereas other expressions do not (happiness, disgust). Furthermore, an expression of anger can be ambiguous unless the entire face manifests anger signals. Similarly, in everyday interaction we are likely to see facial blends in which the eyes may tell one story and other parts of the face may tell another story. And some clues to expressions of emotion can be derived from gazing patterns—for example, sadness may be accompanied by increased looking downward and generally reducing the amount of gaze.

Communicating the Nature of the Interpersonal Relationship   Gazing and mutual gazing is often indicative of the nature of the relationship between two interactants. Relationships characterized by different status levels may be reflected in the eye patterns. With all other variables held relatively constant, Hearn found that gazing and mutual gazing is moderate with a very high-status addressee, maximized with a moderately high-status addressee, and minimal with a very low-status addressee.[13] Another experiment with a freshman addressing a senior-freshman pair, adds some support to Hearn's work, since the senior consistently received more eye glances.[14] Mehrabian's work shows less visual contact on the part of both males and females (sitting and standing) with low-status addressees.[15] If you perceive a low amount of gazing from a higher-status person, it may be related to interpersonal needs. The higher-status person may not feel the need to monitor your behavior as closely as you monitor his or hers. There will, however, be predictable differences based on how much a person likes another person and how many rewards are derived.

We make more eye contact when we look at something rewarding to us. Efran and Broughton, using male subjects and experimenters, found that their subjects engaged in more visual interaction with the person with whom they had had a friendly conversation just prior to the experiment and who nodded and smiled during the subject's presentation.[16] Exline and Winters report that subjects avoided the eyes of an interviewer and disliked him after he had commented unfavorably on their performance.[17] Using the same verbal communication, Exline and Eldridge found that it was decoded by a subject as being more favorable when associated with more eye gaze than when it was presented with less eye gaze.[18]

Closely related to looking at persons and objects that are rewarding is the factor of positive or negative attitude toward the other person. Generally, we seem to gaze more at people we like, but we also sometimes look long and hard at people we don't like. It makes sense to predict that we will look more at those who like us—if for no other reason than to observe their signs of approval and friendliness for us. Mehrabian asked a group of people to imagine they liked another and to engage this person in conversation. Even in this role-playing situation, increased gazing was associated with increased liking.[19] Wiemann confronted subjects with a simulated employment interview in which the interviewer's gaze was varied across four conditions—100 percent, 75 percent, 25 percent, and 0 percent. When subjects were asked to evaluate the interviewers, the level of "friendliness" decreased as the amount of gaze decreased. However, "applicants" did not seem to evaluate the interviewer's dominance, potency, or confidence as lower with decreasing gaze.[20]

The term *making eyes* is frequently used in the context of a courtship relationship. Several sources confirm an increase in eye behavior between two people who are seeking to develop a more intimate relationship. Rubin's analysis of engaged couples indicated more mutual gaze,[21] and Kleinke et al. found that longer glances or reciprocated glances were perceived as an indicator of a longer relationship.[22] Kleck and Rubinstein varied the physical attractiveness of female confederates by altering makeup and hairstyling and found that male subjects looked more at the attractive confederates.[23] The amount of gazing may increase as relationships become more intimate, but it may also be that after maintaining an intimate relationship for years, gazing may return to levels below those used during more intense stages of development. Argyle and Dean have proposed an intimacy equilibrium model, which suggests that intimacy is a function of the amount of eye gazing, physical proximity, intimacy of topic, and amount of smiling.[24] Argyle believes that the model is more appropriate to established relationships. Other variables might be inserted into the equation—for example, body orientation, the form of address used, tone of voice, facial expression, forward lean, and the like. The central idea behind this proposal is that as one component of the model is changed, one or more of the other components will also change—in the opposite direction; for example, if one person looks too much, the other may look less, move further away, smile less, talk less about intimate matters, and so on. Although this notion has received some support, there are occasions when, rather than complement the other's behavior, we seem to imitate it—that is, gazing will elicit gazing.

When the relationship between the two communicators is characterized by negative attitudes, we might see a decrease in gazing and mutual gazing. But, as we previously suggested, a hostile or aggressive orientation may trigger the use of staring to produce anxiety in others. A gaze of longer than ten seconds is likely to induce irritation—if not outright discomfort—in many situations. We can express our hostility toward another by visually and verbally ignoring him or her—especially when the other person knows that we are deliberately doing so. But we can insult another person by looking at that person too much—that is, by not according him or her the public anonymity that each of us requires at times. There are also times when you can elicit aggressive behavior from others just because you happen to look too long at a stranger's behavior. Sometimes threats and aggressive motions can be elicited by human beings who stare too long at monkeys in a zoo. Desmond Morris, in his popular book *The Naked Ape,* hypothesized that this tendency to produce anxiety in others through staring is the result of our biological antecedents as a species—for example, the aggressiveness and hostility signified by the ape's stare.

Thus, if we are looking for a unifying thread to link gazing patterns motivated by positive and negative feelings toward the other, it would seem to be that *people tend to look at those with whom they are interpersonally involved.* Gazing that is motivated by hostility or affection, then, suggests both an interest and involvement in the interpersonal relationship.

We now consider a number of conditions that seem to influence the amount of gazing: (1) distance, (2) physical characteristics, (3) personal and personality characteristics, (4) topics and tasks, and (5) cultural background.

Conditions Influencing Gaze

Distance.   Gazing and mutual gazing seem to increase as the communicating pair increases the distance between them. In this case, gazing psychologically reduces the distance between the communicators. There may be less visual contact when the two parties are too close together—especially if they are not well acquainted. Reducing one's gaze in this situation, then, psychologically increases the physical distance.

Physical Characteristics.   One would think that when interacting with a person who was perceived as disabled or stigmatized in some way (identified as an epileptic or made to look like an amputee) eye gaze would be less frequent. However, Kleck found that the amount of gazing between normal and disabled interactants did not differ significantly from normal-normal interactions.[25] One possible explanation is that in such situations, the normal person is desperately seeking information that might suggest the proper mode of behavior. This counteracts any tendency to avoid eye gaze.

Personal and Personality Characteristics.   Generally, the relationships between gazing and personality traits are weak. In most cases, however, the meanings attributed to various gaze patterns seem to reflect the message sender's mood, intent, or disposition. Kleck's and Nuessle's study reflects a number of personality characteristics that are commonly associated with gaze and averted gaze.[26] A film of people looking either 15 or 80 percent of the time was shown to observers who were asked to select characteristics that typified the interactants. The 15 percent lookers were labeled as cold, pessimistic, cautious, defensive, immature, evasive, submissive, indifferent, and sensitive; the 80 percent lookers were seen as friendly, self-confident, natural, mature, and sincere. The two traits that seem to show the least correspondence between encoding and decoding are judgments of anxiety and dominance. Observers seem to associate anxiety with too little gazing and dominance with too much gazing. From what we know at this time, these associations are less frequently true than we think. Gazing may more appropriately be associated with efforts to establish dominance or to maintain it when someone seems to challenge one's authority. Further, dominant persons seem to be more apt to control the other person's gazing patterns in reprimand situations—for example, "You look straight ahead when I'm talking to you, soldier!" or "Look at me when I talk to you (chew you out)!" Dependent individuals, on the other hand, seem to use eye behavior not only to communicate more positive attitudes but also to elicit such attitudes when they are not forthcoming.[27] Dependent males made more eye gaze with a listener who provided them with few, as compared to many, social reinforcers, whereas dominant males decreased their eye gaze with less reinforcing listeners.

Extroverts seem to gaze more frequently than introverts and for longer periods of time, particularly while they are talking.[28]

In an early study of aggression, Moore and Gilliland found eye behavior to be a good predictor of aggressiveness:

> Thus the simple behavioristic fact of the ability to look another person in the eye seems to have such a high significance regarding the presence or absence of aggressiveness as to warrant giving it an extremely prominent place in any scoring method devised as a measure of this trait aggressiveness.[29]

These authors also report that an unaggressive person is three times more likely than an aggressive person to be deterred to a considerable degree when stared at.

A number of research studies suggest special gazing patterns (usually less gaze) for autistic, schizophrenic, depressed, and neurotic persons.

Finally, it seems that males and females can be expected to differ in the amount of gaze shown. Females seem to look more than males on almost all measures of gaze frequency, duration, and reciprocity—and such differences have been observed in early elementary school. Henley has observed that although women tend to look at others more than men, they also tend to avert their eyes more than men.[30] One of Henley's students observed another pattern of eye behavior that seems to be enacted primarily by females. This pattern involves a repeated sequence of glancing and glancing away in response to being stared at by a man. Only one male from the thirty observed performed this behavior whereas it was seen in twelve of the thirty females.

Most of the results of these efforts to link gazing patterns to personality and/or personal characteristics may be accounted for by the following: (1) The existing need for affiliation, involvement, or inclusion: Those with high affiliative needs will tend to glance and return glances more often. (2) Other looking motivations: Persons who are highly manipulative and/or need a lot of information in order to control their environment (high Machiavellian types) will predictably look more. (3) The need to avoid unduly high levels of arousal caused by gazing (mutual gazing especially): Autistic children, for instance, are thought to have a high level of arousal and will avoid gaze in order to keep arousal down. (4) A feeling of shame or low self-esteem: The lower level of gaze sometimes seen in adolescents may reflect the well-known uncertainties about ourselves that most of us have experienced during this period.

Topics and Tasks. Common sense would suggest that the topic being discussed and/or the task at hand will affect the amount of gazing. People who have not developed an intimate relationship can be expected to gaze less when discussing intimate topics—providing that other factors such as the need for affiliation or inclusion are controlled. We would expect competitive situations and cooperative situations to elicit different patterns of gaze.

Discussions on topics that cause embarrassment, humility, shame, guilt, or sorrow might be expected to engender gazing less at the other person. Looking away during such situations may be an effort to insulate oneself against threats, arguments, information, or even affection from the other party. You have probably noticed how some men look away rather quickly after having made visual contact with a woman who is not wearing a bra. When subjects were caused to fail at an anagram task and were publicly criticized for their work, they not only reported feeling embarrassed but the amount of their gaze slipped from 30 percent to 18 percent.[31] When people want to hide some aspect of their inner feelings, they may try to avoid visual contact, for example, in situations when you are trying to deceive your partner. Exline and his colleagues designed a fascinating, if not ethically suspect, experiment.[32] A paid confederate induced subjects to cheat on an experimental task. Later the experimenter interviewed the subjects with the supposed purpose of understanding and evaluating their problem-solving methods. For some subjects the experimenter grew increasingly suspicious during the interview and finally accused the student of cheating and demanded an explanation. The subjects included those who scored high on tests of Machiavellianism and those who scored low on such tests. Machiavellianism is often associated with people who use cunning and shrewdness to achieve a goal without much regard for how unscrupulous the means might be. Figure 9.2 shows that the high Machiavellians seem to use gazing to present the appearance of innocence after being accused of cheating; low Machiavellians, on the other hand, continued to look away. Some people will tend to look away from others just to avoid seeing signs of rejection or threat, and mutual gaze during deception could be a source of dissonance since, as has been noted, this signals a free flow of communication and mutual openness.

Another communicative task we all undertake is that of persuasion. Gazing can add emphasis to a particular point, but Mehrabian and Williams report that a person trying to be more persuasive will tend to look more generally.[33] The relationship between actual attitude change in a listener and speaker gazing is not known, but listeners do seem to judge speakers with more gaze as more persuasive, truthful, sincere, and cred-

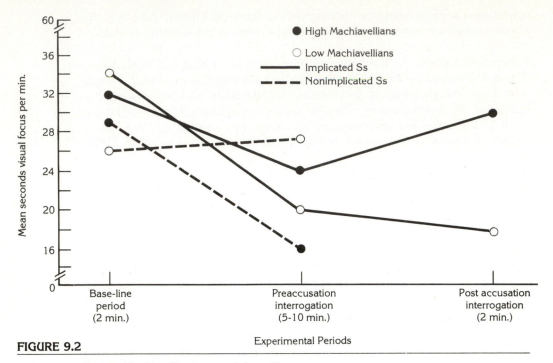

FIGURE 9.2

Experimental Periods

Gazing, Machiavellianism, and deception.

ible. Beebe manipulated the amount of gaze in an informative speech of about seven minutes.[34] Gaze seemed to primarily affect audience ratings on the following characteristics: skilled, informed, experienced and honest, friendly, and kind. Similarly, Wills found that speakers rated as sincere had an average of 63.4 percent eye gaze whereas those who were rated insincere had an average of 20.8 percent.[35]

Cultural Background. Eye behavior will also vary according to the environment in which one learns social norms. Gazing patterns sometimes show differences between "contact" (Arabs) and "noncontact" (Northern Europeans) cultures. The differences may be in duration of gaze rather than frequency; for example, it has been said that Swedes look less frequently, but for longer periods, than the English. Sometimes it is a question of "where" we analyze gaze that differences between cultures are revealed; for example, looking more in public places, and there are rules regarding "whom" you should or should not look at—for example, a person of high status. One report suggests that a conversation between some men in Kenya and their mothers-in-law is conducted by each turning their back on the other. As suggested earlier, we may find different patterns within our own culture—for example, the possible black-white differences in gazing during speaking and listening. Although patterns differ, we may find that perceived extremes in gaze elicit similar meanings in different cultures. For instance, too much gazing may signal anger, threat, or disrespect, whereas too little gaze may signal dishonesty, inattention, or shyness. Additional studies of multicultural perceptions of meaning in gaze patterns remain to be done.

PUPIL DILATION AND CONSTRICTION

Most of us are aware that the pupils of the eyes constrict in the presence of bright light and dilate in the absence of light. In the early 1960s, Hess and his colleagues at the University of Chicago renewed the interest of the scientific community in pupil dilation and constriction as a possible indicator of mental and emotional states. At one point, dozens of universities were conducting pupil dilation research and advertising agencies were testing magazine advertisements, package designs, television pilot films, and television commercials using the results of Hess' pupil dilation measures.

In an early experiment, Hess and Polt presented five pictures to male and female subjects.[36] The pupils of the male subjects dilated more than the pupils of the females when they were shown pictures of female nudes, whereas the pupils of the females dilated more than those of the males when shown pictures of a partially clothed "muscle man," a woman with a baby, and a baby alone. Thus, it seemed that pupil dilation and interest value of the stimulus were related. Hess, Seltzer, and Shlien found the pupils of male homosexuals to dilate more when viewing pictures of males than did the pupils of heterosexual males—who dilated to female pictures.[37] Studies that were subsequently carried out had similar results. For instance, Barlow preselected subjects with particular political preferences—subjects who actively supported either liberal or conservative candidates.[38] He photographed the pupil of the right eye while the candidates watched slides of political figures. There seemed to be a perfect correlation between pupillary response and verbal response. The pupils of white conservatives dilated to slides of George Wallace and constricted to slides of Lyndon B. Johnson and Martin Luther King, and those of black liberals reacted in an exact opposite manner.

Several of Hess's studies suggest that pupil response might be an index of attitudes—that is, that pupils will dilate for positive attitudes and constrict for negative ones. His oft-cited study supporting this theory was the eventual constriction of the pupils of subjects who viewed pictures of concentration camp victims, dead soldiers, and a murdered gangster. In Hess's words: "The changes in emotions and mental activity revealed by changes in pupil size are clearly associated with changes in

195

attitude."[39] His most recent work continues to maintain this position.[40] Hess cites a study that showed photographs such as those in Figure 9.3, in which the woman's pupils were retouched so she had large pupils in one photograph and smaller ones in the other. Although male subjects did not tend to pick either picture as consistently more friendly or attractive, there was a tendency to associate positive attributes with the woman who had larger pupils and negative attributes to the one who had smaller pupils. Woodmansee set out to test Hess's theory. Although he tried to improve on Hess's methodology and measuring instruments, Woodmansee could find no support for pupil dilation and constriction as an index of attitudes toward blacks.[41] Hays and Plax found that their subjects' pupils dilated when they received supportive statements ("I am very much interested in your speech."), but constriction did not follow from nonsupportive statements ("I disagree completely with the development of your speech."[42] One study found dilation from both positive and negative feedback.[43] Other research has found the reflex dilation reaction of the pupil to be associated with arousal, attentiveness, interest, and perceptual orientation—but it does not seem to be an attitudinal index. Tightening muscles anywhere on the body, anticipating a loud noise, using drugs, closing the lids, and exerting mental effort will all alter pupil size. Even the advertising agencies seem to have lost interest in pupils as an involuntary measure of viewer attitudes.

Some of the potential problems facing the testing of advertisements include: (1) The viewer's pupil response may be affected by light and dark colors on the ad itself. (2) It is difficult to know what the viewer is focusing on. In one ad for French fries, viewers' pupils dilated, but subsequent analysis suggested that the dilation may have been the result of a steak that was also shown in the ad. (3) One advertising executive, commenting on the viability of a theory of attitudes and pupil dilation for his products, asked: "How excited can a person get about a laundry detergent?" (4) In some experiments it was noted that the pupils did not immediately return to their predilated state after seeing an arousing picture. Hence, the following stimuli were viewed with eyes that were still partially dilated. (5) Since dilation occurs in response to so many different stimuli, it is difficult to state positively that the dilation is exclusively the result of an attitudinal orientation.

Although pupil dilation reveals emotional arousal, it is still not clear how much people notice it, or how close they have to be to see it. However, at least one study suggests that pupil dilation may be influential in selecting interaction partners—or even dates. Stass and Willis dealt with live subjects rather than with pictures.[44] Subjects were told that they would be in an experiment and they had to choose a partner—one whom they could trust and one who was pleasant and easy to talk to on an intimate basis. The subjects were taken to a room where two

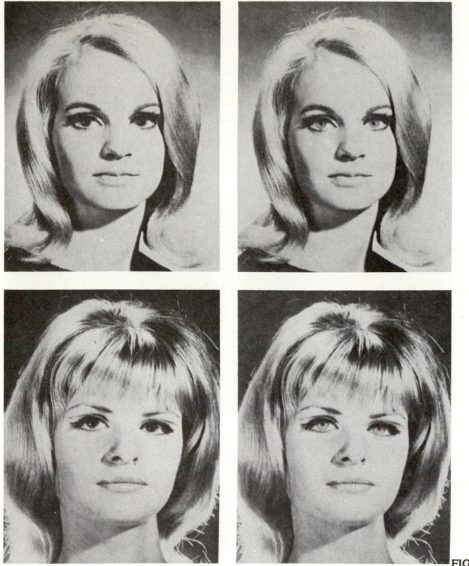

FIGURE 9.3

Some of Hess's stimulus photos with pupil dilation varied.

other persons were waiting. These two persons had previously been independently rated as about the same in general attractiveness. Eye gazing and pupil dilation (through the use of a drug) were varied. Once the naive subject left the waiting room, the experimenter asked him or her to choose one of the persons and give reasons for the choice. Results show that eye gazing is an overwhelming factor in choice making, but pupil dilation is also a factor. A few people mentioned visual contact as a reason for their choice, but none mentioned pupil dilation. Thus, for both women and men, pupil dilation seems to play an influential role as an attraction device for interaction. Perhaps this is not a revelation to those many women who, since the Middle Ages, have put belladonna in their eyes to increase attractiveness; or to those expert romancers who suggest a dimly lighted place to meet.

SUMMARY

Although researchers have examined the size, color, and position of the eyes, eye rings, eyebrows, and eyespots, our major concern was with gaze and mutual gaze. The term *eye contact* was not used because it did not seem to accurately represent the phenomena studied or perceived by the interactants. Gazing serves many interpersonal functions: (1) regulating the flow of communication—opening the channels of communication and assisting in the turn-taking process; (2) monitoring feedback; (3) expressing emotions; and (4) communicating the nature of the interpersonal relationship—for example, variations resulting from status, liking, and disliking.

We also outlined a number of factors that will influence the amount and duration of gaze in human relationships—for example, distance, physical characteristics, personal and personality characteristics, topics and tasks, and cultural background. From this review, we would predict more gazing when:

> you are physically distant from your partner.
> you are discussing easy, impersonal topics.
> there is nothing else to look at.
> you are interested in your partner's reactions—interpersonally involved.
> you are interested in your partner—that is, you like or love the partner.
> you are of a lower status than your partner.
> you are trying to dominate or influence your partner.
> you are from a culture that emphasizes visual contact in interaction.
> you are an extrovert.
> you have high affiliative or inclusion needs.
> you are dependent on your partner (and the partner has been unresponsive).
> you are listening rather than talking.
> you are female.

We would predict less gazing when:

you are physically close.
you are discussing difficult, intimate topics.
you have other relevant objects, people, or backgrounds to look at.
you are not interested in your partner's reactions.
you are talking rather than listening.
you are not interested in your partner—that is, you dislike the partner.
you perceive yourself as a higher-status person than your partner.
you are from a culture that imposes sanctions on visual contact during interaction.
you are an introvert.
you are low on affiliative or inclusion needs.
you have a mental disorder such as autism or schizophrenia.
you are embarrassed, ashamed, sorrowful, sad, submissive, or trying to hide something.

The preceding lists are not exhaustive. Indeed, some of the listed factors are dependent on certain important qualifications—for example, you may have less gaze and mutual gaze when you are physically close—unless you happen to love your partner and want to get as close, physically and psychologically, as you can! The lists are not intended to replace the qualified principles as they appear in the chapter.

The last part of this chapter dealt with pupil dilation and constriction. We reviewed the work of a major writer in this area, Eckhard Hess and others who have pursued his ideas. Pupil dilation has been associated with arousal, attentiveness, mental effort, interest, and perceptual orientation. Aside from Hess's work, however, no support has been found for the idea that pupils reflect attitudinal states. Dilation has been found to occur under conditions that seem to represent positive attitudes, but there is little or no support for the belief that constriction of pupils is associated with negative attitudes toward objects and people. Finally, we examined one study that intimates that pupil dilation may be a factor in our desire to interact with another person.

NOTES

1. M. Worthy, *Eye Color, Sex and Race* (Anderson, S.C.: Droke House/Hallux, 1974).
2. Two excellent summaries of the research in this area include M. Argyle and M. Cook, *Gaze and Mutual Gaze* (Cambridge: Cambridge University Press, 1976), and P. C. Ellsworth and L. M. Ludwig, "Visual Behavior in Social Interaction," *Journal of Communication* 22 (1972): 375–403.

3. M. von Cranach and J. H. Ellgring, "Problems in the Recognition of Gaze Direction," in M. von Cranach and I. Vine (eds.), *Social Communication and Movement* (New York: Academic Press, 1973).

4. G. Nielson, *Studies in Self Confrontation* (Copenhagen: Monksgaard, 1962); M. Argyle and R. Ingham, "Gaze, Mutual Gaze and Proximity," *Semiotica* 6 (1972): 32–49.

5. A. Kendon, "Some Functions of Gaze-Direction in Social Interaction," *Acta Psychologica* 26 (1967): 22–63. Also see M. Argyle, R. Ingham, F. Alkema, and M. McCallin, "The Different Functions of Gaze," *Semiotica* 7 (1973): 19–32.

6. One study, however, suggests that this pattern may be limited to Caucasians. In this study, whites gazed more while listening and blacks gazed more while speaking. See M. LaFrance and C. Mayo, "Racial Differences in Gaze Behavior During Conversations: Two Systematic Observational Studies," *Journal of Personality and Social Psychology* 33 (1976): 547–552.

7. J. Jaffe, D. N. Stern, and C. Perry, " 'Conversational' Coupling of Gaze Behavior in Prelinguistic Human Development," *Journal of Psycholinguistic Research* 2 (1973): 321–329.

8. C. L. Kleinke, A. A. Bustos, F. B. Meeker, and R. A. Staneski, "Effects of Self-Attributed and Other-Attributed Gaze in Interpersonal Evaluations Between Males and Females," *Journal of Experimental Social Psychology* 9 (1973): 154–163.

9. M. E. Day, "Eye Movement Phenomenon Relating to Attention, Thought, and Anxiety," *Perceptual and Motor Skills* 19 (1964): 443–446.

10. P. Bakan, "The Eyes Have It," *Psychology Today* 4 (1971): 64–67; and P. Bakan and F. F. Strayer, "On Reliability of Conjugate Lateral Eye Movements," *Perceptual and Motor Skills* 36 (1973): 429–430.

11. P. Ekman, W. V. Friesen, and S. S. Tomkins, "Facial Affect Scoring Technique: A First Validity Study," *Semiotica* 3 (1971): 37–58.

12. P. Ekman and W. V. Friesen, *Unmasking the Face* (Englewood Cliffs, N.J.: Prentice-Hall, 1975).

13. G. Hearn, "Leadership and the Spatial Factor in Small Groups," *Journal of Abnormal and Social Psychology* 54 (1957): 269–272.

14. J. S. Efran, "Looking for Approval: Effect on Visual Behavior of Approbation from Persons Differing in Importance," *Journal of Personality and Social Psychology* 10 (1968): 21–25.

15. A Mehrabian, *Nonverbal Communication* (Chicago: Aldine-Atherton, 1972).

16. J. Efran and A. Broughton, "Effect of Expectancies for Social Approval on Visual Behavior," *Journal of Personality and Social Psychology* 4 (1966): 103–107.

17. R. Exline and L. Winters, "Affective Relations and Mutual Glances in Dyads," in S. Tomkins, and C. Izard (eds.), *Affect, Cognition and Personality* (New York: Springer, 1965).

18. R. Exline and C. Eldridge, "Effects of Two Patterns of a Speaker's Visual Behavior upon the Perception of the Authenticity of His Verbal Message," paper presented to the Eastern Psychological Association, Boston, 1967.

19. Mehrabian, *Nonverbal Communication.*

20. J. M. Wiemann, "An Experimental Study of Visual Attention in Dyads:

The Effects of Four Gaze Conditions on Evaluations by Applicants in Employment Interviews," paper presented to the Speech Communication Association, Chicago, 1974.

21. Z. Rubin, "The Measurement of Romantic Love," *Journal of Personality and Social Psychology* 16 (1970): 265–273.

22. C. L. Kleinke, A. A. Bustos, F. B. Meeker, and R. A. Staneski, "Effects of Self-Attributed and Other Attributed Gaze in Interpersonal Evaluations Between Males and Females."

23. R. E. Kleck and S. Rubinstein, "Physical Attractiveness, Perceived Attitude Similarity, and Interpersonal Attraction in an Opposite-Sex Encounter," *Journal of Personality and Social Psychology* 31 (1975): 107–114.

24. M. Argyle and J. Dean, "Eye-Contact, Distance and Affiliation," *Sociometry* 28 (1965): 269–304.

25. R. Kleck, "Physical Stigma and Nonverbal Cues Emitted in Face-to-Face Interaction," *Human Relations* 21 (1968): 19–28.

26. R. E. Kleck and W. Nuessle, "Congruence Between the Indicative and Communicative Functions of Eye-Contact in Interpersonal Relations," *British Journal of Social and Clinical Psychology* 7 (1968): 241–246.

27. R. Exline and D. Messick, "The Effects of Dependency and Social Reinforcement upon Visual Behavior During an Interview," *British Journal of Social and Clinical Psychology* 6 (1967): 256–266.

28. N. Mobbs, "Eye Contact in Relation to Social Introversion/Extroversion," *British Journal of Social and Clinical Psychology* 7 (1968): 305–306.

29. R. T. Moore and A. R. Gilliland, "The Measurement of Aggressiveness," *Journal of Applied Psychology* 5 (1921): 97–118.

30. N. M. Henley, *Body Politics: Power, Sex, and Nonverbal Communication* (Englewood Cliffs, N.J.: Prentice-Hall), 1977.

31. A. Modigliani, "Embarrassment, Facework and Eye-Contact: Testing a Theory of Embarrassment," *Journal of Personality and Social Psychology* 17 (1971): 15–24.

32. R. V. Exline, J. Thibaut, C. B. Hickey, and P. Gumpert, "Visual Interaction in Relation to Machiavellianism and an Unethical Act," in R. Christie and F. L. Geis (eds.), *Studies in Machiavellianism* (New York: Academic Press, 1970).

33. A. Mehrabian, and M. Williams, "Nonverbal Concomitants of Perceived and Intended Persuasiveness," *Journal of Personality and Social Psychology* 13 (1969): 37–58.

34. S. A. Beebe, "Eye-Contact: A Nonverbal Determinant of Speaker Credibility," *Speech Teacher* 23 (1974): 21–25.

35. J. Wills, "An Empirical Study of the Behavioral Characteristics of Sincere and Insincere Speakers" (Ph.D. diss., University of Southern California, Los Angeles, 1961).

36. E. H. Hess and J. M. Polt, "Pupil Size as Related to Interest Value of Visual Stimuli," *Science* 132 (1960): 349–350.

37. E. H. Hess, A. L. Seltzer, and J. M. Shlien, "Pupil Response of Hetero- and Homosexual Males to Pictures of Men and Women: A Pilot Study," *Journal of Abnormal Psychology* 70 (1965): 165–168.

38. J. D. Barlow, "Pupillary Size as an Index of Preference in Political Candidates," *Perceptual and Motor Skills* 28 (1969): 587–590.

39. E. H. Hess, "The Role of Pupil Size in Communication," *Scientific American*, 233 November, 1975, 110–112, 116–119.

40. E. H. Hess, *The Tell-Tale Eye* (New York: Van Nostrand Reinhold, 1975). Another historical-critical account of the development of Hess's work can be found in B. Rice, "Rattlesnakes, French Fries, and Pupillometric Oversell," *Psychology Today* 7 (1974): 55–59.

41. J. J. Woodmansee, "The Pupil Response as a Measure of Social Attitudes," in G. F. Summers (ed.), *Attitude Measurement* (Chicago: Rand McNally, 1970). pp. 514–533.

42. E. R. Hays and T. G. Plax, "Pupillary Response to Supportive and Aversive Verbal Messages," *Speech Monographs* 38 (1971): 316–320.

43. M. P. Janisse and W. S. Peavler, "Pupillary Research Today: Emotion in the Eye," *Psychology Today* 7 (1974): 60–63.

44. J. W. Strass and F. N. Willis, Jr., "Eye Contact, Pupil Dilation, and Personal Preference," *Psychonomic Science* 7 (1967): 375–376.

ADDITIONAL READINGS

Argyle, M. and M. Cook. *Gaze and Mutual Gaze.* Cambridge: Cambridge University Press, 1976.

Coss, R. G. "Reflections on the Evil Eye." *Human Behavior* 3 (October 1974): 16–22.

Hess, E. H. *The Tell-Tale Eye.* New York: Van Nostrand Reinhold, 1975.

Rice, B. "Rattlesnakes, French Fries, and Pupillometric Oversell," *Psychology Today* 7 (1974): 55–59.

Worthy, M. *Eye Color, Sex and Race.* Anderson, S.C.: Droke House/Hallux, 1974.

10

THE EFFECTS
OF VOCAL CUES
THAT ACCOMPANY
SPOKEN WORDS

I understand a fury in your words, but not the words　　　SHAKESPEARE, **Othello**, *Act IV*

Ideally, this chapter should not be read, and should not even have been written! Instead, this chapter should be a sound recording, which would give you a greater appreciation for the vocal nuances that are the subject of this chapter, or, as the cliché goes, "how something is said rather than what is said." However, the dichotomy set up by this cliché is misleading, because how something is said is frequently what is said.

Some responses to vocal cues are elicited because we deliberately try to manipulate our voice in order to communicate various meanings. Robert J. McCloskey, a major spokesman for the State Department during the Nixon Administration, reportedly exemplified such behavior:

> McCloskey has three distinct ways of saying, "I would not speculate": spoken without accent, it means the department doesn't know for sure; emphasis on the "I" means "I wouldn't, but you may—and with some assurance"; accent on "speculate" indicates that the questioner's premise is probably wrong.[1]

Most of us do the same kind of thing when we emphasize a particular word in a message. Notice how different vocal emphases influence the interpretation of the following message:

1. *He's* giving this money to Herbie.
  1a. HE is the one giving the money; nobody else.

2. He's *giving* this money to Herbie.
   2a. He is GIVING, not lending, the money.
3. He's giving *this* money to Herbie.
   3a. The money being exchanged is not from another fund or source; it is THIS money.
4. He's giving this *money* to Herbie.
   4a. MONEY is the unit of exchange, not a check or wampum.
5. He's giving this money to *Herbie*.
   5a. The recipient is HERBIE, not Eric or Rod.

We manipulate our voice to indicate the end of a declarative sentence (by lowering our voice) or a question (by raising it). Sometimes we consciously manipulate our voice, so that the vocal message contradicts the verbal one. In certain situations, this may be perceived as sarcasm. For instance, you can say the words, "I'm having a wonderful time" so that they mean "I'm having a terrible time." You may say "I'd much rather hear Gordon Lightfoot than Willie Nelson," while your voice says, "I can't think of anything worse than listening to Gordon Lightfoot." If you are perceived as being sarcastic, the vocal cues you have given have probably superseded the verbal cues.

Vocal cues seem to exert a great deal of influence on listener perceptions—particularly with certain classes of information or for certain kinds of responses. Generally, these responses are based on stereotypes associated with various vocal qualities, intonations, characteristics, and the like.

VOCAL CUES AND SPEAKER RECOGNITION

You may have had this experience: A person calls you on the telephone and, apparently assuming you will recognize his or her voice, does not provide any verbal content that would help you identify that person, for example, you pick up the phone and say: "Hello." The voice on the other end says: "Hi, how ya doin'?" At this point you realize two things: (1) The greeting suggests an informality found among people who are supposed to know each other, and (2) you don't know who it is! So you try to extend the conversation without admitting your ignorance, hoping that some verbal clue will be given or that you'll eventually recognize the caller's voice. As a result, you say something like, "Fine. What have you been up to?"

Each time we speak we produce a complex acoustic signal. That signal is not exactly the same each time we speak (even if it is the same word); nor is the signal you produce exactly the same as the one produced by other speakers. The knowledge that there are greater differences between the voices of two different speakers than the voice of a single speaker at two different times has led to considerable interest in the process of identifying speakers by their voices alone.

There are three primary methods of identifying speakers: (1) listening, (2) visual comparison of spectrograms (voiceprints), and (3) recognition through machine analysis of the speech signals.

After reviewing an extensive body of literature in this area, Hecker argues that the recognition accuracy for listening compares very favorably with the other two techniques.[2] However, many variables will affect accuracy, such as familiarity with the speaker, the judge's desire to accurately identify the speaker, the type of spectrogram used, the amount of training of the judges, the amount of noise or masking accompanying or distorting the signal, the method of identification and discrimination used by the judge, the duration of the speech sample, the number of phonemes represented in the sample, the psychological state or bias of the hearer or reader, and so on.

Even when listeners accurately pinpoint a speaker's voice, they aren't able to explain the perceptual bases for their decision, that is, we don't know what features of the voice listeners are reacting to. Listeners probably utilize very few of the many characteristics of the voice in speaker recognition attempts.

Law enforcement and judicial agencies have had a special concern in identifying speakers objectively from their vocal characteristics. At the famous trial of Bruno Hauptmann, the accused kidnapper of the Lindbergh baby, Lindbergh claimed that he recognized Hauptmann's voice as that of the kidnapper, even though it had been about three years since he had last heard it. Although it is not beyond the realm of possibility that such an identification could have been accurate, McGehee found that accuracy in voice recognition tends to drop off sharply after three weeks, and after five months it dips to about 13 percent.[3] Uncertainties of this nature have encouraged a search for more objective methods to recognize voices. One such attempt to gather more objective data on voice recognition is to get a visual picture of a person's speech, a spectrogram.

Some people have made strong claims for the accuracy and reliability of spectrographic analysis, but the experimental data only reminds us that we still face human error in the interpretation of the visual data. The interpreter's skill becomes particularly relevant when one looks at Figure 10.1, which shows two similar spectrograms—admittedly featuring only one word—but sufficient to point out that our reliance on spectrograms as evidence at trials must be weighed very carefully.[4] Spectrograms are not entirely like fingerprints. No two voices are exactly alike, but depending on the voice sample obtained and the equipment used, two different voices may appear very similar. Fingerprints, unlike voices, however, will show little variability from one time to the next—unless smudges or smears have occurred. In one study, speakers were

FIGURE 10.1

Similar spectrograms of the word *you* uttered by two arbitrarily selected speakers.

asked to produce the same sentence using their normal voice and a number of "disguises"—speaking like an old person, using a hypernasal voice and a hoarse voice, speaking at a slow rate, and using a disguise of one's own choosing.[5] These voice samples were then submitted to spectrographic analysis by experts who were paid fifty dollars if they achieved the highest accuracy of identification. The experts matched normal voices with about 57 percent accuracy, but all the disguised voices significantly interfered with identification, with the least accuracy being achieved when the speakers chose their own disguise.

VOCAL CUES AND PERSONALITY JUDGMENTS

Numerous research efforts have been aimed at determining whether certain personality traits are expressed in one's voice and whether others are sensitive to these cues. The results of these studies have been mixed. It is common to find: (1) a great amount of agreement among judges of the voices regarding the presence of certain personality characteristics; (2) little agreement between the judges' personality perceptions and the speaker's actual score on personality tests; and (3) for some voices and some personality traits, a very high correspondence between the judges' perceptions and actual criterion measures (personality traits). Kramer, in his interpretation of this data, makes several worthwhile observations:[6] First, the criterion measures are also frequently imperfect measures—that is, a judge may rate a voice as representative of a particular personality trait and, when matched with a score on a personality test taken by that speaker, the two measures only correlate as much as would be predicted by chance. However, since the personality test is not a totally accurate measure, there may be a higher correspondence than this data seems to indicate. Second, Kramer points out that almost all these studies have used a speaker giving a monologue to which the judges respond. Some personality characteristics associated with vocal cues may only "come out" in dialogue form—a possibility that has not been adequately tested. Finally, Kramer points out that the research has generally ignored differences among listeners with respect to such things as personality, culture, and developmental and psychophysical traits, which may have a profound impact on the listener's accuracy in perceiving personality traits based on vocal cues. It would also seem highly desirable to obtain acoustical records on spectrograms to find out how acoustically similar voices are perceived.

One of the more complete studies in this area was conducted by Addington, who recognized that stereotyped judgments of vocal cues regularly occur and decided to explore the specific nature of these stereotypes.[7] Male and female speakers simulated nine vocal characteristics, and judges responded to the voices by rating them on forty personality characteristics. Judges were most reliable in rating masculine-feminine, young-old, enthusiastic-apathetic, energetic-lazy, and good-looking-ugly. The least reliable ratings occurred in judging extroverted-introverted, honest-dishonest, law abiding-criminal, and healthy-sickly. Addington factor-analyzed his personality data and concluded that the male personality was generally perceived in terms of physical and emotional power, whereas the female personality was apparently perceived in terms of social faculties. Table 10.1 summarizes Addington's results. Addington concluded his study by raising the question of the extent to which these stereotyped impressions of personality are maintained in the face of conflicting personality information. Another question concerns the nature of the relationship between a given personality impression and vocal cue. For example, Addington's research indicated that increased pitch variety led to more positive personality impressions, but is it not possible that at some point, increasing pitch variety could become so exaggerated as to evoke negative perceptions? These questions await further study.

Closely related to the studies of an individual's personality inferred from the voice are the many attempts made to show how people evaluate

TABLE 10.1
Simulated Vocal Cues and Personality Stereotypes

SIMULATED VOCAL CUES*	SPEAKERS	STEREOTYPED PERCEPTIONS
Breathiness	Males	Younger, more artistic
	Females	More feminine, prettier, more petite, more effervescent, more high-strung, and shallower
Thinness	Males	Did not alter listener's image of the speaker; no significant correlations
	Females	Increased social, physical, emotional, and mental immaturity; increased sense of humor and sensitivity
Flatness	Males	More masculine, more sluggish, colder, more withdrawn
	Females	More masculine, more sluggish, colder, more withdrawn
Nasality	Males	A wide array of socially undesirable characteristics
	Females	A wide array of socially undesirable characteristics
Tenseness	Males	Older, more unyielding, cantankerous
	Females	Younger; more emotional, feminine, high-strung; less intelligent
Throatiness	Males	Older; more realistic, mature; sophisticated; well adjusted
	Females	Less intelligent; more masculine; lazier; more boorish, unemotional, ugly, sickly, careless, inartistic, naive, humble, neurotic, quiet, uninteresting, apathetic. In short, "Cloddish or oafish" (Addington)
Orotundity	Males	More energetic, healthy, artistic, sophisticated, proud, interesting, enthusiastic. In short, "hardy and aesthetically inclined." (Addington)
	Females	Increased liveliness, gregariousness, esthetic sensitivity, and "increasingly proud and humorless" (Addington)
Increased Rate	Males	More animated and extroverted
	Females	More animated and extroverted
Increased Pitch Variety	Males	More dynamic, feminine, esthetically inclined
	Females	More dynamic and extroverted

*For descriptions of these cues, see P. Heinberg, *Voice Training for Speaking and Reading Aloud* (New York: Ronald Press, 1964), pp. 152—181.

From D. W. Addington, "The Relationship of Selected Vocal Characteristics to Personality Perception," *Speech Monographs* 35 (1968):492-503.

various dialects and accents. You may recall that Liza Doolittle in Lerner and Loewe's *My Fair Lady* based on Shaw's *Pygmalion* spent considerable time and effort trying to correct her dialect so that she could rise in social standing. (Professor Higgins: "Look at her—a pris'ner of the gutters; Condemned by ev're syllable she utters." Act 1, Scene 1, *My Fair Lady*). Liza's training, according to one study, was most appropriate—suggesting that if we expect a speaker to reflect a nonstandard and/or "lower-class" dialect and the speaker actually presents him/or herself in accord with standard or "upper-class" models, the evaluation will be very positive. The reverse was also true, speakers who were expected to speak "up" and instead spoke "down", were evaluated negatively.[8] Obviously, there is a fine line between "adapting to your audience" and severely violating expectations of your own background.

Although some of the studies that form the foundation for the following conclusions seemed to use stimuli which represented something more than just vocal cues, they still represent a significant corpus of material that is relevant to our understanding of vocal cues. Although there are some exceptions, dialects other than the one spoken by the listener/evaluators ordinarily receive less favorable evaluations than those considered "standard." Generally, these negative responses occur because the listener associates the speaker's dialect with an ethnic or regional stereotype and then evaluates the voice in accordance with the stereotype. Typical of this type of response are studies that found the following: (1) Chicano English speakers were rated lower on success, ability, and social awareness by English-speaking students; (2) native-born Americans rated Europeans (speaking English) less positively than other native-born speakers; (3) teachers tended to label a child as "culturally disadvantaged" especially if the speech exhibited perceived irregularities in grammar, silent pausing, and pronunciation; and (4) "standard" dialects were preferred and judged more competent than "nonstandard"—regardless of who spoke—except that standard dialects were more often associated with white speakers than with black.[9]

Do regional varieties of speech in the United States differ in prestige value? Some people in Maine, Louisiana, New York City, Arkansas, and Michigan rated twelve voice samples of American dialects and one foreign accent.[10] The most unfavorably regarded of these were the foreign accent and the example of "New Yorkese." Although this study is about thirty years old, some current dialect or accent stereotype may influence your own judgments of a speaker's status today. Certainly many people had a chance to test their stereotypes of Southern dialect as they evaluated the speech of President Carter. Miller's work appears to be the only current effort to go beyond the theory that dialects evoke stereotypes of groups that influence the judgment of that dialect. This study provides some support for the notion that aspects of certain dialects may be evaluated independently of the stereotype—that is, some listeners may respond negatively to a French-Canadian speaker because of a negative stereotype and/or because of some dislike of the dialect itself.[11]

VOCAL CUES AND JUDGMENTS OF PERSONAL CHARACTERISTICS

Over forty years ago Pear did his pioneering work on vocal cues and judgments of personal characteristics.[12] Using nine speakers and over four thousand radio listeners, he found that a speaker's age could be estimated fairly accurately, the speaker's sex could be estimated with remarkable accuracy, the speaker's birthplace could be estimated with little accuracy, and occasionally the speaker's vocation was estimated with surprising accuracy. The actor and clergyman were consistently identified from among the nine professions represented. Since the time of Pear's study, others have been interested in judgments based on vocal cues of such characteristics as body type, height, weight, age, occupation, status or social class, race, sex, education, and dialect region.

Nerbonne found that listeners were able to differentiate accurately between male and female, black and white, and big and small speakers; among twenty-to-thirty-year-old, forty-to-sixty-year-old, and sixty-to-seventy-year-old speakers (age differentiation being easiest from spontaneous cues); among speakers with less than a high school education, high school graduates, and college graduates; and among speakers from eastern, southern, and General American dialect regions.[13] For some reason, the age and dialect of the speakers were more accurately judged in Nerbonne's study when the aural cues were provided by telephone speech rather than under conditions simulating face-to-face conversation. A student of mine doubted the validity of distinctions between blacks and whites on the basis of voice alone—particularly if the characteristics of the social community in which the speakers were born and raised were kept constant—conducted an informal telephone survey of blacks and whites who were raised from childhood in the same neighborhood in Milwaukee. Her results showed no more than chance accuracy in making such distinctions. Thus, although black and white speakers can sometimes be distinguished by their vocal cues at high levels of accuracy, at other times such identifications will be very difficult. For instance, West Indian blacks in a community in England were misattributed as white 8 percent of the time when their voice samples were judged.[14]

Weitz, in a slightly different approach, looked at interracial interaction and voice tone.[15] She found that voice tone seemed to be a better predictor of "friendliness" for whites interacting with blacks than overtly expressed verbal attitudes. Weitz has also speculated that in crossed-sex interactions, vocal tones may also help identify underlying attitudes, such as patronizing, friendly, or hostile.

Listeners who heard six recorded vowels of twenty speakers were able to identify the sex of the speaker 96 percent of the time when the tape was not altered in any way. Accuracy of identification decreased to 91 percent for a filtered tape and to 75 percent for a whispered voice sample.[16] Women and men may sometimes be identified on the basis of their intonation patterns. Some believe, for instance, that women might end a sentence on a higher pitch, relative to where they started the sentence, than men. Pitch may be another basis for discrimination. Again, the nature of the vocal stimuli will be most influential in determining exactly how well we can discriminate male from female voices. For instance, males and females interacting may manifest different vocal cues than when they present monologues or interact with a member of the same sex.[17] The topic of discussion may also affect voice production and perceptions, and if, as we noted earlier with black speakers, there is a gradual narrowing of differences as adaptations to the social community are made, we might speculate that the vocal tones of working women in predominantly male organizations may be harder to distinguish—particularly if the sample is taken in the work milieu. Instead of children shaping their voices to sound like the adult version of their sex,[18] this may be an instance of adults acquiring some vocal characteristics of the opposite sex. It may also be that females whose voices are at some variance with a traditional female-stereotyped voice are selectively hired by male employers for traditionally male-held jobs.

The literature on height and weight judgments based on vocal cues is mixed; some studies report accuracy and others do not. One source of variance might be the range allowed for an accurate answer; for example, we would predict greater accuracy if we had to guess a person's height within five inches than within two inches. As long as the response category is not too discriminating, height and weight can probably be judged with greater than chance accuracy from vocal cues.[19] When Lass and his colleagues asked people to estimate the exact height and weight of a speaker, however, the average difference between actual height (for all speakers—male and female) and estimated height (for all speakers) was only .80 inches. The weight discrepancy was only 3.48 pounds, even though the height and weight of the speakers was not limited to a narrow range. As judges we might attach various heights and weights to certain vocal characteristics. Test your own stereotypes and compare them with your friends. Would you associate an extremely low-pitched voice with a heavier person? Does loudness suggest a weight category for you? Think of people you know who are very tall, very short, very light, and very heavy. Would your reaction to an unknown voice be influenced by your experience with, and memory of, these other people? These are only a few of the many characteristics that influence our judgments; others include breathiness, rate, intonation, and resonance.

When listeners are asked to match voice samples with photographs, we again find that the task is performed with better than chance accuracy—but again, the accuracy level will depend heavily on the preciseness of the judgment to be made.[20] Fay and Middleton studied body type as one variable that might be associated with vocal cues.[21] Unfortunately, they did not verify the actual body types of the speakers by precise measurements (only observed guesstimates), so it is advisable to weigh their findings with caution. Listeners were asked to write in the body type they thought fit the voice they heard. Listeners heard nine different speakers and were asked to determine whether they were ectomorphic, endomorphic or mesomorphic (See Chapter Five). Fay and Middleton report that the endomorphic and ectomorphic types were judged with far more than chance accuracy whereas the athletic type was judged at about chance accuracy. It seems that for extreme body types, vocal stereotypes may have some validity.

Judgments of occupation from vocal cues also seems to vary from study to study. Generally the judges agree with one another, but their judgments do not always match the actual occupations. Some early studies reported a fairly consistent identification of occupation from voices, but Fay and Middleton only found the voice of a preacher identified at a rate better than chance—and it was frequently mistaken for the voice of a lawyer.[22]

Several studies show age to be fairly accurately assessed from vocal cues. Davis concluded her research by saying: "the results of this study seem to indicate clearly that voice alone can suggest age to the listener."[23] Several studies, which investigated pitch of males during infancy, childhood, adolescence, early adulthood, and middle and advanced age, indicate a general lowering of pitch level from infancy through middle age. Then a reversal occurs, and pitch level rises slightly with advancing age. Mysak found that males in his 80–92-year-old study group were characterized by higher measures of average fundamental pitch levels than males aged 65–79.[24] Mysak found that age 80 is a very sensitive dividing line in terms of pitch change, and that pitch changes were explained by physical changes and increasing tension. A similar, but less complete, series of studies have been completed on the developing female voice. McClone and Hollien, using research methods similar to Mysak's, found no significant difference in the mean pitch level of two groups of women (aged 65–79 and 80–94).[25] The data on pitch from the 65–79 group was compared with data gathered by another investigator on some young adult women. Since there were no differences in the pitch of their voices, McClone and Hollien concluded that the speaking pitch level of women probably varies little throughout adult life, even though data for middle-aged women was not compared. If, as some gerontological studies suggest, our voices change in pitch and flexibility, rate, loudness, vocal quality, articulatory control, and the like, this may give clues to age of which we are largely unaware. We may also be responding to other vocal characteristics that have not been reported in these developmental studies—they only give us possible clues.

Other studies show listeners to be amazingly accurate in judging social class or status on the basis of voice alone. Harms obtained independent scores from nine speakers on the Hollingshead Two Factor Index of Status Position.[26] The speakers were then categorized as either high-, middle-, or low-status. Each speaker recorded a forty-to-sixty-second conversation in which he responded to questions and statements like "How are you?" "Ask for the time," and so on. Adult listeners rated the speakers according to status and credibility. The results indicate that these listeners were not only able to identify the speakers' status, but many of them said that they made their decision after only ten to fifteen seconds of listening to the recording. The responses also showed that those perceived as high in status were also perceived as most credible. This finding is consistent with other studies of status and vocal cues. Ellis even conducted a study in which he told speakers to try to fake status and imitate an upper-class speaker.[27] Listener judgments still correlated .65 with independent measures of status for these speakers. As has been previously intimated, it appears that we learn to talk like those around us—those in our neighborhoods, those in our vocational environment, and those in our educational environments.

If voice and status are so intimately related, the following dialogue from *The Selling of the President 1968* takes on a definite note of realism: "The announcer who was to do the opening called to ask if his tone was too shrill. 'Yeah, we don't want it like a quiz show,' Roger Ailes said. 'He's going to be presidential tonight so announce presidentially.' "[28]

VOCAL CUES AND JUDGMENTS OF EMOTION

Would you know if someone was happy? sad? afraid? "Of course I would," you say. What if we removed this person from your sight? "Sure," you say. "The kinds of things the person says will tell me whether he or she is happy, sad, angry, or afraid." What if we eliminated any words to which you might respond so that the voice is the only stimulus for judging emotional expressions? "Maybe" you say. Some researchers might be more optimistic, but "maybe" may, indeed, be the best answer.

Starkweather, in 1961, summarized a series of studies that attempted to specify the relationship between the voice and judgments of emotion. His conclusion reiterated the frequent finding in studies of personality judgments from vocal cues—consistent agreement among the judges.

> Studies of content free speech indicate that the voice alone can carry information about the speaker. Judges agree substantially, both when asked to identify the emotion being expressed and when given the task of estimating the strength of the feeling. Judgments appear to depend on significant changes in pitch, rate, volume and other physical characteristics of the voice, but untrained judges cannot describe these qualities accurately.[29]

Three years later, Davitz seemed to suggest that such judgments are not only reliable but also valid: "Regardless of the technique used, all studies of adults thus far reported in the literature agree that emotional meanings can be communicated accurately by vocal expression."[30]

Several methods have been used to eliminate or control the verbal information that usually accompany vocal cues. Accuracy may vary depending on the method used. Some studies attempt to use what is assumed to be "meaningless content." This usually takes the form of having the speaker say numbers or letters while trying to convey various emotional states. Other studies have attempted to control the verbal cues by using "constant content." In other words, a speaker reads a standard passage while attempting to simulate different emotional states. The assumption underlying this technique is that the passage selected is neutral in emotional tone. Some of the more recent studies have used electronic filtering to eliminate verbal content. A low-pass filter holds back the higher frequencies of speech upon which word recognition depends, so that the finished product sounds much like a mumble you might hear through a wall. One common problem with the electronically filtered technique is that some of the nonverbal vocal cues may be eliminated in the filtering process, creating an artificial stimulus. Another method that eliminates the continuity and rhythm of the speaking voice, but still maintains the affective tone and emotional information, is randomized splicing.[31] With this method, the voice is recorded on tape, cut into short segments, and pasted back together in random order to mask the speech content.

We previously noted the merit of the answer "maybe" to a question concerning our ability to judge emotional expression from vocal cues. One reason for this qualified answer involves the differing methods by which such observations may be made. Other reasons for equivocation include:

(1) Speakers vary in their ability to produce expressed emotion. Several studies show distinct differences in perceived accuracy between speakers as a result. In the Davitz and Davitz study, one speaker's expressions were correctly identified only 23 percent of the time

whereas another speaker communicated accurately well over 50 percent of the time.[32] Some researchers who studied speakers from vastly different socioeconomic levels suggest that there are differences in the "affective tone" of these speakers. It is clear that there are distinct differences in encoding behavior for emotional expressions, but we know very little about this phenomenon from empirical studies conducted so far.

(2) We also know that listeners vary in their ability to perceive emotional expressions. In the Davitz and Davitz study, listeners ranged from 20 percent correct to over 50 percent correct. Again we have limited information on the correlates of listener sensitivity to vocal cues. The best available information suggests the following: (a) Listeners who are sensitive to emotions expressed vocally by others are also likely to be able to express emotions accurately to others and to identify their own vocal expressions of feelings accurately; (b) listeners who are able to accurately express emotions vocally are likely to be able to accurately express emotions facially as well; (c) sensitive listeners must be able to make auditory discriminations; (d) sensitive listeners must have some abstract symbolic ability; (e) listeners who are sensitive to feelings expressed vocally must have a knowledge of vocal characteristics of emotional expressions; (f) sensitive listeners should score well on tests of verbal intelligence; (g) general intellectual ability is a valuable asset for listeners who are sensitive to vocal cues, but a high IQ is not a guarantee of emotional sensitivity; and (h) sensitive listeners must have had exposure to a wide range of emotional expressions carried by the voice.[33] Some researchers talk about a "general factor" of sensitivity that influences a wide range of behaviors involved in nonverbal emotional communication, but most agree that it only accounts for a small part of the total sensitivity to any one feature—like the voice. Snyder finds that some people are more conscious of, and have more control over, their expressive behavior. He calls this process "self-monitoring." Extensive testing brought Snyder to the conclusion that people who are high in self-monitoring behavior are better able to intentionally express emotions in both vocal and facial channels. There also seems to be a tendency for high self-monitors to be better judges of the expressed emotions of others.[34]

(3) Several studies show vast differences in the accuracy of judging emotional vocal expressions—depending on the emotions being tested. One study found that anger was identified 63 percent of the time whereas pride was only identified correctly 20 percent of the time. Another study found that joy and hate were easily recognized, but shame and love were the most difficult to recognize. The similarity of some feelings may account for some of the difference. Certain errors are consistent in some studies; for example, fear is mistaken for nervousness, love is mistaken for sadness, and pride is mistaken for satisfaction. Some have suggested that when two subjectively similar feelings are sought

to be communicated, the "stronger" of the two is perceived more accurately and more often. Another possible explanation is that we have not been socially trained to deal with the finer discriminations involved in two "similar" emotions. General semanticists frequently remind us of our tendency to communicate in polar extremes like black-white, hot-cold, good-bad, and the like. Perhaps such verbal behavior has influenced the way we perceive nonverbal emotional expression. It is also possible that as we develop, we rely on context to discriminate emotions with similar characteristics. Thus, when confronted with such cues and no context, we find discrimination difficult.

(4) Finally, we must consider that the context of everyday communication will not duplicate the often well-controlled environment in the laboratory. Your ability to identify a given emotion expressed vocally will be influenced by the context (conversational and/or environmental), how well you know the other person, supplementary cues given through other channels (visual), and so on.

If one of the necessary requirements for developing sensitivity to emotional vocal expressions is knowledge of the vocal characteristics of emotional expression, it would seem worthwhile to outline these characteristics. Unfortunately, the development of such a dictionary of emotions—defined by nonverbal vocal characteristics—is extremely difficult. The same emotion may be expressed differently by different people at different times. Several isolated studies do provide some information on the vocal characteristics associated with various vocalized emotional states, but few generalizations can be made from these studies. Rather than report these isolated findings, we have reproduced the scoring table (Table 10.2) developed by Davitz that represents, as well as anything, a composite statement of vocal cues associated with various emotional expressions.[35] The table was developed to test subjects on their knowledge of vocal characteristics.

This table should not be interpreted as a summary of research or as "fact." It simply represents one way of devising the Emotion-Vocal Cue Dictionary. Any shortcomings you find in Table 10.2, and any exceptions you find, only serve to demonstrate the difficulty in developing such a compendium.

In addition to its role in personality and emotional judgments, the voice also seems to play a part in retention and attitude change, which has been primarily studied in the public speaking situation.

VOCAL CUES, COMPREHENSION, AND PERSUASION

Typical prescriptions for use of the voice in delivering a public speech include (1) Use variety in volume, rate, pitch, and articulation. The probabilities of desirable outcomes are less when one uses a constant rate,

TABLE 10.2
Characteristics of Vocal Expressions Contained in the Test of Emotional Sensitivity

FEELING	LOUDNESS	PITCH	TIMBRE	RATE	INFLECTION	RHYTHM	ENUNCIATION
Affection	Soft	Low	Resonant	Slow	Steady and slight upward	Regular	Slurred
Anger	Loud	High	Blaring	Fast	Irregular up and down	Irregular	Clipped
Boredom	Moderate to low	Moderate to low	Moderately resonant	Moderately slow	Monotone or gradually falling	—	Somewhat slurred
Cheerfulness	Moderately high	Moderately high	Moderately blaring	Moderately fast	Up and down; overall upward	Regular	
Impatience	Normal	Normal to moderately high	Moderately blaring	Moderately fast	Slight upward	—	Somewhat clipped
Joy	Loud	High	Moderately blaring	Fast	Upward	Regular	
Sadness	Soft	Low	Resonant	Slow	Downward	Irregular pauses	Slurred
Satisfaction	Normal	Normal	Somewhat resonant	Normal	Slight upward	Regular	Somewhat slurred

From *The Communication of Emotional Feeling* by J. R. Davitz. Copyright © 1964 by J. R. Davitz. Used with permission of McGraw-Hill Book Company.

volume, pitch, and articulation. Being constantly overprecise may be as ineffective as being overly sloppy in your articulation. Although it has not been formally studied, when vocal variety is perceived as rhythmic or patterned, it may no longer be variety and this decreases the probabilities of desirable outcomes. (2) Decisions concerning loud-soft, fast-slow, precise-sloppy, or high-low should be based on what is appropriate for a given audience in a given situation. (3) Excessive nonfluencies are to be avoided. How are these prescriptions reflected in the research on vocal cues?

Vocal Cues, Comprehension, and Retention.   Several studies tend to support the prescriptions for vocal variety in increasing audience comprehension or retention. Woolbert, in perhaps the earliest study of this type, found that large variations of rate, force, pitch, and quality produced high audience retention when compared with a no-variation condition.[36] Glasgow, using prose and poetry, established two conditions for study: "good intonation" and "monopitch."[37] Multiple-choice tests, following exposure to these differing vocal samples, showed that monopitch decreased comprehension by more than 10 percent for both prose and poetry. Diehl, White, and Satz, using similar methods, however, found that several ways of varying pitch did not significantly affect comprehension scores.[38] Other research data suggests that moderately poor vocal quality, pitch patterns, nonfluencies,[39] mispronunciation,[40] and even stuttering[41] to not interfere significantly with comprehension although listeners generally find these conditions unpleasant. Diehl and McDonald found that simulated breathy and nasal voice qualities significantly interfered with comprehension, but that simulated harsh and hoarse voice qualities did not appear to have a very negative effect.[42] All of these studies indicate that listeners are rather adaptable; it probably takes constant and extreme vocal unpleasantnesses to affect comprehension—and even then, the listener may adapt to the extent that he or she retains important information being communicated. Poor vocal qualities probably contribute more to a listener's perception of the speaker's personality or mood than to a decrease in comprehension.

The study of speaking rate only yields additional evidence of listener flexibility and lack of impact on comprehension of seemingly "poor" voice-related phenomena. The normal speaking rate is between 125 and 190 words per minute. Some believe that comprehension begins to decrease once the rate exceeds 200 words per minute, but experts in speeded speech place the level of significant decline in comprehension at between 275 and 300 words per minute. Obviously, there are wide differences in individual ability to process information at rapid rates. The inescapable conclusion from studies of speech rate, however, is that we can comprehend information at much more rapid rates than we ordinarily have to cope with. In an experiment in which individual listeners were allowed to vary the rates of presentation at will, the average choice was one and one-half times normal speed.[43]

Vocal Cues and Persuasion. It is clear we can communicate various attitudes with our voice alone—for example, friendliness, hostility, superiority, and submissiveness. What contribution, if any, then do vocal cues make toward changing people's attitudes? We know that we can sometimes be persuaded by ordinarily positive words spoken in negative tones—for example, disliking someone who calls you "honey" in a nasty voice.

Mehrabian and Williams conducted a series of studies on the nonverbal correlates of intended and perceived persuasiveness.[44] Extracting only findings on vocal cues, the following seem to be associated with both "increasing intent to persuade and decoded as enhancing the persuasiveness of a communication": more intonation, more speech volume, higher speech rate, and less halting speech. One might think that frequent nonfluencies would work against attitude change, but this does not seem to be the case. In a speech characterized by 0, 50, 75, 100, and 125 nonfluencies of five types ("ah," sentence change, repetition, tongue slip, and stutter), Sereno and Hawkins found no significant differences in audience attitude changes after exposure to the various versions of the speech.[45]

Considerable evidence from the persuasion literature suggests that a speaker's perceived credibility may profoundly affect his or her persuasive impact. Some studies show that communicators with "good delivery" are consistently observed to have higher credibility at the end of the speech than those with poor delivery. Therefore, it is not surprising to find Pearce asking whether vocal cues alone affect judgments of credibility—and hence, potential for achieving audience attitude change.[46] Pearce developed a speech arguing that marijuana is pleasant, useful, and not harmful and had it recorded by a professionally experienced actor using two different styles of delivery. One type of delivery epitomized a "scholarly, dispassionate, yet very involved person, serious about his subject." This version had a smaller range of inflections, greater consistency of rate and pitch, less volume, and generally lower pitch than the second version. The second type of delivery epitomized a "person who was passionately involved in his subject, unalterably committed to his position, and highly emotional." This version had more pauses, used primarily the upper portion of the speaker's pitch range, and had more variations in volume than the first type. Pearce says that neither type of delivery was what he would call extreme. Each represented good, but different delivery techniques used by spokesmen in society. The tapes were electronically filtered to eliminate the influence of the speaker's words and were used as vocal stimuli for three studies. The results of these studies indicate that the vocal cues affected judgments about trustworthiness, dynamism, and likeableness, but not competence. Furthermore, the conversational style elicited higher ratings on several socioeconomic characteristics and honesty, and was perceived as more person-oriented than the dynamic-vocalic delivery style. Although no evidence from this study suggests that style of delivery had a direct effect on the effectiveness of the message in changing audience attitudes toward the topic, a later study did show that initial credibility (induced through an introduction) and vocal cues did affect the message's persuasive impact.[47] Although many studies do show dramatic effects of speaker credibility in creating attitude change, high credibility will not necessarily ensure a corresponding attitude change.

The previously mentioned Sereno and Hawkins study, which found that large numbers of nonfluencies did not seem to affect audience attitude change, also seems to show that increasing numbers of nonfluencies do have an impact on ratings of speaker credibility. As nonfluencies increase, ratings for a speaker's competence and dynamism decrease, but not ratings on trustworthiness. This finding was confirmed by Miller and Hewgill.[48] Another study found that speech rate seemed to function as a general cue that augmented credibility ratings, and that rapid speech was more likely to enhance persuasion or attitude change than slower speech.[49]

At this point you may legitimately ask, "So what?" What if we know the voice's potential for eliciting various responses related to comprehension, attitude change, and speaker credibility? In real-life situations, there will be visual cues, prior publicity and experiences with the speaker, verbal cues, and a multitude of other interacting factors that will greatly reduce the importance of vocal cues. In short, vocal cues do not operate in an isolated fashion in human interaction as they do in the experiments reported in this section. Vocal cues do not operate alone, but we do not know what their role is in context—they may even be more influential. As was pointed out earlier, a book which focuses only on nonverbal communication distorts reality by not integrating the role of verbal and nonverbal cues. The study of vocal cues also distorts reality. However, in this case, it is necessary to divide the process and study the component parts to understand them better—so that when we develop methods for studying more complex phenomena, we will know a little more about the nature of the parts we are putting together.

VOCAL CUES AND TURN-TAKING IN CONVERSATIONS

Thus far we have talked about the role of vocal cues in communicating interpersonal attitudes, emotions, and information about oneself. Vocal cues also play an important role in managing the interaction. Vocal cues are part of a system of cues that help us structure our interactions—that is, who speaks, when, to whom, and for how long. Turn-taking, or "floor apportionment," rules may have as much to do with how a conversation "comes off" or is perceived as the actual verbal content of the interaction.[50] Most of us can recall instances when turn-taking rules played a significant role in our responses—for example, when a long-winded speaker wouldn't let you get a word in edgewise, when a passive respondent refused to "take the conversational ball" that you offered, when you were confronted with an "interrupter," or those awkward moments when two people were talking simultaneously. Vocal cues compose only some of the signals we use to manage our turn-taking; these other cues were discussed in previous chapters. We do know that we only rarely explicitly verbalize this information—for example, "OK, Lillian, I'm finished talking. Now it's your turn to talk." Vocal signals may be a part of the following management behaviors:

Turn-Yielding. To "yield" a turn means to signal that you are finished and the other person can start talking. Sometimes we do this by asking a question—causing the pitch of our voice to rise at the end of our comment. Another unwritten rule by which most of us operate is that questions require (or demand) answers. We can also drop our pitch (sometimes with a drawl on the last syllable) as we do when we finish a declarative statement that concludes our monologue. If the cues are not sufficient for the other person to start talking, we may have to add a "trailer" on the end. The "trailer" may be just silence or it may take the form of a filled pause—for example, "ya know," "so, ah," or "or something" to reiterate the fact that you are yielding, and to fill a silence that might otherwise indicate the other's insensitivity to your signals (or your own inability to make them clear).

Turn-Requesting. We can also show others that we want to say something through the use of some vocal cues. Although an audible inspiration of breath may not be a sufficient cue by itself, it does help to signal turn-requesting. The mere act of interrupting or simultaneous talking (without a knowledge of the verbal content) may signal an impatience to get the speaking turn. Sometimes you can inject vocalizations during normal pausing of the other speaker. These "stutter starts" may be the beginning of a sentence ("I . . . I . . . I . . .") or they may just be vocal buffers (Ah . . . Er . . . Ah . . ."). Another method used to request a turn is to assist the other person in finishing quickly. This can be done by increasing the rapidity of one's responses—much like the increased rapidity of the head nods when people are anxious to leave a situation in which the other person has the floor. These "back-channel" cues are vocalizations like "Uh-huh," "Yeah," and "Mm-hmm," but the message from the rapid use of these cues is "Get finished so I can talk."

Turn-Maintaining. Sometimes we want to keep the floor to show our status or to avoid unpleasant feedback, or perhaps because of some exaggerated sense of importance attached to our own words and ideas. Common vocal cues in these instances may include: (1) increasing volume and rate when turn-requesting cues are sensed, (2) increasing the frequency of filled pauses, and (3) decreasing the frequency and duration of silent pauses. Although Lalljee's and Cook's research does not support the use of pauses for control,[51] Rochester cites several studies that give support to the following: (1) More filled pauses and fewer silent pauses are found more often in dialogue and in monologue, (2) more filled pauses and fewer silent pauses are not found when people want to break off speaking, and (3) more filled pauses and fewer silent pauses are more likely when the speaker lacks visual means of controlling the conversation.[52]

Turn-Denying. There may also be instances when we want the other person to keep talking—to deny the turn when it is offered to us. The back-channel cues noted previously may serve to keep the other person talking by giving reinforcement for what is being said. The rate with which these cues are delivered, however, is probably slower than when we are requesting a turn. And just remaining silent may dramatically communicate a turn denial. Silence and pauses are the subjects of our next section.

HESITATIONS AND PAUSES

Spontaneous speech is actually highly fragmented and dicontinuous. Goldman-Eisler says that even when speech is at its most fluent, two thirds of spoken language comes in chunks of less than six words—strongly suggesting that the concept of fluency in spontaneous speech is an illusion.[53] Pauses between speech range in length from milliseconds to minutes, and seem to be subject to considerable variation based on individual differences, the kind of verbal task, the amount of spontaneity, and the pressures of the particular social situation. Pauses are not evenly distributed throughout the speech stream.

Analysis of spontaneous speech shows that only 55 percent of the pauses occur at grammatical junctures, whereas oral readers of prepared texts are highly consistent in pausing at clause and sentence junctures.

Types of Pauses. The two major types of pauses are the unfilled pause (silent) and the filled pause. A filled pause is simply filled with some type of phonation such as "um," "uh," stutters, false starts, repetitions, and slips of the tongue. A variety of sources associate filled pauses with a range of generally undesirable characteristics. Some people associate filled pauses and repetitions with emotional arousal and others feel that filled pauses may reduce anxiety, but jam cognitive processes. Goldman-Eisler found, in four studies, that unfilled pausing time was associated with "superior (more concise) stylistic and less probable linguistic for-mulations," whereas higher rates of filled pauses were linked to "infe-rior stylistic achievement (long-winded statement) of greater predicta-bility."[54] Livant found that the time required to solve addition problems was significantly greater when the subject filled pauses than when he or she was silent.[55] Several experimenters reached similar conclusions—that when speakers fill pauses they also impair their performance. Thus, in a heated discussion you may maintain control of the conversation by filling the pauses, but you may also decrease the quality of your contri-bution. Too many filled or too many unfilled pauses may receive nega-tive evaluations from listeners. Lalljee found that too many unfilled pauses by the speaker caused listeners to perceive the speaker as anx-ious, angry, or contemptuous; and that too many filled pauses evoked perceptions of the speaker as anxious or bored.[56] Specialized receivers (like counselors) may have different reactions. For example, variations in filled and unfilled pauses did not affect counselors' perceptions of a patient's genuineness or anxiety, but unfilled (three to seven seconds) pauses seemed to make the counselor think that the ensuing message was revealing more about the person.[57]

Reasons Why Pauses Occur.   During the course of spontaneous speech, we are confronted with situations that require decisions as to what to say and what lexical or structural form to put our speech in. One school of thought relates hesitancy in speech to the uncertainty of predicting the cognitive and lexical activity while speaking. The speaker may be reflecting on decisions about the immediate message or may even be projecting into the past or future—that is, "I don't think she understood what I said earlier" or "If she says no, what do I say then?" Working on the assumption that these hesitation pauses were actually delays that resulted from processes taking place in the brain whenever speech ceased to be the automatic vocalization of learned sequences, Goldman-Eisler conducted an experiment designed to "make thought construction an indispensable and controlled part of the speaking process." Subjects were presented with cartoons and were given tasks of describing and interpreting. It was found that pause time while "interpreting" was twice as long as while "describing." It was also observed that with each succeeding trial (a reduction in spontaneity), there was a decline in pausing. Another possible explanation for some pausing behavior in-volves what is described as disruption behavior. Instead of representing time for planning, the pause may indicate a disruption caused by an emotional state that may have developed from negative feedback or time pressures. These disruptions may take many forms; fears about the sub-ject matter under discussion, desire to impress the listener with one's verbal and/or intellectual skills, pressure to perform other tasks simul-taneously, pressure to produce verbal output immediately, and so on.

Further study of pauses and breathing suggests that the cognitive and lexical decision processes are also regulators of the incidence of breathing during speech. While reading passages of prose aloud, speakers took breaths exclusively at the gaps occasioned by grammatical junctures. During spontaneous speech, approximately one third of the breaths were taken at gaps that were in the nongrammatical category. The frequency and length of pauses may also be the result of certain predispositions to certain listeners, adaptations to certain audience situations, the number of potential speakers, and one's desire to speak.

Silence.   Most of the hesitations and pauses that have been discussed are of relatively short duration. Sometimes silence may be extended. Silences may be imposed by the nature of the environment—for example, in churches, libraries, courtrooms, or hospitals; they may be imposed for the duration of a given event—for example at a funeral, during the playing of taps, when praying, or when singing the national anthem; or they may be self-imposed—remaining quiet in the woods to hear other sounds or enjoying with a lover the mutual closeness that silence may bring. Silence can mean virtually anything—anything that can be said verbally at least. Silence is charged with those words that have just been exchanged; words that have been exchanged in the past; words that have not or will not be said, but that are fantasized; and words that may actually be said in the future. For this reason it would be absurd to provide a list of meanings for silence. The meaning of silence, like the meaning of words, can only be deduced after careful analysis of the communicators, subject matter, time, place, culture, and the like.

Some of the many interpersonal functions served by silence[58] include: (1) punctuation or accenting—drawing attention to certain words or ideas; (2) evaluating—providing judgments of another's behavior, showing favor or disfavor, showing agreement or disagreement, or attacking (for example, not responding to a comment, greeting, or letter); (3) revelation—making something known or hiding something by being silent; (4) expression of emotions—the silence of disgust, sadness, fear, anger, or love; (5) mental activity—showing thoughtfulness and reflection or ignorance through silence.

SUMMARY

Generally, this chapter should have left you with the overall impression that vocal cues frequently play a major role in determining responses in human communication situations. You should be quick to challenge the cliché that vocal cues only concern how something is said—frequently they *are* what is said. What is said might be an attitude ("I like you" or "I'm superior to you"), it might be an emotion, it might be the coordination and management of the conversation, or it might be the presentation of some aspect of your personality, background, or physical features. Vocal cues will, depending on the situation and the communicators, carry a great deal of information in some message classes and perhaps little in others.

As a communicator and observer, you should also recognize the important role vocal stereotypes play in determining responses. Whether judges are trying to estimate your occupation, sociability, race, degree of introversion, body type, or any of various other qualities about you, they will be very apt to respond to well-learned stereotypes. These stereotypes may not accurately describe you, but they will be influential in the interaction that takes place between you and the judge. Almost all the research reviewed in this chapter demonstrated considerable agreement among judges. So far it is difficult to identify any personality trait that seems to be judged with consistent accuracy, which is partly the result of the imperfect nature of the personality measures. Moreover, a particular person, judging a particular voice, may be very accurate in judging the personality behind that voice. Our judgments of large groups of people are also influential in our judgments of a single person's vocal personality. Although it is not uncommon for you to perceive negatively a person speaking a dialect other than your own, speakers who try to correct for speech differences and severely violate expectations for their speech may also be perceived negatively. There is considerable support for the idea that a voice may evoke an ethnic stereotype that will then overlay one's perceptions of an individual's voice; however, one study suggests that we may also react to vocal aspects of the dialect itself which we either like or dislike.

Accurate judgments (beyond chance) of age, sex, and status from vocal cues alone are fairly consistently reported in the literature. Furthermore, we seem to be able to identify specific speakers from their voice alone, but recently greater attention has been given to spectrographic and electronic means of speaker identification.

Although studies of judgments of emotions from vocal cues have used different methods, different emotions, listeners with differing sensitivities, and speakers with differing abilities for portraying the emotions, the results of the studies have been remarkably consistent. We can make highly accurate judgments of emotions and feelings from wordless vocal messages, although we should consistently remind ourselves that any given individual may vocally express the same emotion differently on different days, in different situations, and with different provoking stimuli.

There is some indication that moderately poor vocal behaviors do not interfere with a listener's comprehension of a message, and that if we use variety in the volume, pitch, and rate of our speech we may increase our chances of achieving audience comprehension. Unchanging, constant vocal behavior (particularly at the extremes) may be less advantageous in achieving audience comprehension.

Preliminary findings suggest that the voice may also be important in some aspects of persuasion. Nonfluencies do not seem to affect attitude change, but more intonation, higher rate, more volume, and less halting speech seem related to intent to persuade and perceived persuasiveness. The credibility of the speaker plays an important role in persuasion in some situations, and some decisions concerning credibility (trustworthiness, dynamism, likeableness, and competency) are made from word-free samples of the voice alone. Increasing nonfluencies also tend to impair credibility.

Vocal cues also help us manage the give-and-take of speaking turns. In turn-yielding, turn-requesting, turn-maintaining, and turn-denying we can use vocal cues to make our intensions clear.

Hesitations or pauses also play an important role in spontaneous speech. Such pauses, ordinarily between one and two seconds long, may be greatly influenced by the other interactant, the topic being discussed, and the nature of the social situation. Several reports suggest that "impaired performance" in a number of areas may result from an excessive use of filled pauses. Pauses may be the overt manifestation of time used to make decisions about what to say and how to say it, or they may represent disruptions in the speech process.

Taken together, these findings show that vocal cues alone can give much information about a speaker and that our total reaction to another individual is at least somewhat colored by our reactions to these vocal cues. Our perceptions of vocal cues combine with other verbal and nonverbal stimuli to mold conceptions used as a basis for communicating. Perhaps future study will provide some information on how our responses to our own voices affect our self-images and hence, our communication behavior. First, however, we must give more attention to voices manifested in naturalistic interaction—particularly with partners other than strangers. Some of these results may need modification as we look at spontaneous speech at different stages in relationships.

NOTES

1. *Newsweek*, October 5, 1970, p. 106.
2. M. H. L. Hecker, "Speaker Recognition: An Interpretive Survey of the Literature," *ASHA Monographs*, Number 16 (Washington: American Speech and Hearing Association, 1971).
3. F. McGehee, "The Reliability of the Identification of the Human Voice," *Journal of General Psychology* 17 (1937): 249–271.
4. P. Ladefoged and R. Vanderslice, "The Voiceprint Mystique," *Working Papers in Phonetics*, 7, November 1967, University of California, Los Angeles.
5. A. R. Reich, K. L. Moll, and J. F. Curtis, "Effects of Selected Vocal Dis-

guises upon Spectrographic Speaker Identification," *Journal of the Acoustical Society of America* 60 (1976): 919–925.

6. E. Kramer, "Personality Stereotypes in Voice: A Reconsideration of the Data," *Journal of Social Psychology* 62 (1964): 247–251.

7. D. W. Addington, "The Relationship of Selected Vocal Characteristics to Personality Perception," *Speech Monographs* 35 (1968): 492–503.

8. F. E. Aboud, R. Clement, and D. M. Taylor, "Evaluational Reactions to Discrepancies Between Social Class and Language," *Sociometry* 37 (1974): 239–250.

9. A Bradford, D. Ferror, and G. Bradford, "Evaluation Reactions of College Students to Dialect Differences in the English of Mexican-Americans," *Language and Speech* 17 (1974): 255–270. A. Mulac, T. D. Hanley, and D. Y. Prigge, "Effects of Phonological Speech Foreignness upon Three Dimensions of Attitude of Selected American Listeners," *Quarterly Journal of Speech* 60 (1974): 411–420; F. Williams and G. W. Shamo, "Regional Variations in Teacher Attitudes Toward Children's Language," *Central States Speech Journal* 23 (1972): 73–77; F. Williams, "The Psychological Correlates of Speech Characteristics: On Sounding 'Disadvantaged,'" *Journal of Speech and Hearing Research* 13 (1970): 472–488; J. Buck, "The Effects of Negro and White Dialectical Variations upon Attitudes of College Students," *Speech Monographs* 35 (1968): 181–186.

10. W. Wilke and J. Snyder, "Attitudes Toward American Dialects," *Journal of Social Psychology* 14 (1941): 349–362.

11. D. T. Miller, "The Effect of Dialect and Ethnicity on Communicator Effectiveness," *Speech Monographs* 42 (1975): 69–74.

12. T. H. Pear, *Voice and Personality* (London: Chapman and Hall, 1931).

13. G. P. Nerbonne, "The Identification of Speaker Characteristics on the Basis of Aural Cues" (Ph.D. diss., Michigan State University, 1967).

14. H. Giles and R. Y. Bourhis, "Voice and Racial Categorization in Britian," *Communication Monographs* 43 (1976): 108–114. Some of the vocal features to which judges may respond or look for in making such identifications can be found in F. S. Dubner, "Nonverbal Aspects of Black English," *Southern Speech Communication Journal* 37 (1972): 361–374.

15. S. Weitz, "Attitude, Voice, and Behavior: A Repressed Affect Model of Interracial Interaction," *Journal of Personality and Social Psychology* 24 (1972): 14–21.

16. N. J. Lass, K. R. Hughes, M. D. Bowyer, L. T. Waters, and V. T. Broune, "Speaker Sex Identification from Voiced, Whispered and Filtered Isolated Vowels," *Journal of the Acoustical Society of America* 59 (1976): 675–678.

17. N. N. Markel, L. D. Prebor, and J. F. Brandt, "Biosocial Factors in Dyadic Communication: Sex and Speaking Intensity," *Journal of Personality and Social Psychology* 23 (1972): 11–13.

18. J. Sachs, P. Lieberman, and D. Erickson, "Anatomical and Cultural Determinants of Male and Female Speech," in R. W. Shuy and R. W. Fasold (eds.), *Language Attitudes: Current Trends and Prospects* (Washington, D.C.: Georgetown University Press, 1973), pp. 74–84.

19. L. J. Lass and M. Davis, "An Investigation of Speaker Height and Weight Identification," *Journal of the Acoustical Society of America* 60 (1976): 700–707.

20. N. J. Lass and L. A. Harvey, "An Investigation of Speaker Photograph

Identification," *Journal of the Acoustical Society of America* 59 (1976): 1232–1236.

21. P. Fay and W. Middleton, "Judgments of Kretschmerian Body Types from the Voice as Transmitted over a Public Address System," *Journal of Social Psychology* 12 (1940): 151–162.

22. P. Fay and W. Middleton, "Judgment of Occupation from the Voice as Transmitted over a Public Address System," *Sociometry* 3 (1940): 186–191.

23. P. B. Davis, "An Investigation of the Suggestion of Age Through Voice in Interpretative Reading" (M.A. thesis, University of Denver, 1949), p. 69.

24. E. D. Mysak, "Pitch and Duration Characteristics of Older Males," *Journal of Speech and Hearing Research* 2 (1959): 46–54.

25. R. E. McClone and H. Hollien, "Vocal Pitch Characteristics of Aged Women," *Journal of Speech and Hearing Research* 6 (1963): 164–170.

26. L. S. Harms, "Listener Judgments of Status Cues in Speech," *Quarterly Journal of Speech* 47 (1961): 164–168. This study was replicated with similar results in J. D. Moe, "Listener Judgments of Status Cues in Speech: A Replication and Extension," *Speech Monographs* 39 (1972): 144–147.

27. D. S. Ellis, "Speech and Social Status in America," *Social Forces* 45 (1967): 431–451.

28. J. McGinniss, *The Selling of the President 1968* (New York: Trident Press, 1969), p. 155.

29. J. A. Starkweather, "Vocal Communication of Personality and Human Feelings," *Journal of Communication* 11 (1961): 69.

30. J. R. Davitz. *The Communication of Emotional Meaning* (New York: McGraw-Hil, 1964), p. 23.

31. K. R. Scherer, "Randomized Splicing: A Note on a Simple Technique for Masking Speech Content," *Journal of Experimental Research in Personality* 5 (1971): 155–159. Also see K. P. Scherer, J. Koivumaki, and R. Rosenthal, "Minimal Cues in the Vocal Communication of Affect: Judging Emotions from Content-Masked Speech," *Journal of Psycholinguistic Research* 1 (1972): 269–285.

32. J. R. Davitz, and L. Davitz, "The Communication of Feelings by Content-Free Speech," *Journal of Communication* 9 (1959): 6–13.

33. Davitz, *The Communication of Emotional Meaning.*

34. M. Snyder, "Self-Monitoring of Expressive Behavior," *Journal of Personality and Social Psychology* 30 (1974): 526–537.

35. Davitz, *The Communication of Emotional Meaning,* p. 63.

36. C. Woolbert, "The Effects of Various Modes of Public Reading," *Journal of Applied Psychology* 4 (1920): 162–185.

37. G. M. Glasgow, "A Semantic Index of Vocal Pitch," *Speech Monographs* 19 (1952): 64–68.

38. C. F. Diehl, R. C. White, and P. H. Satz, "Pitch Change and Comprehension," *Speech Monographs,* 28 (1961): 65–68.

39. V. A. Utzinger, "An Experimental Study of the Effects of Verbal Fluency upon the Listener" (Ph.D. diss., University of Southern California, 1952). Utzinger found that varying degrees of fluency ranging from four to sixty-four breaks in two minutes did not affect recall.

40. R. J. Kibler and L. L. Barker, "Effects of Selected Levels of Misspelling

and Mispronunciation on Comprehension and Retention," *Southern Speech Communication Journal* 37 (1972): 361–374.

41. H. N. Klinger, "The Effects of Stuttering on Audience Listening Comprehension" (Ph.D. diss., New York University, 1959).

42. C. F. Diehl and E. T. McDonald, "Effect of Voice Quality on Communication," *Journal of Speech and Hearing Disorders* 31 (1956): 233–237.

43. D. B. Orr, "Time Compressed Speech—A Perspective," *Journal of Communication* 18 (1968): 288–292.

44. A. Mehrabian and M. Williams, "Nonverbal Concomitants of Perceived and Intended Persuasiveness," *Journal of Personality and Social Psychology* 13 (1969): 37–58.

45. K. K. Sereno and G. J. Hawkins, "The Effect of Variations in Speakers' Nonfluency upon Audience Ratings of Attitude Toward the Speech Topic and Speakers' Credibility," *Speech Monographs* 34 (1967): 58–64.

46. W. B. Pearce and F. Conklin, "Nonverbal Vocalic Communication and Perceptions of a Speaker," *Speech Monographs* 38 (1971): 235–241. Also see W. B. Pearce, "The Effect of Vocal Cues on Credibility and Attitude Change," *Western Speech* 35 (1971): 176–184.

47. W. B. Pearce and B. J. Brommel, "Vocalic Communication in Persuasion," *Quarterly Journal of Speech* 58 (1972): 298–306.

48. G. R. Miller and M. A. Hewgill, "The Effect of Variations in Nonfluency on Audience Ratings of Source Credibility," *Quarterly Journal of Speech* 50 (1964): 36–44.

49. N. Miller, G. Maruyama, R. J. Beaber, and K. Valone, "Speed of Speech and Persuasion," *Journal of Personality and Social Psychology* 34 (1976): 615–624.

50. J. M. Wiemann and M. L. Knapp, "Turn-Taking in Conversations," *Journal of Communication* 25 (1975): 75–92. Also see S. Duncan, Jr., "Toward a Grammar for Dyadic Conversation," *Semiotica* 9 (1973): 24–46.

51. M. G. Lalljee and M. Cook, "An Experimental Investigation of the Function of Filled Pauses in Speech," *Language and Speech* 12 (1969): 24–28.

52. S. R. Rochester, "The Significance of Pauses in Spontaneous Speech," *Journal of Psycholinguistic Research* 2 (1973): 51–81.

53. F. Goldman-Eisler, *Psycholinguistics: Experiments in Spontaneous Speech* (London and New York: Academic Press, 1968).

54. F. Goldman-Eisler, "A Comparative Study of Two Hesitation Phenomena," *Language and Speech* 4 (1961): 18–26.

55. W. P. Livant, "Antagonistic Functions of Verbal Pauses: Filled and Unfilled Pauses in the Solution of Additions," *Language and Speech* 6 (1963): 1–4.

56. M. C. Lalljee, "Disfluencies in Normal English Speech" (Ph.D. diss., Oxford University, 1971).

57. M. J. Fisher and R. A. Apostal, "Selected Vocal Cues and Counselors' Perceptions of Genuineness, Self-Disclosure, and Anxiety," *Journal of Counseling Psychology* 22 (1975): 92–96.

58. J. V. Jensen, "Communicative Functions of Silence," *ETC* 30 (1973): 249–257. Also see T. J. Bruneau, "Communicative Silences: Forms and Functions," *Journal of Communication* 23 (1973): 17–46.

ADDITIONAL READINGS

Giles, H. and P. F. Powesland. *Speech Style and Social Evaluation*. New York: Academic Press, 1975.

Kramer, E. "Judgment of Personal Characteristics and Emotions from Nonverbal Properties." *Psychological Bulletin* 60 (1963): 408–420.

———. "Personality Stereotypes in Voice: A Reconsideration of the Data." *Journal of Social Psychology* 62 (1964): 247–251.

Mahl, G. F. and G. Schulze. "Psychological Research in the Extralinguistic Area." In T. Sebeok, A. S. Hayes, and M. C. Bateson (eds.). *Approaches to Semiotics*. The Hague: Mouton, 1964.

Ostwald, P. F. *Soundmaking*. Springfield, Ill.: Charles C Thomas, 1963.

11

THE ABILITY TO SEND AND RECEIVE NONVERBAL SIGNALS

Americans are characteristically illiterate in the area of gesture language.   W. LA BARRE

As previously noted, the subject of nonverbal communication has received a great deal of attention in the last decade. Elementary, secondary, and college students are exposed to entire courses devoted to an understanding of nonverbal behavior, and adults can purchase any number of books and pamphlets at local newsstands that, with varying degrees of fidelity, introduce readers to this fascinating world without words. Thus, it is reasonable to assume that the Americans referred to in the La Barre quotation are not currently nonverbally "illiterate." However, as we look around, we readily note that some people seem to be more sensitive to nonverbal cues than others, and that some people seem more proficient at expressing their feelings and attitudes nonverbally. It is also clear that, as with verbal cues, the ability to send and receive those nonverbal cues accurately is essential for developing social competence—whether it be in the office, the courtroom, the barroom, or the bedroom, or whether we want to effectively bridge gaps in social class and/or culture. If we accept the premises that one's ability to communicate nonverbal message is important and that some people are more effective in doing so than others, we might legitimately inquire how these people became effective and if the same ability can be developed in others.

DEVELOPING THE NONVERBAL SKILLS

Most of the ability we have in sending and receiving nonverbal signals is derived from "on-the-job training," the job, in this case, referring to the process of daily living. In short, we learn (not always consciously) nonverbal skills by imitating and modeling ourselves after others and by adapting our responses to the coaching, feedback, and advice of others. This feedback is not necessarily "about" our behavior but often takes the form of a response to our behavior. Feedback, then, may refer to a person who says, "Well, you don't look happy" or, without making such a statement, your partner may just respond to you as a person who is not happy. Through feedback we increase our awareness of ourselves and others—for example, "Can't you see I don't like you!" We not only learn what behaviors to enact, but how they are performed, with whom, when, where, and with what consequences. Naturally, some of us have more and better "helpers" than others; some of us seek help more than others. You can practice nonverbal sending and receiving frequently, but without regular, accurate feedback, you may not improve your ability.

Ultimately, the development of your nonverbal skills will depend on the following: (1) *Motivation.* The more you desire to learn nonverbal skills, the greater is your chances of doing so. Often this motivation will develop when you feel that such skills will help improve the nature of your career or personal life. (2) *Attitude.* People enter learning situations with productive or unproductive attitudes—for example, "I can do this" versus "I can't do this," or "This will be fun" versus "This will be tedious." You may be highly motivated, but unproductive attitudes toward the learning situation will inevitably lessen the learning outcome. (3) *Knowledge.* The development or reinforcement of any skill is partly dependent on an understanding of the nature of that skill. We seem to unconsciously obtain a lot of nonverbal knowledge from watching others as we develop. Some of this knowledge is only known to ourselves when we hear or read about it from another source. This "consciousness-raising" may be an important ingredient in making future adaptations. (4) *Experience.* Skills cannot be learned in isolation. With the proper guidance and useful feedback, practice will assist you in developing nonverbal skills. The greater the variety of one's experiences, the greater are the opportunities for increased learning. Any given experience may provide useful information for future skill development even if you are ineffective in that particular situation.

With this overview of some common methods and some general prerequisites for nonverbal skill development, we now turn to another approach to the same issue. This approach seeks to understand the characteristics of people who are effective or ineffective senders and receivers of nonverbal signals. Most of the research that is relevant to nonverbal skills has been conducted within this framework.

PROFILES OF NONVERBAL SENDERS AND RECEIVERS

A variety of methods may be used to test a person's nonverbal abilities. For encoding or sending ability, the person is usually asked to record a sentence or series of letters while expressing different emotional/attitudinal states. For facial encoding, the person is asked to facially express a series of emotional and/or attitudinal states. Buck shows a series of "emotionally loaded" color slides to his subjects that are categorized as scenic, sexual, maternal, unpleasant, and unusual.[1] The subjects' facial reactions to the slides can then be assessed. In this case, "senders" probably differ in the degree of conscious intent from senders who are asked to portray a particular expression. The issue of posed versus spontaneous behavior is discussed later in this chapter. Decoding or receiving ability is usually assessed by asking people to identify the emotional or attitudinal state expressed by another person—either "live" or on film, videotape, photograph, or audio recording. The social psychologist Robert Rosenthal and his associates have developed what is perhaps the most comprehensive method for testing nonverbal decoding ability, which Rosenthal calls the Profile of Nonverbal Sensitivity (PONS).[2] The PONS test is a forty-five-minute black and white sound film, which contains 220 numbered auditory and visual segments to which the viewers are asked to respond. Each segment is a two-second excerpt from a scene portrayed by a North American woman. There are five scenes that portray a positive-dominant affect or attitude—for example, "admiring a baby"; five scenes that portray positive-submissive behavior, such as "being interviewed for a job"; five scenes that portray negative-dominant behavior, such as "being angry at someone for making a mess"; and five scenes that portray negative-submissive behavior—for example, "showing someone that your feelings have been hurt." Each scene is presented to viewers in eleven different ways:

Face only
Body only (neck to knees)
Face plus body
Electronically filtered speech only*
Randomized splicing of speech only*
Face plus electronically filtered speech
Face plus randomized splicing of speech
Body plus electronically filtered speech
Body plus randomized splicing of speech
Face and body plus electronically filtered speech
Face and body plus randomized splicing of speech

A receiver or viewer obtains a score for particular channels and combinations of channels in addition to a total score. The test has been

---

*See Chapter 10 for descriptions of these techniques.

administered to several thousand people of different ages, occupations, and nationalities. For this reason, the results of the PONS test are used here as the primary basis for answering our questions about decoding abilities: (1) What are the characteristics of people who are skilled at receiving nonverbal signals? and (2) What factors affect the accuracy with which people receive nonverbal signals?

Characteristics of Skilled Nonverbal Receivers.　Perhaps the most consistent finding, from PONS and other research efforts, is that females tend to score higher than males at receiving nonverbal signals. This finding was found from females in grade school up through the middle twenties. Rosenthal examined forty-three independent studies of adults and children and found females to have an advantage in their ability to judge nonverbal cues in thirty-three of them. Although some studies showed no difference between male and female nonverbal receiving ability, rarely do males, as a group, score higher than females in these studies.

Studies of the effect of age generally show a gradually increasing skill at decoding nonverbal cues from kindergarten age until it levels off between the ages of twenty and thirty. Older age groups have not been tested. Independent studies of the ability to accurately decode vocal cues[3] and facial expressions[4] support the PONS results. Typically, younger children will score better on tests of vocal discrimination than on visual discrimination.

In two studies, the race of the receiver did not provide any particular advantage or disadvantage in accurately judging facial expressions.[5] The results from several groups of students who took the PONS test tend to refute the notion that intelligence or academic ability characterizes effective nonverbal receivers. Neither IQ, SAT (Scholastic Aptitude Test) scores, class rank, nor scores on vocabulary tests had much relationship to this nonverbal ability. Thus, you may do well in school, where most criteria for success are based on verbal ability, but this does not mean that you will also be able to accurately interpret nonverbal signals.

People who do well on the PONS test also seem to have the following personality profile: better adjusted, more interpersonally democratic and encouraging, less dogmatic, and more extroverted. In addition, skilled nonverbal receivers were judged more popular and interpersonally sensitive by others, such as by their acquaintances, clients, spouses, and supervisors. Snyder would probably include what he calls "self-monitoring" as a characteristic of accurate decoders of nonverbal information in both face and voice.[6] Self-monitors are sensitive to, and exert strong control over, their own behavior, but they are also sensitive to the behaviors of others—using these cues as guidelines for monitoring their own self-presentation.

Certain groups also tend to have better scores on the PONS decoding experience. In order, the top three groups tested so far include actors, students studying nonverbal behavior, and students studying visual arts. Buck's research on the interpretation of facial expressions found students who were fine arts majors and business majors to be better receivers than science majors—that is, students in biology, chemistry, math, and physics.[7] Business executives who took the PONS test did not seem to show the same expertise in receiving nonverbal signals that Buck's business majors did. Business executives and teachers showed significantly less ability than clinical psychologists and college students, who were significantly lower than the top three groups previously mentioned. It should be remembered that these are group scores. Individual teachers, supervisors, and clinicians who were rated excellent at their jobs did well on the PONS instrument. Finally, it seems that parents (particularly mothers) of preverbal children have more nonverbal receiving sensitivity than married nonparents.

The PONS test has also been administered to people from over twenty different nations. As might be expected, people from countries most similar to the United States in language and culture (modernization, widespread use of communications media) scored highest. Some of the scores from foreign nations were high enough, however, to suggest a multicultural component. In a related venture, word-free voice samples of Cree Indians and white, English-speaking Canadian residents were also judged along ethnic and cultural lines.[8] Each group was more accurate in perceiving the emotional content in the voice samples made by members of their own group. As stated in earlier chapters, some cultures use and pay more attention to certain types of nonverbal behavior and would naturally be expected to show more proficiency in those areas than a culture that deemphasized a particular behavior or channel of communication.

Although a vast amount of research suggests that similarity rather than dissimilarity is the key to selecting friends and romance partners, Rosenthal and his colleagues found what seems to be an interesting exception. Romantic partners were more similar on their PONS scores to randomly selected peers than they were to each other! And, the more dissimilarity in nonverbal sensitivity, the greater is the level of reciprocal verbal disclosures, suggesting that effectiveness in the verbal modality may be used to offset a lack of proficiency in the nonverbal mode. Some people argue that differences of this type are related to the dependency shown in the relationship, with the more dependent member showing more sensitivity because he or she has the most to gain. Although this finding is intriguing, we do not know how much of a difference will affect the relationship's stability. Most authors have predicted an increased reliance on nonverbal cues and an increased proficiency of reading them with a specific other person in a long-term, intimate relationship.[9]

There is also some indication that people can improve their scores in receiving ability on the PONS test with practice. One study suggests that physiological arousal may be advantageous for judging emotions in the faces of others.[10] Passive receivers, then, seem to be less effective than those who get actively involved in the task.

Like any skill, nonverbal decoding ability is affected by any number of factors, some of which reside within the characteristics of people that reveal differences between groups of people. Some of these factors reside within the person being judged or the situation in which the judging takes place. The following review considers only those factors that have been examined by researchers using PONS or other tests and does not pretend to detail all the potential sources of variations in one's accuracy in identifying nonverbal signals.

Factors Affecting Nonverbal Receiving Accuracy. You may think that the particular channels (face, voice, and the like) that are tested will make a difference in a person's nonverbal receiving accuracy. Indeed, several studies do show that emotions and attitudes of liking/disliking are more accurately perceived in the face than in the voice. And, although you may be better able to recognize many emotions and attitudes if you get both audio and visual cues, some messages may be more effectively communicated in one mode than in another—for example, vocal cues may be more effective for communicating anxiety and seductiveness than other individual communication channels.[11] Furthermore, if you are accurate in recognizing facial signals, you will probably also be accurate in perceiving vocal ones. This does not deny the possibility that some people may have a preference for, and rely more heavily, on a particular channel. Beldoch's work extended beyond the traditional facial/vocal dichotomy.[12] He obtained word-free tape recordings of twelve emotions, asked musicians to write and record short musical renditions of the same twelve emotions, and, finally, asked artists to create abstract art they felt captured the emotions under consideration. The results support the idea that one's ability to accurately decode feelings in one medium may carry over to other media. Similarly, accuracy in perceiving nonverbal signals may vary according to whether expressions are posed (usually higher) or spontaneous, but if you do well in decoding posed expressions, you'll probably do well in decoding the other,[13] as has been indicated in some preliminary work with a still-photo version of the original PONS. It is clear that some emotional and attitudinal states are more difficult to judge than others. Negative nonverbal messages, some argue, may even be more readily conveyed than positive ones. Guber says that if you (as a judge) have had prior experience in the expression-inducing situation, your accuracy will supersede those who have not had such experiences.[14] Thus, we find variations in accuracy attributed to the channel of communication and the type of message, but we also find several indications of individual consistency across conditions.

Although Eiland and Richardson found that differences in the sex, age, and race of the person expressing a facial emotion would significantly affect judgments of accuracy, this is not a consistent finding.[15]

We might also speculate, as did the PONS researchers, that the amount of time a receiver was exposed to a nonverbal signal would affect his or her accuracy in identification. The PONS materials were presented to people with the exposure time varied—for example, 1/24 of a second, 3/24 of a second, and so on. Although accuracy of judging nonverbal signals did increase as the exposure time increased, the differences in accuracy observed are probably minimal when the exposure times reach higher levels. Some people, it seems, achieve high levels of accuracy with minimal exposure time, and perceive and process this nonverbal information very quickly. It is even speculated that these persons may "see too much" and as a result have less satisfying interpersonal relationships.

We now turn to our next two questions, which relate to encoding or sending ability: (1) What are the characteristics of people who are skilled at sending nonverbal signals? and (2) What factors affect the accuracy with which people send nonverbal signals?

Characteristics of Skilled Nonverbal Senders. Although we do not have the wide-ranging results for encoding patterns that the PONS test gave us for decoding, some trends in sending or encoding nonverbal signals seem evident. For instance, females seem to manifest greater encoding skills than males.[16] This sex-related difference in sending ability has not been found with children between the ages of four and six years old.[17]

Some personality characteristics have also been associated with accurate senders of nonverbal information. Like receivers, high "self-monitors" are better able to send emotional information through facial and vocal channels.[18] "Internalizers" are poorer stimuli for others to judge than "externalizers."[19] Internalizers are people who tend to repress their emotional reactions—to "keep their feelings inside." Buck's personality profile for younger children shows many of the same characteristics we reviewed earlier for decoders.[20] Children who were effective senders were extroverted, outgoing, active, popular, and somewhat bossy and impulsive. Ineffective senders tended to play alone, were introverted, passive, shy, controlled, and rated as cooperative.

Two studies suggest that lower physiological arousal tends to be associated with more accurate nonverbal sending ability.[21]

Some studies have addressed the question of what factors will affect nonverbal sending ability, but like the studies of sender characteristics, these are few in number.

Factors Affecting Nonverbal Sending Ability. A study that obtained both spontaneous and posed expressions from the same people found that accuracy in sending transcends the question of intent.[22] That is, if a person's spontaneous facial expression to pleasant stimuli ("The Carol Burnett Show") and unpleasant stimuli (gory accident scene) was clearly expressed and interpreted, the same person would show skill in performing posed expressions. The type of message (positive/negative; dominant/submissive; type of emotion) will also affect one's accuracy in sending, with the more extreme emotional experiences often being more accurate.

We are now ready to address the final question for this chapter: Are skilled encoders also skilled decoders and vice versa?

The Relationship Between Sending and Receiving Skills.   As far back as 1945, Knower reported evidence that suggested that effective senders of facial and vocal expressions of emotions were also effective receivers.[23] Since then, several other studies have reported a similar conclusion. Levy, for instance, found a strong relationship between one's ability to send vocal emotional signals, to interpret vocal signals of others, and to interpret vocal signals of others, and to interpret his or her own vocal cues.[24] These researchers hypothesize a "general communication ability," which means that, although separate skills are involved in sending and receiving, a general ability seems to overlap these separate skills. In other words, effective senders are often effective receivers and vice versa.

Some researchers have found no relationship between sending and receiving ability with nonverbal signals. The study by Lanzetta and Kleck is frequently cited as support for this position because a negative relationship between sending and receiving ability was found—that is, people who were accurate senders were poor receivers and vice versa.[25] College-age males were videotaped as they responded to a series of red and green lights. The red light signaled the advent of a shock. These subjects and others were then asked to discriminate between shock and no-shock trials by viewing the videotaped reactions.

Zuckerman and his associates tried to sort through the studies that supported and denied a relationship between encoding and decoding abilities with nonverbal cues.[26] Their own study of facial and vocal emotions and their analysis of other studies support a general communication ability that is superimposed with abilities related to specific emotions. Studies that did not find that sending and receiving skills were interrelated tended to measure a single emotion and were more apt to deal with spontaneous expressions. It boils down to this: *If a person is skilled at sending, the same person is probably also skilled at receiving (and vice versa), but for any given emotion the person may show very different levels of expertise.*

Even though we may demonstrate accuracy in sending or receiving nonverbal signals, our receiving skills may be higher than our sending skills. Odom and Lemond speculated that the production of facial expressions, for instance, may never attain the same level of accuracy we have in interpreting facial expressions of emotion.[27] This idea was an outgrowth of their analysis of the sending and receiving skills of kindergarten and fifth-grade children. Six of the eight emotions tested with these children showed differences in sending and receiving ability—with sending ability lower.

SUMMARY

This chapter dealt with nonverbal skills—how to develop them and the characteristics of people who have such skills. This area is just beginning to receive scientific exploration, and few firm conclusions can be made. We have a fair grasp of various methods for developing social skills in general, but specific procedures for developing specific nonverbal skills have received little attention. At present, we can only say that nonverbal skill development will accrue with a strong desire or motivation to improve, with positive and productive attitudes toward the learning situation, with an adequate understanding of the knowledge related to nonverbal behavior, and with guided experience and practice in a variety of situations.

The second part of this chapter examined people and conditions associated with effectiveness in nonverbal sending and receiving. Most of the research in this area has focused on questions of decoding or receiving ability. The most comprehensive and widely tested instrument was developed by Rosenthal and his colleagues at Harvard University and is called the Profile of Nonverbal Sensitivity (PONS). The results of this eleven-channel test and other research probes provided the following information about nonverbal receiving skills: (1) As a group, females generally tend to be better decoders than males; (2) decoding skills tend to increase up to the mid-twenties; (3) there seems to be a minimal relationship between intelligence and other verbal measures and nonverbal decoding ability; (4) the personalities of effective decoders seem to reflect extroversion, popularity, self-monitoring, and judgments of interpersonal effectiveness by others; (5) actors, students of nonverbal behavior, and students in visual arts tend to score well on tests on nonverbal decoding ability, but anyone from an occupational group who is rated excellent on his or her job can be expected to do well at nonverbal decoding; (6) tests using facial, body, and vocal stimuli from subjects in the United States tend to elicit the highest scores from cultures most similar to the United States, but accuracy scores tend to suggest the possibility of a multicultural component in decoding nonverbal behavior; and (7) physiological arousal and practice also seem to improve one's decoding ability. We also discussed how one's accuracy in decoding may vary as a result of the channel in which the information was presented, whether the expressions were posed or spontaneous, what characteristics the stimulus person had, and how long the behavior was seen or heard. In spite of these possible variations, some evidence suggests that if you are proficient at decoding one channel of information, you will be proficient in others, and if you are proficient at decoding posed expressions you will be proficient at decoding spontaneous ones.

Our discussion of sending or encoding skills was abbreviated because little empirical work has focused on sending ability. The little work done so far has found that (1) females are also skilled senders; (2) skilled senders are also extroverted, popular, monitor their own behavior carefully, do not internalize their emotions, and show decreased physiological arousal. If you can send accurate spontaneous expressions there is an indication that you will also accurately send posed expressions—and vice versa.

Generally, "good" encoders are also "good" decoders and vice versa. But for any given emotion, a person may show very different sending and receiving abilities. Thus, some have proposed that there is a general communication ability that is superimposed with specific abilities tied to particular message classes.

NOTES

1. R. Buck, R. E. Miller, and W. F. Caul, "Sex, Personality and Physiological Variables to the Communication of Affect via Facial Expression," *Journal of Personality and Social Psychology* 30 (1974): 587–596.
2. R. Rosenthal, J. A. Hall, M. R. DiMatteo, P. L. Rogers, and D. Archer, *Sensitivity to Nonverbal Communication* (Baltimore, Md.: Johns Hopkins University Press, 1979).
3. L. Dimitrovsky, "The Ability to Identify the Emotional Meaning of Vocal Expressions at Successive Age Levels," in J. R. Davitz (ed.), *The Communication of Emotional Meaning* (New York: McGraw-Hill, 1964).
4. G. S. Gates, "A Test for Ability to Interpret Facial Expressions," *Psychological Bulletin* 22 (1925): 120; and M. L. Hamilton, "Imitative Behavior and Expressive Ability in Facial Expressions of Emotions," *Developmental Psychology* 8 (1973): 138.
5. Gates, "A Test for Ability"; and R. Eiland, and D. Richardson, "The Influence of Race, Sex and Age on Judgments of Emotion Portrayed in Photographs," *Communication Monographs* 3 (1976): 167–175.
6. M. Snyder, "Self-Monitoring of Expressive Behavior," *Journal of Personality and Social Psychology* 30 (1974): 526–537.

7. R. Buck, "A Test for Nonverbal Receiving Ability: Preliminary Studies," *Human Communication Research* 2 (1976): 162–171.

8. D. C. Albas, K. W. McCluskey, and C. A. Albas, "Perception of the Emotional Content of Speech: A Comparison of Two Canadian Groups," *Journal of Cross Cultural Psychology* 7 (1976): 481–490.

9. M. L. Knapp, *Social Intercourse: From Greeting to Goodbye* (Boston: Allyn & Bacon, 1978).

10. J. T. Lanzetta and R. E. Kleck, "Encoding and Decoding of Nonverbal Affect in Humans," *Journal of Personality and Social Psychology* 16 (1970): 12–19.

11. K. L. Burns and E. G. Beier, "Significance of Vocal and Visual Channels in the Decoding of Emotional Meaning," *Journal of Communication* 23 (1973): 118–130.

12. M. Beldoch, "Sensitivity to Expression of Emotional Meaning in Three Modes of Communication," in R. Davitz (ed.), *The Communication of Emotional Meaning* (New York: McGraw-Hill, 1964).

13. M. Zuckerman, J. A. Hall, R. S. DeFrank, and R. Rosenthal, "Encoding and Decoding of Spontaneous and Posed Facial Expressions," *Journal of Personality and Social Psychology* 34 (1977): 966–977.

14. G. Guber, "Recognition of Human Facial Expressions Judged Live in a Laboratory Setting," *Journal of Personality and Social Psychology* 4 (1966): 108–111.

15. R. Eiland and D. Richardson, "The Influence of Race, Sex and Age and Judgments of Emotion Portrayed in Photographs," *Communication Monographs* 43 (1976): 167–175.

16. Buck et al., "Sex, Personality and Physiological Variables . . ."; and S. Zaidel and A. Mehrabian, "The Ability to Communicate and Infer Positive and Negative Attitudes Facially and Vocally," *Journal of Experimental Research in Personality* 3 (1969): 233–241.

17. R. Buck, "Nonverbal Communication of Affect in Children," *Journal of Personality and Social Psychology* 31 (1975): 644–653.

18. Snyder, "Self-Monitoring of Expressive Behavior."

19. R. Buck, V. Savin, R. Miller, and W. Caul, "Communication of Affect Through Facial Expressions in Humans," *Journal of Personality and Social Psychology* 23 (1972): 362–371.

20. Buck, "Nonverbal Communication of Affect in Children."

21. Lanzetta and Kleck, "Encoding and Decoding of Verbal Affect in Humans"; and Buck et al., "Sex, Personality and Physiological Variables. . .".

22. Zuckerman et al., "Encoding and Decoding of Spontaneous and Posed Facial Expressions."

23. F. H. Knower, "Studies in the Symposium of Voice and Action: V. The Use of Behavioral and Tonal Symbols as Tests of Speaking Achievements," *Journal of Applied Psychology* 29 (1945): 229–235.

24. P. K. Levy, "The Ability to Express and Perceive Vocal Communication of Feelings," in J. R. Davitz (ed.), *The Communication of Emotional Meaning* (New York: McGraw-Hill, 1964).

25. Lanzetta and Kleck, "Encoding and Decoding of Verbal Affect in Humans."

26. M. Zuckerman, M. S. Lipets, J. H. Koivumaki, and R. Rosenthal, "Encoding and Decoding Nonverbal Cues of Emotion," *Journal of Personality and Social Psychology* 32 (1975): 1068–1076.
27. R. D. Odom and C. M. Lemond, "Development Differences in the Perception and Production of Facial Expressions," *Child Development* 43 (1972): 359–369.

ADDITIONAL READINGS

Beier, E. G. "Nonverbal Communication: How We Send Emotional Messages." *Psychology Today* (1974): 53, 55–56.

Davitz, J. R. (ed.). *The Communication of Emotional Meaning.* New York: McGraw-Hill, 1964.

Rosenthal, R., D. Archer, M. R. DiMatteo, J. Koivumaki, and P. Rogers. "Body Talk and Tone of Voice: The Language Without Words." *Psychology Today* 8 (1974): 64–68.

12

OBSERVING AND RECORDING NONVERBAL BEHAVIOR

Why do you keep looking at me that way, Daddy?

ERIC KNAPP, AGE NINE

Examine Figure 12.1. What do you see? Write down your observations.

Given such an open-ended or unstructured task, it is likely that you, as an observer, will report such findings as a brick structure; abstract modern art; a line drawing; a group of squares, rectangles, and other odd shapes; nothing; a bunch of lines; a maze; and so forth. If, however, you were instructed to be particularly observant of letters of the alphabet, it is highly probable that you (the observer) would see the capital letter E when confronting this stimulus. In Figure 12.1 the vertical and horizontal lines acted as visual interference or "noise" and kept the letter E well concealed. Interference in human observational situations can be far more distracting if we attempt to examine it without any sense of perspective—or system for observing. We need to know what to look for and how to record it if we want to look at it later. One could certainly argue that rigid adherence to a particular observational scheme will eventually bias what we see—making us unable to notice behaviors that are not on our list. Although this can happen and we should be careful to avoid it, we need to start somewhere; we need to give some order to a very complex set of events.

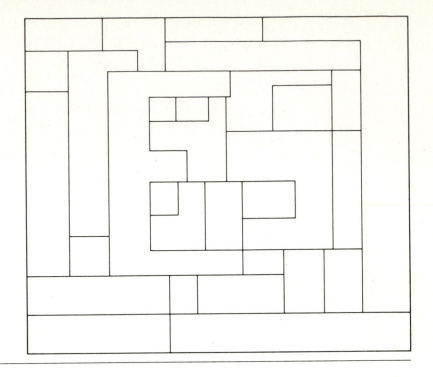

FIGURE 12.1

THE OBSERVER

We are all observers. The process of observation may be more critical to some occupations and leisure time activities than others, but we are all involved: the lawyer and the jury; the sales representative and the customer; the doctor and the patient; the teacher and the student; the actor and the audience; the personnel manager and the job applicant; the minister and the congregation; and in the daily observations of parents, children, lovers, friends, and TV personalities. But some of us observe human behavior more accurately than others. It is not wholly clear why some people seem to make more insightful observations than others, but we can offer a few ideas based on our own experience. The effective observer should be able to maintain a delicate balance between assuming the knowledgeable role as an expert in his or her field and the ignorance and wide-eyed naiveté of a child. When you are feeling very confident about your understanding of what is taking place around you, it is time to shift the emphasis to that of the child; when you feel a great deal of chaos and disorder in your observation field, it is time to shift to that of the expert. Just as effective speakers are highly motivated to have their audience understand their ideas, an effective observer probably has a strong interest and drive to understand the behavior of the observed. This does not mean, however, that the observer can't achieve a sense of detachment from those being observed when necessary.

Effective observers probably have had a variety of educational and personal experiences. This experiential base assists the observer in processing complex and fleeting ongoing stimuli and in putting isolated observations in their proper perspective later. Put another way, the observer should have the skills necessary for slow, careful, detailed work and the skills necessary to see unifying threads and broad concepts that tie the many isolated observations together. This, then, also suggests a need for patience and perseverance. And, finally, if people are going to be effective observers of others, it seems reasonable that they will also show some skill at self-insight—seeing and accepting both the positive and negative qualities in themselves. Not everyone will agree with this last point. We just don't know if those who are best at understanding themselves are also the best at understanding others, or whether those who are skilled at observing and interpreting the behavior of friends are equally proficient at similar processes with strangers.

Another approach to determine the characteristics of successful observers is to look at the information they seek and obtain. The following list can be useful to observers of any human transaction. At times some of the following information will contribute to observer bias, but the information may be necessary at some point to fully interpret the observations: (1) Find out about the participants—age, sex, position or status, relationship to each other, previous history, and the like. (2) Find out about the setting of the interaction—kind of environment, relationship of the participants to the environment, expected behavior in that environment, and so on. (3) Find out about the purposes of the interaction—hidden goals, compatibility of goals, and so on. (4) Find out about the social behavior—who does what to or with whom, form of the behavior, its intensity, toward whom it is directed, what initiates it, apparent objective of the behavior, effect on the other interactants, and so forth. (5) Find out about the frequency and duration of such behavior—when it occurs, how long it lasts, whether it recurs, frequency of recurrence, how typical such behavior is in this situation, and so on.

The Fallibility of Human Perception.   It is not unusual for several observers of the same event to see very different things; nor is it unusual for one observer to see very different things in the same event at two different times. Sometimes an observer will perceive a sequence of action as one perceptual unit, whereas another may see the same sequence as several units—or only part of a unit. The following are but some of the factors that may contribute to differences in perception—factors that successful observers must be aware of and take into account.

We must first recognize that our perceptions are structured by our own cultural conditioning, education, and personal experiences. Adults teach children what they think are critical dimensions of others by what they choose to talk about and make note of. Thus, we form associations that inevitably enter into our observations. For instance, we may be unable to see what we consider to be contradictory traits of behaviors in others—that is, can you conceive of a person who is both quiet and active? wealthy and accessible? short and romantic? Another aspect of this internally consistent world view that may affect our observations concerns preconceived notions about what we will see; for example, "My observations will take place in a nursing home. Therefore, the people I will observe will be old, noncommunicative, sick, inactive, and so on." Admittedly, such expectations and stereotypes can sometimes be helpful; sometimes they prevent accurate observations. In the United States, we are taught to rely primarily on our visual and auditory systems for reliable information, missing, at times, useful data derived from other senses like touch and smell.

We should also be aware that we will sometimes project our own qualities on to the object of our attention—after all, if it is worth being a part of us, it must be true of others. We do reverse the process sometimes when we want to see ourselves as unique—for example, "I am a rational person, but most people aren't." This interaction between our own needs, desires, or even temporary emotional states and what we see in others sometimes causes us to see only what we want to see or to miss what may be obvious to others. This is the process known as *selective perception*. To show the mental gyrations that we can perform in the pursuit of selective perception, let us assume that we have observed a mother slapping her child—a mother who was previously perceived to be incapable of such an act. We can ignore the stimulus—for example, "She's a wonderful mother, so she couldn't have been slapping her child"; we can reduce the importance of the contradictory information—for example, "Kids can be exasperating sometimes, and it's understandable that parents have to 'get tough' sometimes—besides it wasn't a hard slap"; we can change the meaning of the inconsistency— "It couldn't have been slapping because the child would have recoiled more and cried harder—it must have been a 'love tap' "; we can reinterpret previously observed traits to fit the contradictory information— "I always felt that her 'wonderful mother' image was just a front and this slapping incident only confirms it"; or we can infer new traits in the person—"I think she is an energetic, committed, and generous person, but she may be quick-tempered and overly punitive." Thus, it is not uncommon that observations that contradict what we believe to be true will often be twisted into a shape so that they "make sense" to us. When adults observe animals or infants, it is difficult to resist analyses that are deeply rooted in adult human activity. Because we have these perceptual biases, it is important that observers check their observations against the independent reports of others—or check the consistency of their own observations at several different points over an extended period of time.

We must also recognize that our perceptions will be influenced by what we choose to observe. We probably do not use the same criteria for observing our friends, our parents, and strangers. To see our own children or our spouse as others do is about as difficult as hearing a tape recording of ourselves as others do. We may attribute more positively perceived behaviors to our friend's personality and negatively perceived behaviors to situational constraints. Familiarity can assist observation or it can create observational "noise"—but it does affect our perceptions. Furthermore, some phenomena will cause us to zero in on one particular kind of behavior, observing it very closely but missing simultaneous behaviors occurring elsewhere. The behavior receiving the scrutiny may be bigger or more active or just more interesting, or we may monitor deviant behavior more closely than normative or expected behavior. When observing a conversation, we cannot possibly attend to everything as it happens. Sometimes we will look for, see, respond to, and interpret a particular set of cues and at other times the same cues will go unnoticed or disregarded. Observers will sometimes fall prey to the natural tendency to follow the conversational speaking turns, viewing the speaker and missing other nonverbal events associated with the nonspeaker. And some phenomena are so complex, so minute, or so frequent that observer fatigue becomes a major concern.

Even if two people observe the same event and attach similar meanings to it, they may choose to express their observations differently. Others may suspect that the two observers saw two different things. It is the difference between describing a facial expression as happiness, joy, delight, pleasure, or amusement, or it might be the difference between saying, "She struck him" versus "She pushed him." Hence, the language we use to express our perceptions can be an important variable in judging the accuracy of those perceptions.

Observers must also be sensitive to the possible influence of order effects. Sometimes we will observe some feature of another's behavior that will influence the perceptions of what follows, and sometimes it is a person's last act that causes us to reanalyze and reinterpret all the behavior that preceded it.

Finally, we must be concerned about factual, nonevaluative descriptions of behavior, and the interpretations we give to these descriptions. At the most basic level, we can say that a successful observer is careful not to confuse pure description with the inferences or interpretations about the behavior. Failure at the "inference stage" is aptly illustrated by the familiar story of the scientist who told his frog to jump and, after a few minutes, the frog jumped. The scientist recorded this behavior and amputated one of the frog's hind legs. Again he told the frog to jump. He repeated his instruction "Jump!" several times and, in time, the frog made a feeble attempt to jump with one hind leg. Then the scientist cut off the other hind leg and repeatedly ordered the frog to jump. When no jumping behavior occurred, the scientist recorded in his log: "Upon amputation of one of the frog's hind legs, it begins to lose it's hearing; upon severing both hind legs, the frog becomes totally deaf." Another valuable lesson to be drawn from this story concerns the problem of simple explanations for complex behavioral acts. It is very tempting to note when someone seems to avoid eye contact with you that this suggests that he or she is hiding something from you. We should constantly be on guard against such simple cause-effect explanations of observed behavior. Only after considering the total context of the event can we even begin to make inferences about why such behavior occurred—even then, we only speak with varying degrees of probability—never with complete certainty.

When observers do wish to make interpretations of observed behaviors, considerable caution must be exercised. For instance, let us suppose you observed me from a distance and you saw me using what you thought was an inordinate number of illustrators. Whether this was just my usual communicative "style" or whether it was the result of the situation (for example, talking to a person who didn't speak my language very well) would not be clear until you obtained further information. Sometimes we are faced with the question of whether a behavior is attributable to a person's personality or to something in the immediate situation. We might look for a situational cause for some "undesirable" behavior, but if we don't find a plausible explanation, we may attribute it to the person's personality with even more confidence. We should, however, recognize that we could have missed the situational cause, being unable to view the situation as the participant does. If we err in any direction, we are probably more likely to attribute actions to enduring dispositions of others and to minimize situational demands. If a behavior is a part of a person's personality and is carried from place to place, our predictions about this person are made considerably easier.

The preceding perceptual tendencies are only some of the matters that a successful observer must be aware of, adapt to, and account for.

THE OBSERVATIONAL RECORD

What should we observe? What categories of behavior should be coded? The behaviors you choose to study will vary with the object of your concern—for example, deception, turn-taking, leave-taking, and so on. Initial categories will probably be developed by the observer's own informal observation. Achieving precision of these category descriptions is a difficult, but important task. For instance, touching may be a behavior that one wishes to code. Yet, there may be vast differences in the touch of an open palm lightly placed on the shoulder of the other interactant and the hard touch of a closed fist on the other's jaw! Hence, one not only has to be aware of possible differences in strength of touch but place of touch, kind of touch (open or closed fist), duration of touch, and frequency of touch must also be considered. The amount of category specificity is largely dependent on the observer's purposes and hypotheses, but nonverbal observers should at least be aware of differences that may make a difference before they start coding. As we have seen, such information may have a profound impact on interpreting the data and inferences made from it. For instance, one may code the frequency of verbal reinforcers such as "Yeah," "right," or "Uh-huh," and conclude that one party was giving a lot of support to the other. However, we know that the same words can be said in a sarcastic fashion (with the addition of certain vocal cues), which changes the interpretation completely; we also know that such verbal devices are also used to "get the floor" when conversational openings are otherwise absent.

In the development of categories for observation it may be tempting to assume common referents for "common" behaviors. In one study in which smiling behavior was to be coded, it seemed like there was little need to describe exactly what was meant by a smile. However, out of twelve nonverbal behaviors coded for that study, the lowest agreement among the observers was on the frequency of smiling. Less time was spent specifying (visually and verbally) what constituted a smile, and the reliability obtained from the observers was understandably low. The more intangible or abstract the behavior to be coded, the more your reliability among observers is likely to suffer. In any case, observers and coders should be given a thorough training program prior to performing their tasks. They should be given a thorough description of the behavior to be coded and enough time to practice on events that closely approximate their eventual task.

Closely intertwined with the development of categories is the method of recording the behaviors. Efficiency is always an important criterion in recording procedures, but equally important is the criterion of accuracy. For instance, it would be efficient to simply record whether a given behavior occurred or did not occur; however, the subtleties of some nonverbal behaviors demand scales of various lengths to record the degree to which a given behavior was performed. One must determine, for instance, whether it is important to record that a "forward lean" occurred (yes/no) or what degree of forward lean occurred (ten degrees, thirty degrees, forty-five degrees, and so on) or how long a forward lean occurred (one to five seconds, six to ten seconds, eleven to fifteen seconds, and so on) or at what point in the interaction the forward lean occurred (first ten seconds of the interaction, last ten seconds, and so on) or all four. Such judgments can only be made in a specific context, but it is very tempting to select a bipolar scale when a five- or seven-point scale would provide more accurate data. Furthermore, the intensity and significance of an event may be lost if all the behaviors in your category system are given the same weight.

Working with Visual Records.   You might want to obtain permanent visual records of the subject of your observations for any number of reasons.

For all the promise that film and videotape offer to the observation of nonverbal behavior, they are not without problematic issues and potential sources of error.

First, and perhaps the most basic, is the influence of a camera on the behavior of the observed. In laboratory settings, the camera can be hidden, or, if this is not possible or desirable, you can assume that the initial anxiety of being filmed will dissipate after a few minutes when the people get used to the camera. This assumption should be checked, however, because people may get used to the camera at different rates, some may try to perform naturally, and some may never be comfortable in front of the camera.

A second issue concerns how the action, event, or individual is filmed. For instance, camera angles can affect the meaning we attach to a situation—for example, a person can be made to look shorter by filming from a higher angle; a close-up may cause a given behavior to assume an exaggerated importance—like the familiar close-up of a person's hands seen in so many television newcasts; rapidly shifting from scene to scene may give an illusion of speed that does not accompany the actual event; and so on. In short, meanings can be in the movement patterns of the camera as well as in the movement patterns of those being filmed.

After many hours of viewing visual materials, you may get the uneasy feeling that you are observing and recording minute behaviors that may have relatively little real-life impact—if any at all. You wonder whether the interacting parties are cognizant of fleeting movements, which, only with the advantage of replays, you are able to observe. You are uncomfortable with the knowledge that videotapes or films represent something short of an accurate representation of what actually took place and wish they did more. Somehow we need to obtain supplementary "natural state" feedback from interactants to determine which of the many behaviors we examine are attended to. Some may question the relevance of looking at micromomentary facial expressions, eyebrow flashes, and pupil dilation by asking the question: "Are such behaviors perceived in everyday human interaction?" Even if the answer is no, this does not suggest that such research is unimportant or even irrelevant, but it raises the question of observational priorities for those concerned with understanding human communication. And, it reiterates the need to establish observational categories that are meaningful to human interaction.

Many potential sources of error are rooted in the viewing behavior of coders who examine visual records. If a coder is given a list of ten or twelve nonverbal behaviors to code, which range from head movements to foot movements, it is inevitable that intercoder reliability will suffer. To correct for this, areas of observation can be broken down into smaller portions and coders can focus on this one area. In some cases, too much focus may cause an observer to miss important co-occurring behavior. We also have a tendency to follow a conversation like a Ping-Pong match—shifting our head from side to side as the speaking turns shift. If the observer is asked to focus on the behavior of one interactant, looking only at the talker will surely bias the observations.

Finally, there are far too many problems concerning the technical use of videotape and film to detail here, but there are numerous and all too easy ways to obtain poor quality videotape and film. Since sharp resolution of the picture is so critically important in the observation of nonverbal behavior, it is worth investigating seemingly mundane problems like the type and size of videotape or film, and the type of recorder and playback unit that will provide the best overall quality.

A GLOBAL ANALYSIS OF HUMAN COMMUNICATION

A number of highly technical systems used by researchers have not been reviewed. If you are interested in the categories and notations used for observing vocal cues,[1] kinesics,[2] proxemics,[3] dance,[4] classroom behavior,[5] verbal behavior,[6] and verbal/nonverbal behavior,[7] you are referred to the original works.

In an effort to avoid some of the pitfalls of current notational systems, and to summarize or bring together some of the material in this book, the following categories for a "global analysis" are proposed. This method is not designed for sophisticated research purposes. It is designed for those who want to acquire a general framework for looking at interpersonal transactions, and to provide a general feel for the judgments needed to observe an act of human communication. The number of questions within each category should act only as starters for observations. You will think of other important questions that have been omitted. Some of the questions included will probably seem very insignificant for interpreting some situations—and very important for others. You will also note that not all of the questions concern directly observable elements; some require inferences.

To use such a "global analysis" it is recommended that you first read all the questions in all the categories to give yourself a general perspective of the bases for observing communication events. Then you may wish to take one or two categories at a time to perfect observational skills in those particular areas—observing only those dimensions in several encounters and adding to the questions already suggested. After having worked with the separate categories for some time, try observing a communication event using all nine categories. Compare your observations with those of another observer and the two (or more) communicators if possible. The discussion of your observations may be more valuable than any notation system that might be proposed at this time.

GLOBAL ANALYSIS: INITIAL PHASE
(Recording First Impressions)

The Environment.   Are there any environmental stimuli likely to affect this interaction? Is the temperature going to be a factor? How about the number of other people around the two interactants? How will these other people influence what the two interactants may do—even if they do not say anything? Will the colors and general decor influence this interaction? How much space is available between and around the communicators? What architectural factors, such as chairs (soft-hard), tables, walls, and desks, may influence what happens? Out of all the available places in the immediate environment, why did the interactants choose the exact place they did? Does it seem like a familiar environment for both parties? Do they appear to feel at home? What behavior can be expected in this environment?

The Participants.   Will the sex of the participants likely affect the interaction and, if so, how? Will age have any influence on what happens? How about the status or authority relationships involved? How do the participants look? Is attractiveness going to be a factor? Will hairstyle or body size affect the interaction and, if so, how? What is the role of dress in this interaction? Does the participants' dress meet expectations for the environment and their roles and mutual expectations? Can any odors be detected? Are the participants aware of them? Are there any differences in education, occupation, or socioeconomic status that may affect the communication behavior? How? Does race or cultural background play any major part in interpersonal behavior in this situation? Will artifacts such as lipstick, glasses, and the like, affect participant reactions to any significant degree? What is the relationship of these two participants to one another? Do they have any previous experience with each other that will likely be influential here? Do they seem to like each other? Why? Do the participants enter this transaction with compatible goals or purposes? What information do the participants bring to this subject on this occasion?

As an observer, you must recognize that some of these initial observations and hypotheses may change as the interaction progresses—a woman may remove her glasses, a man may take off his ring, or attitudes may not be as similar as predicted. Observers should be prepared to note such changes.

GLOBAL ANALYSIS: INTERACTION PHASE
(Recording Ongoing Verbal-Nonverbal Responses)

Touching Behavior.   Is there any physical contact at all? If so, does it seem to be deliberate or accidental? Does this action seem to be motivated by some specific purpose—for example, reinforcing a point? If there is no contact, why? Did the situation call for contact or no contact? Was contact made only at special times during the interaction? How frequent was the contact? How long did it last? Who initiated the contact? What was the apparent effect on the person being touched?

Facial Expressions.   Do either or both communicators have a relatively consistent facial expression in this situation? Are they generally communicating one attitude or emotion with their facial expressions? Were there gross changes at certain points in the conversation? What might have accounted for such gross facial changes—verbal or nonverbal behavior? Were there times when one person's facial expression elicited a similar expression from the other person? Did you see any "micro-momentary" or fleeting facial expressions that suggested attitudes contrary to those being expressed verbally? At what points did you notice expressions that would generally be described as frowning or sad, smiling and happy, angry, anxious, impatient, bored, puzzled, serious, or surprised? Did the facial expressions differ in intensity at various points in the transaction? Did the facial expression seem genuine? If so, why? If not, why not?

Eye Behavior.   Is there generally a lot of visual contact or not very much? Why? Does one person look away more than the other? Why? Do one or both participants seem to stare or extend eye contact beyond "normal" limits? Is there a pattern to the places a person looks when he or she does not look at the other person? If so, can you explain why this pattern may occur? Is there any excessive blinking by one or both parties? At what points is eye gaze more evident and not evident? What effect does eye gaze or lack of it seem to have on the other participant?

Posture-Position.   Do both participants assume the same posture? Why? Are both standing or sitting? If one participant is standing, and one is sitting, how does this relate to their respective roles in this situation? Does the assumed position seem to be relaxed or tense? Does this change during the course of interaction and, if so, why? Are one or both participants leaning back or leaning forward? What does this suggest? Are the participants facing head-on, at an acute angle, at an obtruse angle, or side by side? Have they arranged their bodies to block others from entering their conversation? What is the relative distance used for communicating—close, medium, or far? Do leg and arm positions communicate impenetrability or coldness? Do leg positions suggest inclusion? Are one person's changes in posture matched by the other person? How long do the participants maintain a given posture? Why do they change?

Vocal Behavior. Are both participants using the appropriate level of loudness for the situation? Does one person have an unusually soft or loud voice? What is the effect on the other person? Is talking rate a factor in this situation? How? Are there times when you perceive an incongruity between vocal cues and verbal statements? What is the effect on the other participant? Do one or both participants have fairly deep voices? Do they have fairly high voices? Are there periods of silence beyond normal pauses? Why? Do vocal cues such as laughing or groaning play a significant part? What about a quivering or quaking voice during periods of nervousness? Does vocal quality such as hoarseness seem to affect the total impression of one or both of the participants? Are there excessive nonfluencies? With what effect?

Physical Movement. What were the significant movements in the event? Did head nodding play a major part? How? How about hand gestures? Did one participant seem to be moving in on the other while the other moved back? Was there generally a lot of movement or not too much? Why? Did hand or finger movements play a part? How? Did hand or foot cues suggest clues to deception? How about foot tapping? Were there major changes in posture? How frequent were they? Did you observe any cues for terminating the conversation—for example, a participant looking at his or her watch; making motions to get up or move out the door, taking a deep breath, frequently looking around and out the window, and the like?

Verbal Behavior. Here we look at some familiar, typical types of verbal responses. Consider: (1) What was the general style of one or both participants? Can it be generally characterized in any one or two categories? (2) What specific kinds of remarks elicited what specific kinds of nonverbal behavior? In other words, what seemed to be the effect of certain verbal responses on the initiator's nonverbal behavior and on the receiver's verbal and nonverbal responses? Some common response types include: disagreement about content; agreement about content; advice about feelings; advice about action; ambiguous responses; interrupting responses; personal attacks; defensive responses; evaluative responses; supportive responses; questions; opinions; tension release through jokes and the like; tangential responses; irrelevant responses; expression of own feelings—positive or negative; interpretive responses; request for clarification of feelings; request for clarification of content.

A final, but important, note. A book devoted entirely to nonverbal communication might be considered misleading in that nonverbal systems should not be portrayed as separate processes, independent from verbal behavior. To overcome this danger, we have stressed the integral relationship between verbal and nonverbal systems whenever possible. But an equally misleading view of the nonverbal communication process may result from the organization of this book into seemingly separate categories of behavior. Even our "global analysis" reflects this apparent separation. We could not leave any discussion of these various categories without further noting that even within the nonverbal system, the dynamics cannot be ignored.

SUMMARY

In this chapter we reviewed some general principles of observing human communication behavior. We started by examining some of the characteristics of people who seemed to be insightful observers. One characteristic we pursued in some depth was an understanding of the process of human perception. "Good" observers would familiarize themselves with possible sources of observer distortion and would adapt accordingly. In this treatment of human perception we discussed how we sometimes project our own needs, desires, and expectations onto those we are observing, how we sometimes perceive only those things that will make sense to our own view of human behavior, how what we observe first may affect later observations—and vice versa, how the expressions of our observations can be a source of perceived bias, and how we must be careful to distinguish observed "facts" from inferences.

We also discussed various aspects of visual records. We suggested several advantages in obtaining such records but cautioned against possible pitfalls. It was noted that the methods of filming can inject meaning into the visual documents that may bias interpretations of them. We also offered some suggestions regarding what to film and how to view these visual records.

The last part of this chapter presented a nine-category "global analysis" system that may significantly increase verbal and nonverbal sensitivity to social interaction. The global analysis gives some structure to guide initial observations and, it is hoped, will stimulate additional ideas that can be applied and adapted to almost any encounter.

NOTES

1. G. L. Trager, "Paralanguage: A First Approximation," *Studies in Linguistics* 13 (1958): 1–12. For a detailed application of this system, see R. E. Pittenger, C. F. Hockett, and J. J. Danehy, *The First Five Minutes* (Ithaca, N.Y.: Martineau, 1960).

2. R. L. Birdwhistell, *Kinesics and Context* (Philadelphia: University of Pennsylvania Press, 1970); D. Efron, *Gesture and Environment* (New York: King's Crown Press, 1941); and D. Efron, *Gesture, Race and Culture* (The Hague: Mouton, 1972). A. Kendon and J. Ex. "Progress Report of an Investigation into Aspects of the Structure and Function of the Social Performance in Two-Person Encounters," cited in M. Argyle, *Social Interaction* (New York: Atherton Press, 1969), pp. 123–126. A. Mehrabian, "Methods and Designs: Some Referents and Measures of Nonverbal Behavior," *Behavior Research Methods and Instrumentation* 1 (1969): 203–207.

3. E. T. Hall, "A System for the Notation of Proxemic Behavior," *American Anthropologist* 65 (1963): 1003–1026; and E. T. Hall, *Handbook for Proxemic Research* (Washington, D.C.: Society for the Anthropology of Visual Communication, 1974).

4. A. Hutchinson, *Labanotation: The System of Analyzing and Recording Movement* (New York: Theater Arts Books, 1970).

5. B. M. Grant and D. G. Hennings, *The Teacher Moves: An Analysis of Nonverbal Activity* (New York: Columbia Teachers College Press, 1971). Also P. Amidon, *Nonverbal Interaction Analysis* (Minneapolis, Minn.: P. S. Amidon and Associates, 1971). N. A. Flanders, *Interaction Analysis in the Classroom: A Manual for Observers* (Minneapolis, Minn.: University of Minnesota, 1960).

6. R. Bales, *Interaction Process Analysis* (Reading, Mass.: Addison-Wesley, 1950). W. B. Stiles, "Verbal Response Modes and Dimensions of Interpersonal Roles: A Method of Discourse Analysis," *Journal of Personality and Social Psychology* 36 (1978): 693–703.

7. R. Harrison, "Verbal-Nonverbal Interaction Analysis: The Substructure of an Interview," paper presented to the Association for Educational Journalism, Berkeley, California, 1969. Also see J. Frahm, "Verbal-Nonverbal Interaction Analysis: Exploring a New Methodology for Quantifying Dyadic Communication Systems" (Ph.D. diss., Michigan State University, 1970).

ADDITIONAL READINGS

Brandt, R. M. *Studying Behavior in Natural Settings*. New York: Holt, Rinehart and Winston, 1972.

Collier, J. *Visual Anthropology: Photography as a Research Method*. New York: Holt, Rinehart and Winston, 1967.

Hastorf, A. H., D. J. Schneider, and J. Polefka. *Person Perception*. Reading, Mass.: Addison-Wesley, 1970.

Lofland, J. *Analyzing Social Settings*. Belmont, Calif.: Wadsworth, 1971.

Webb, E. J., D. T. Campbell, R. D. Schwartz, and L. Sechrest. *Unobtrusive Measures*. Chicago: Rand McNally, 1966.

Weick, K. E. "Systematic Observational Methods," in G. Lindzey and E. Aronson (eds.). *Handbook of Social Psychology*, 2nd. ed. Reading, Mass.: Addison-Wesley, 1968, vol. 2.

SUBJECT INDEX

(Acknowledgments continued from copyright page)

Perception of Faces," *Journal of Personality* 25 (1956):142-158 by permission of Duke University Press. Copyright 1956 by Duke University Press.

Figure 9.2: R. V. Exline, J. Thibaut, C. B. Hickey, and P. Gumpert, "Visual
Interaction in Relation to Machiavellianism and an Unethical Act," in R.
Christie and F. L. Geis (eds.) *Studies in Machiavellianism* (New York: Ac-
ademic Press) 1976.

Figure 9.3: E. H. Hess, "The Role of Pupil Size in Communication," *Scientific
American* 233 (Nov., 1975) p. 111.

Figure 10.1: P. Ladefoged and R. Vanderslice, "The Voiceprint Mistique,"
Working Papers in Phonetics, 7, November, 1967, University of California,
Los Angeles.

264